HEALING THE HURT

TIM CORMIER

CONTENTS

RADICAL CHANGE THROUGH THE POWER OF CHRIST

A MAN'S SEARCH FOR MEANING, AND HIS DANGEROUS
LIFE, FILLED WITH ADDICTION

let me go. Without their sacrifice, love, and kind words, I simply would have just disappeared.

My sister Carol, and her prayers.

Finally, I dedicate this book to the hurting people who are hearing voices and are in addiction, this is for you. Every word written in this book is coming from a heart that hurt like yours does, and that hurts for you. These are words meant to be oxygen for your lungs, food for your hunger, life for your death, and hope for your hopelessness.

ACKNOWLEDGMENTS

I want to acknowledge Ravi Kamath for proofreading, and grammatically editing the first draft of this manuscript. To Mike Murdock and his testimony in my darkest of hours. To Bill Winston and his powerful message, "Speak the Word Only." To Jachin Dardar for his mentorship, and theological expertise.

Thank you Bryon Quertermous for providing the content edit, and for referring me to Frankie Blooding at Real Indie Author who helped bring this book to world.

INTRODUCTION

This book was written for people who are experiencing emotional pain and suffering as well as the addict. It discusses mental anguish and addiction from the perspective of one who lived within its clutches. It is a chronicled record of my life in short and precise moments. It is not my full story in depth. It is factual and true, but a lot of the detailed horrors of sin and perversion are kept out on purpose. I did not want to glorify or expand on more than what was necessary; if it would not serve helpful to someone in recovery or glorify God, it was kept out. I was 43 when my family and ministry were destroyed through separation and divorce. I had been married for 23 years. At 43, I became an addict and lost everything important to me. I lived that way for the next twelve years. In this book, you get the whole story, in excerpts.

This book was written as God gave it to me, and with each principle, my deliverance and biography are intertwined together. My deliverance is in chronological order, but my life story is not. As God would set me free and the strongholds of Satan were destroyed, you will see how my past was finally put to rest. These chapters are meant to be studied and reread. They are filled with much valuable information. The book was written to help you overcome the inner pain from experiences of hurtful trauma, destructive internal voices of anger and bitterness, clinical depression, doubt in yourself and God. I believe that this book if read in humility and prayer, will give you power to defeat any type of addiction or controlling substance.

To the addict,

What you see right now is chaos, confusion, and disorder. It might seem like a sane view, but it is a deceptive misconception. For those of you who see it as it is, you are already deep in addiction's final stages. You have already lost almost everything of value in your life, maybe everything. You possibly no longer have your kids, a driver's license, a job, or even a permanent place to stay. You have lost all respect for yourself and are living in the stages of denial. The different stages of denial are a reality. Little by little you are losing your authentic self and are doing things that you never dreamed you would be doing. The alcohol or the drug steals a little part of you every day. A little honesty, loyalty, morality, and self-esteem goes with each passing day.

In the early stages of my drug use, everything seemed exciting and pleasurable. It opened a carefree world filled with unpredictable adventure for me. It was filled with people, and I was never alone. In a world where anything goes. It had no boundaries and order to it. The people were inviting, fun, and uninhibited. That was a delusional picture. A sane, honest view would have given me a totally different perspective. But hurting people do not always see things clearly and objectively. At the time, I was vulnerable. I was in need. I was broken. There are many reasons people do drugs or alcohol. I wrote this book for all of my previous friends who are still in the fight and for you. It was birthed in me through my own experience of recovery and freedom. No one starts using with the idea to become addicted. The lifestyle can be just as addictive as the drug. If you are not ready for a change spiritually, this book is not for you.

If you are ready for God to deliver you completely and ready to give Him the authority to work change in your life, this is the book for you! I truly believe the principles in this book will produce a freedom in you that you have never experienced. If you are in recovery now, these pages will give you strength to complete your journey of healing. If you are skeptical and have doubts, I understand. I too thought that I would never be completely restored to a healthy and productive life. I had tried many times and failed. That is why this information is so important. This is a book of hope. This is a book about freedom. Your freedom.

When writing this book, I felt inadequate, and I was humbled. I knew these words were being born from the most awesome experience I had ever encountered. God was leading me to do it. It had been in the making from the very start. In my spirit. When faith dawned, I sat down and began to write. The words just poured out of my soul. I knew the Holy Spirit inspired these words. I cannot take the credit for them. They were from Him. He deserves the credit, the honor, and all the praise.

Sincerely, Tim

SURRENDER

TO HIM WHO THE SON SETS FREE IS FREE INDEED.

METHADDICTSHELP, FACEBOOK POST

MARCH 24, 2016

FINALLY, WHEN I CAME TO THE VERY END OF MYSELF, ALONE, HIGH, NOWHERE TO GO, AND WITH ALL MY BELONGINGS IN MY CAR WITH ME.... I HAD DROVE AND DROVE AROUND FOR HOURS THAT DAY CALLING MY SO - CALLED FRIENDS FOR A PLACE TO STAY WITH NO RESPONSE. I PRAYED, AND ASKED GOD TO HELP ME....I TOLD HIM THAT I WOULD LIVE FOR HIM IF HE COULD HELP ME OVERCOME MY ADDICTION , FIND ME A JOB , AND A PLACE TO STAY....EVENTUALLY I PULLED OVER AT A CAR WASH ABOUT 10 PM AND REFUSED TO GET HIGH AGAIN ALTHOUGH I STILL HAD SOME LEFT HIDDEN IN MY CAR........GIVING MYSELF TO CHRIST TO DO WHATEVER HE WANTED WITH ME I FELL ASLEEP ONLY TO BE AWAKEN BY A POLICE OFFICER A COUPLE OF HOURS LATER ...I SEEN THE OFFICER GET REAL EXCITED WHEN SHE REALIZED WHO SHE HAD AND CALLED FOR BACKUP, IMMEDIATELY TWO MORE OFFICERS PULLED UP AND THEY ARRESTED ME AND HELD ME WITHOUT BAIL AND A PHONE CALL FOR THREE DAYS AND THEN EXPEDITED ME TO

ANOTHER JAIL ABOUT HUNDRED MILES AWAY IN ANOTHER PARISH WHERE I WAS HELD FOR SEVERAL FELONY CHARGES THERE...I KNEW I BELONGED IN PRISON BUT I JUST BEGAN TO PRAY AND TOLD GOD IF HE COULD HELP ME I WOULD SERVE HIM THE REST OF MY LIFE....THEN GOD BEGAN TO PERFORM MIRACLE AFTER MIRACLE AND HERE I AM HELPING PEOPLE FROM ALL OVER THE WORLD...A FREE MAN , SANE , DELIVERED, PROSPEROUS, MARRIED, FILLED WITH LOVE AND GRATITUDE RATHER THAN BITTERNESS, HATE, ANGER, LUST , DEPRESSED, AND LONELY. THIS COULD BE YOU ...JUST ASK CHRIST FOR HELP...MESSAGE US FOR PRAYER WE LOVE YOU...AND SO DOES GOD......TPC. (UNEDITED)

104,215 PEOPLE REACHED

5.2K LIKES

1,172 SHARES

632 COMMENTS

I started this book off with the principle of "Surrender" because it is the initial gateway to freedom for anyone who is struggling with addiction or the open door to all spiritual freedom with God. Surrendering to your Creator is the source of all growth. Real growth cannot be achieved outside of an authentic connection with God.

The heralded Alcoholics Anonymous (AA) slogan, "first things first," carries a lot of weight with me. God knows I went to enough of those burdensome meetings to hear a lot of those slogans. I was forced to go to these meetings and get counseling and psychiatric help by a drug program designed by DISA in order to go back to work after violations of employment drug policies. I manipulated and lied to counselors, paid for a therapist, and attended multiple AA meetings from parent groups, prison groups, women's groups, and groups where there was no one under the age of 60. Eventually, I got my drug violations removed after hundreds of dollars spent on counseling sessions, drug testing, time off work, and a lot of lying on my part. I had to lie to these people, or it would have kept going on forever. I wasn't ready. Until a person is ready to stop using, they will continue to use, and there is nothing anyone else can do about it.

Until an individual in addiction experiences enough regret, pain, and sorrow, they will never want change. A person must experience an epiphany—a sudden and striking realization. They must feel regret and see the danger of the never-ending hopeless chaos of addiction. Individuals must come to the understanding that their lives are unmanageable and their addiction is uncontrollable before they will ever think about surrendering their will to God. Most of all, they must see that they have become powerless to change on their own. When I finally realized that I was powerless and that all my efforts were futile, a new world opened up to me. I had tried many times to beat this thing before and failed. I also had a deep hurt and anger in me that would always point back to my only way of escape, being high. Broken people need to be healed. Some of us are just simply broken, and until the brokenness is healed, we will always be in addiction. I suspect many of us were never an addict, just broken.

For years, I was an angry man. Angry and disappointed with God, I blamed God for not protecting me, guarding my family, and was bitter toward Him. I hurt continually, and I felt like God had abandoned me. I had a chip on my shoulder and was very bitter. It was hard for me to cope with daily life. I was hurt and felt lonely in a crowded room. Even when I had a woman in my bed, it just wouldn't go away. I had gone for two years without being able to sleep normally. I couldn't read a newspaper during that time. I was unable to watch my favorite sports on television. Normal things that I once cared for didn't matter to me. My yard was unkempt. **All I ever felt was loneliness, rejection, anger, hurt, and pain. It was at that time I was introduced to meth.**

I was on the job as a welder and would just fall asleep in the middle of a big industrial construction project. A coworker told me my life was in danger and he could give me something that would make me feel alive and filled with energy. It did, and I became addicted immediately. That's how fast it got a hold of me. I didn't realize it at the time, but its powerful effect was more than I could handle. I had never smoked or taken any drugs before that; it was my first experience. **Meth became my answer. It took me, and I gave in willingly. I used almost every day for twelve years. It destroyed everything in my life. I couldn't beat it.**

It was then, after twelve years of devastation, crime, and bitterness that I began to remember about my life before depression and meth. How peaceful and meaningful it had been when I walked with God. During those twelve years, the only preacher I ever saw was Dr. Mike Murdock. He would just appear at key moments of clarity in my chaotic addicted life and periodically on some television program in the early morning hours. In a motel room, I would listen and think of what my life could have been. Ever so gently, God would speak to me as I listened. Little by little God began to speak to me and tell me how much He loved me. But I was so afraid. Afraid that I couldn't live without meth. I tried. I failed many times.

I knew I was an addict by the way I felt when I was sober. I knew I needed healing. I was too angry and broken to live sober on my own. I was driving my car around for hours, thinking and talking to God. I was in a spiritual struggle. It had been going on for days. I had been high for days. I began to see God in a unique way. I recalled some of the things Dr. Murdock would say on television. I remembered Dr. Murdock talking about being recently divorced and living in a house empty of furniture; sheets tacked above his windows for curtains and without even a kitchen table. He was broke and divorced, and people were telling him the same things they told me. However, he kept serving and giving to God. I could see him prosperous and smiling, talking about his love for the person of the Holy Spirit. To this day, I still can picture him sitting at his piano singing, smiling, with tears in his eyes, talking about a wonderful and good God.

I could also hear my dad's voice speaking in my mind. He would say, "Son, God is not through with you. In the end, He is going to bless you. God's hand is on your life. You are called by Him. He loves you." There was a heavy conviction in my car, and in my mind, there was a war raging. I was debating within myself whether God would love me enough to help me. Would God legitimately help me and heal my brokenness and addiction? Help me get on my feet and set me free from this crazy hurt and emotional pain that I continually felt? The psychology behind my change in mindset was truth coming from the conviction of the Holy Spirit.

I realized that I could not even distinguish where my hurt was coming from, and even if God were to heal me emotionally of the wounds in my spirit, the chaotic lifestyle of addiction would steal its freedom from me. The more the battle raged in my mind, the greater my longing for a restored place of meaning and purpose. My life had come to a place where it didn't make sense to keep running from God. I also knew it would take a miracle to recover the things I lost. I understood running from God and doing things my way had not helped but rather had only made things worse. That enlightenment highlighted the biggest problem I faced. My addiction and the continued downward spiral of devastation it causes. My addiction to a lifestyle, and the adrenaline that a 1400% dopamine rush could give.

Finally, while parked in a car wash, I just gave in. I was through— through with it all— and said, "God, I'm through. I cannot live this way any longer. I give you my life to do with however you want. I will serve you. I will not get high anymore. I give you complete control over my life, and surrender everything to you. Jesus, please heal me, forgive me. Forgive me for blaming you for all of those things that happened to me. I know now that it wasn't you. Please set me free. I accept and believe in your sacrifice on the cross, and that by your own blood that was shed on that cross, I am forgiven. I am going to just trust in you from this point on in my life. I surrender my life into your hands."

And right there in that car wash, I surrendered to God. Finally, I could rest. It was like a heavy weight had been lifted from me. **The peace of God filled my car, I was no longer in a spiritual struggle, my mind was at ease, and I felt calm and restful. I fell asleep, right there in that car wash.**

Do you want to finally rest? In Matthew 11:28 (NLT), Then Jesus said, "Come to me, all of you who are weary and carry heavy burdens, and I will give you rest." Do you want to finally be at peace with yourself and with God? In John 14:27 (NLT), Jesus said, "I am leaving you with a gift—peace of mind and heart. And the peace I give is a gift the world cannot give. So don't be troubled or afraid." Today could be your first day of recovery, and you can begin to experience the miracle-working power of God in your life just like I did. I wrote this book for you. God gave me to you as a gift. He put a love in my heart for you. But more than that, much more.

He gave you the most precious gift in the world, His Son. He died for you so that you could be free from addiction and oppression. In Luke 4:18 (KJV), Jesus said, "The Spirit of the Lord is upon me, because he hath anointed me to preach the gospel to the poor; he hath sent me to heal the brokenhearted, to preach deliverance to the captives, and recovering of sight to the blind, to set at liberty them that are bruised," Do you want your broken heart to be healed? Do you want to be delivered today? Then just surrender. Surrender now.

Just say, "Jesus, I surrender my life to you. I completely give you myself. I am powerless over my pain and addiction. Thank you for dying for my sins on the cross and loving me."

Pray it again, slowly.

Now, think slowly about surrendering to Him, and say it using the words from your mind and heart—words from you to Him. Just say Jesus, I ....

Now, softly thank Him. Thank you, Jesus. Thank you, heavenly Father.

If you prayed that prayer and meant it, Jesus is now carrying your burden and lives inside of you. Your sins and mistakes are forgiven. You now have a champion fighting for you, and He will never leave you nor forsake you. You are now a child of God. It is just that simple. Jesus, I give you my heart, all of me, and I trust and rely on you, your word, your strength, and your power.

Surrender is a simple step of faith and confessing the Lordship of Christ. The white flag of surrender is given to Christ.

Ephesians 2:8 (KJV) says, "For by grace are ye saved through faith; and that not of yourselves: it is the gift of God:"

John 3:16 (KJV) says, "For God so loved the world, that he gave his only begotten Son, that whosoever believeth in him should not perish, but have everlasting life."

Romans 10:9-10 (KJV) says, "That if thou shalt confess with thy mouth the Lord Jesus, and shalt believe in thine heart that God hath raised him from the dead, thou shalt be saved. For with the heart man believeth unto righteousness, and with the mouth confession is made unto salvation."

The word of God (Bible) promises salvation, eternal life, and right standing with God through believing in Christ and His resurrection. **The good news is that by trusting in God's Son, we are saved by God's grace through faith. When we confess publicly and privately to Jesus, Lord of our lives, we have favor with God that requires no good works of our own.** We are not saved based on what we feel. You might not feel anything after you prayed that prayer. Sometimes the feelings, and fruits of joy, come later. The point the scripture makes is that you are saved by what you believe, not feel. What you confess, and who you become, grants you favor, not what you feel. You now have access to God's favor and blessing in your life simply by believing in the Son of God, Jesus.

From the moment we confess the lordship of Christ and believe in His resurrection, we have righteousness (right standing with God), and He grants us favor and partnership in all our affairs. **The greatest gift a man can have is favor with power and influence in this life. When that power has no equal and is superior to every other in the universe, then we have a significant and superior advantage in our struggles to achieve and be productive.** But far more valuable, and important, the grace of God reaches into the fourth dimension ——our inward man, the inward spiritual, emotional, and mental internal parts of who we are. God's favor and grace are able to overcome our circumstances and work healing and give strength to our spirit and soul. God's favor is His promise to do that.

God loves the unqualified. The only requirement God has for blessing you is you being human. You are pre-qualified and meet all the requirements necessary to have faith and enjoy the grace of God just by being human. The word of God says that he has given to every man the measure of faith.

Romans 12:3 (KJV) says, "For I say, through the grace given unto me, to every man that is among you, not to think of himself more highly than he ought to think; but to think soberly, according as God hath dealt to every man the measure of faith."

To surrender to God in faith and confess Him Lord is "being born-again"

Notice that Jesus said to truly see the kingdom of God and have it revealed to you completely, you must be born again. He was talking about being born of the spirit.

John 3:1-8 (KJV) says, "There was a man of the Pharisees, named Nicodemus, a ruler of the Jews: The same came to Jesus by night, and said unto him, Rabbi, we know that thou art a teacher come from God: for no man can do these miracles that thou doest, except God be with him. Jesus answered and said unto him, Verily, verily, I say unto thee, Except a man be born again, he cannot see the kingdom of God. Nicodemus saith unto him, How can a man be born when he is old? can he enter the second time into his mother's womb, and be born. Jesus answered, Verily, verily, I say unto thee, Except a man be born of water and of the Spirit, he cannot enter into the kingdom of God. That which is born of the flesh is flesh; and that which is born of the Spirit is spirit. Marvel not that I said unto thee, Ye must be born again. The wind bloweth where it listeth, and thou hearest the sound thereof, but canst not tell whence it cometh, and whither it goeth: so is every one that is born of the Spirit."

The Holy Spirit is invisible to man, but just like the wind is very powerful, He becomes the agent of change in you. Your spirit is considered dead (it is existent, but separated from God) until God gives it life. Your spirit is like a broken radio receiving only partial signals, and Christ has rewired the internal settings so that you can adequately receive the signals your heavenly Father is sending you. That is what happened when you surrendered and committed to Christ. You simply believed and trusted in Him and gave Him your life. He, in return, gave you eternal life. Jesus said that although you were born in the flesh, you needed to be born in the "spirit." **Your spirit had to be made alive toward God, connected to Him in order to hear the "life words" that your heavenly Father would speak to you and to have spiritual understanding to comprehend it.** Just like the powerful winds that blow upon this earth, they are invisible, yet we do feel their power and see their influence and effects upon the trees and the waves of the ocean. We even harness the wind and create electricity with it. It is a powerful source of energy that can be felt, cool entire deserts, and propel great windmills. **So is the power of the Holy Spirit! He lives inside you and changes your heart, soul, and mind. We cannot see Him, but we most certainly can feel the joy and peace He brings.**

John 3:16 (KJV) says, "For God so loved the world, that he gave his only begotten Son, that whosoever believeth in him should not perish, but have everlasting life."

Colossians 2:13 (NLT) says, "You were dead because of your sins and because your sinful nature was not yet cut away. Then God made you alive with Christ, for he forgave all our sins."

When you surrendered to God, you made Him Lord. You acknowledged your need for His control in your unmanageable life. Praise God! That is what you have done. That is why you are already growing and hearing what God has to say; it is being revealed to you through your spirit. Your spirit has come alive. It has been "born again." You now have a second chance at life, this time with the power of God and the ability to connect with Him spiritually.

Surrender is an act of repentance

Acts 3:19 (ESV) says, "Repent therefore, and turn back, that your sins may be blotted out."

Repentance means to have a change of mind, and turn from your sins. It is the act of turning from something. When you surrender your life to God, that's what you are doing: turning from a life of mistakes and bad choices. If you are turning to God, you are turning from something or someone else. It is having a change of mind, direction, and focus. Turning to God requires you to turn from acting independently from Him. It is admitting that you have lost your way and sought meaning and fulfillment on your own, independently from the one who created you. It is coming to the understanding that relying upon oneself for happiness without God is unsuccessful. I found out that all of my basic needs of acceptance, love, and fulfillment can only come from my Creator. That real joy and satisfaction come from within through the gift of God's presence and direction. When rebellion, sin, and the pride of independent behavior leave you empty, hurting, and clinically depressed, it is God, and only God, who knows you intricately and has uniquely designed you, that can fix you. It is my testimony that God gave me true value and purpose and healed my brokenness when I repented, or had a change of mind and turned to God rather than away from Him.

Surrender: its full meaning in a person's life

Since I had known God as a young man, I knew what the word "surrender" meant and what it implied. The idea of repentance with all of its implications was not foreign to me. It meant to completely cease resistance to the authority of God and submit my will to Him and His eternal truth, the word of God. In doing that, I would now be free to live under the protection of God and His law, which set me free from the power of Satan, and mental anguish, so that I could pursue life again. The word surrender means to cease resistance to someone and submit to their authority. When General Douglas MacArthur officially accepted Japan's surrender on September 2, 1945, it meant that all fighting was over; Japan's war against America was over. It also meant that their government and its rule over its people had ended. They had to submit entirely, completely, and wholeheartedly to the United States Government.

We now had complete control over them. Of course, we were a

good nation with good intentions, and we respected them. We even helped them rebuild their war-battered country. It is the same with God. He is in the restoration and recovery business. But first, you must give Him total authority and control. Once He is in control of your thoughts and actions, He becomes a partner in your success. When your actions are God-directed, they become His responsibility. He has all power. All of heaven is now making sure you will succeed. You must be like Japan. They could have rebelled and not let us help them in the reconstruction of their nation, but they didn't. They allowed General MacArthur and the allied forces to occupy their territory and make political and social reforms to help establish a free and open democratic nation. To surrender means that you cease all fighting with God and totally submit to His will and authority.

To surrender is to be humble

James 4:10 (NLT) says, "Humble yourselves before the Lord, and he will lift you up in honor."

James 1:5-8 (KJV) says, "If any of you lack wisdom, let him ask of God, that giveth to all men liberally, and upbraideth not; and it shall be given him. But let him ask in faith, nothing wavering. For he that wavereth is like a wave of the sea driven with the wind and tossed. For let not that man think that he shall receive any thing of the Lord. A double minded man is unstable in all his ways."

Surrendering involves submitting yourself unto God in humility and placing a higher value on God's ability and wisdom. All you have to do is be humble. Being humble is acknowledging that you need your heavenly Father's help. **Humility recognizes your own weaknesses and has a modest view of your ability and sense of importance. Coming to God in need opens the door for Him to lift you up in honor. It is a realization of your**

need for God's power and wisdom. Dr. Murdock said in one of his teachings, "You can have an experience with God and not have the expertise of God." Humility will cause one to seek God's expertise in all their affairs. What good would having an experience with God, no matter how wonderful it might be, without having the expertise of God in your life that could manage your unmanageable life back to a place of wholeness? To just have an experience and not know how to keep it and grow from there? He went on to say, "The purpose of the expertise of God is to protect your experience with God." When I heard this, I knew God was talking to me. A true surrender is humble enough to accept God's wisdom or expertise in your life. If you are not humbly receiving God's word and instructions on how to live, you haven't really surrendered.

If you prayed with me, then you must humbly ask God for wisdom to protect your experience. Wisdom is the expertise, skill, and knowledge of God. **Humility is what opens the door to wisdom.** If you ask in faith, He will show you how. James says to ask in faith, expecting God to give you the wisdom you need. It shouldn't be that hard to believe. Why not have faith? **You have believed in a lot of people and principles that were not as reliable or credible.** You have doubted God for a long time now and doubted His word. That means you have placed your faith somewhere else. Where has that gotten you? Why not be humble and just believe? How could expectation in God's word hurt you?

Your expectation in the people around you possesses a high potential for risk, yet you do it. Why? Because of the potential for reward. The potential for reward is far greater with God. People continually let you down. Even when you get to a place where your level of expectation is diminished, you keep on trying. You do it, because of the value that others add to your life, even though they are not perfect. I'm just saying, give God a legitimate chance. Just being humble enough to ask God for His wisdom is the first step toward recovery. Your faith will bring stability and consistency. Faith drives out all fear. Faith will allow you to ask God for help and wisdom. When you surrender in humility asking God for the wisdom of His expertise, He will freely give it.

Surrender is an attitude

Psalm 37:7-9 (GW) says, "Surrender yourself to the LORD, and wait patiently for him. Do not be preoccupied with {an evildoer} who succeeds in his way when he carries out his schemes. Let go of anger, and leave rage behind. Do not be preoccupied. It only leads to evil. Evildoers will be cut off {from their inheritance}, but those who wait with hope for the LORD will inherit the land."

So, God's Word says, when we surrender, we must let go of anger, and our mind must not be preoccupied with negative thoughts of others. We must have an attitude that puts our hope in God. God tells us that a person who has the right attitude and puts his trust in God will inherit His promises, and acquire land. Land is symbolic of material wealth and prosperity.

Surrendering to God means forsaking a negative attitude and trusting Him. It means to rest from your way of thinking, forsaking anger and fretting over the outcome. That's God's responsibility. It means that after you have done the right thing to be still and wait for God to come through. Anger, worry, and faithlessness lead back to evil-doing and addiction. Once hopelessness sets in, giving up becomes easy. That "I don't care" attitude leads right back to drug use. Why not? Nothing is ever going to change. Why not use again? It's all I have left. But the word of God says that if you wait, even if it looks bad, you will inherit what God has promised. You must have the attitude of a person who has surrendered all of your anxiety and cares to the Lord your God. Your attitude should be one that surrenders the outcome to God.

1 Peter 5:7 (NLT) says, "Give all your worries and cares to God, for he cares about you."

Surrender is not inactivity

James 1:22-23 (NLT) says, "But don't just listen to God's word. You must do what it says. Otherwise, you are only fooling yourselves. For if you listen to the word and don't obey, it is like glancing at your face in a mirror."

James 2:14-20 (KJV) says, "What doth it profit, my brethren, though a man say he hath faith, and have not works? can faith save him? If a brother or sister be naked, and destitute of daily food, And one of you say unto them, depart in peace, be ye warmed and filled; notwithstanding ye give them not those things which are needful to the body; what doth it profit? Even so, faith, if it hath not works, is dead, being alone. Yea, a man may say, thou hast faith, and I have works: shew me thy faith without thy works, and I will shew thee my faith by my works. Thou believest that there is one God; thou doest well: the devils also believe, and tremble. But wilt thou know, O vain man, that faith without works is dead?"

You might ask how surrendering to God requires action? **The very concept of surrendering implies the act of compliance. It is the act of yielding, and conforming to God. It is a willingness to submit, in obedience, to who you have surrendered when it necessitates it. It requires an effort on your part.** It doesn't require perfection, talent, skill, or above average intelligence—just action. The ability to act on His word when you surrender. If you fail to act, God has nothing to bless! All you must do is follow His instructions. Just have the ability to let go of your way of doing things, and cooperate with your heavenly Father. God can only bless an effort. Where there is no effort, there are no miracles. James said that if you don't act, it is like looking in the mirror and seeing yourself, but the person who cooperates with God in his behavior and actions sees God when they look in the mirror. You see a person living and acting as God would.

When God is in control of your actions, He becomes responsible for their consequences. You become His servant and laborer. He then rewards you. He guarantees your success. After all, God would never be involved in an unsuccessful venture. You must ask God to lead you in your everyday life. Spend time alone, in His presence, reading His word, and listening for His voice. The Holy Spirit will immediately start dealing with you about your moral behavior. God will begin teaching you time management, putting first things first, and living one moment at a time. If you are willing to change, God will bless you! If you see God in your actions, and **looking in the mirror reminds you of the progress you have made, then you are looking at a success story in the making.**

Surrender requires patience

James 1:4 (AMP) says, "But let endurance and steadfastness and patience have full play and do a thorough work, so that you may be [people] perfectly and fully developed [with no defects], lacking in nothing."

Hebrews 10:36 (KJV) says, "For ye have need of patience, that, after ye have done the will of God, ye might receive the promise."

I surrendered all my time to God. It belonged to Him. A true surrender requires you to give God your time and put all things in His hands and schedule. I still do not get in a hurry to do anything. I always wait on God. Even when writing this book. I waited until the Holy Spirit completely birthed it in my spirit. If you can stay humble and patient, God will restore everything that you lost while you were in bondage to Satan and his control under sin. Patience is to endure, to persevere, to continue in the course of action with success coming in small doses. It is the capacity to accept delay, or to tolerate delay, without getting upset or angry. It is basically surrendering "time" to God. I had lived so long doing things my way, trying to get things done on my own schedule, that I was glad to let go and let God. When I surrendered, I surrendered my worries. I started enjoying life. The results would no longer be in my hands and control. They would be placed where they belonged, in a safe, reliable place, God!

Surrender with patience equals freedom and enjoyment! Time with God will complete you, fully develop you, and bring you to a place of no need. Needy people are people that have unmet desires and are filled with doubts about what the future will bring. They are not living in the presence of God. God is the only one that can fulfill your desires and complete you. After you have been thoroughly equipped, God will bless you. You will be the beneficiary of all of His promises.

You have to remember I was in jail the first few days of my essential surrendering to God. Wherever you might be, just sit back and take pleasure in this time with God. It is going to be the most rewarding experience of your life. I still think of that year I spent sleeping on a borrowed couch as the most wonderful and precious time of my life. I remember when God delivered me. I was fresh out of jail. It took eleven months before I could move on with my life. I prayed and read the word of God continually. My closest friend and only friend opened his home to me in Houston. God had this planned. It was a divine appointment. My friend was not a Christian at the time, but God was speaking to him, and he didn't even know it. He knew I needed privacy and protection. He even told my girlfriend, Jennifer, I had died. Of course, I didn't know he did it at the time. I found out a couple of days later.

But in reality, I had died; I was a new man. The old guy, full of addiction and pain, was gone. I had a special peace with me. Nothing else mattered. I had no need. For the first time in many years, I was happy. I loved my girlfriend, but I did not hurt without her. Did you hear that? My love for God was stronger than any other need I had. When God was ready, I moved on. What God did for me was nothing short of a miracle. He later saved my girlfriend and my best friend. I married her, and my best friend is on my board of directors. God is now using all of us in a great way to help people from all over the world. All because I waited. If God did it for me or any other person, He will do it for you. There is no favoritism with God.

Romans 2:11 (AMP) says, "For God shows no partiality [undue favor or unfairness]; with Him one man is not different from another."

Patience is the ability to wait without panic. To be able to endure suffering and hardship so that you can receive the promises of God. Patience is a blessing from God. It is a product that comes from abiding in Christ.

John 15:5 (KJV) says, "I am the vine, ye are the branches: He that abideth in me, and I in him, the same bringeth forth much fruit: for without me ye can do nothing."

Abiding in fellowship with Jesus produces spiritual fruit. Fellowship is being open and friendly with Jesus in conversation, having shared interests, goals, likes, and dislikes, to work with each other in open dialog. When there is a lack of fellowship with Jesus, your life will lose the ability to connect to your life source of patience. Fellowship makes waiting easy. Patience requires engaging with your heavenly Father. **It allows God time to develop strength and maturity in your life so that He can fulfill His promises in you.**

2

COMMITMENT

METHADDICTSHELP, FACEBOOK POST
JANUARY 10, 2016

SO IF YOU JUDGED ME RIGHT...YOU WOULD HAVE HAD TO BE PROPHETIC , OR FILLED WITH FAITH IN THE POWER OF CHRIST....AT ONE TIME I HAD BEEN MARRIED A LONG TIME THEN DIVORCED, AND THEN MARRIED AGAIN FOR 2 WEEKS AND TO LEAVE FOR CIGARETTES TO NEVER COME BACK....TO BE STRONGLY HOOKED ON METH AND OTHER DRUG ADDICTIONS...LOSING MY HOME TWICE...BEING HOMELESS, JOBLESS, STRUNG OUT SLEEPING IN PARKING LOTS, ARRESTED MANY TIMES, ACCUMULATING 11 FELONY CHARGES, INVOLVED IN ILLEGAL ACTIVITIES, SURROUNDED BY VIOLENCE AND BEING VIOLENT, WAKING UP WITH WOMEN THAT I DIDN'T EVEN KNOW , BEING SO HIGH THAT I HAD TO BE WATCHED AND LED AROUND LIKE A CHILD, PARTYING FOR MONTHS , STAYING IN $4,000 NIGHT ROOMS , AND CLOSING DOWN STRIP CLUBS, TO BE BROKE THE NEXT DAY , AND THEN FRESH OUT OF JAIL WALKING DOWN THE ROAD WITH NO RIDE , NO PHONE, NO MONEY...BUT THIS TIME WITH THE MIRACLE

WORKING POWER OF JESUS.....AND IN JUST 2 YEARS' TIME WITH HIS HELP , BECOMING A SOURCE OF HELPING PEOPLE AROUND THE WORLD AND A BLESSING TO EVERYONE AROUND ME IS PHENOMENAL..... LIVING DEBT FREE, AND BECOMING THE FOUNDER OF METHADDICTSHELP, AND PRESIDENT OF RECOVERY MINISTRIES, IN WHICH WE HELP ADDICTS FREE OF CHARGE...AMAZING GRACE !!.... I BELIEVE THIS COULD BE YOU ...MESSAGE US FOR PRAYER............TPC. (UNEDITED)

122,412 PEOPLE REACHED

4,100 LIKES

964 SHARES

503 COMMENTS

After my surrender to Christ, I pulled into a car wash and fell asleep. Then, after being awakened by a police officer, I was booked and put in jail. I knew I was going to be there a long time. I knew no one would bail me out, and I felt like I deserved prison. I was alone. But something was different. I did not have anxiety and unrest. Also, I did not hurt inside. I was different. I felt that God was with me in that empty jail cell. I fell asleep immediately. The next morning when I awakened, I started to feel uneasy and worried. I was not allowed a phone call. I also did not know which warrants they had used to arrest me. I didn't know my charges, which could range from a host of illegal activities. I did not even know if they found the drugs in my used BMW. I had seen them search it with a fine-tooth comb, but didn't know anything else. I was dealing with a lot of uncertainty. I paced the floor nervously. I knew this time, there would be no get-out-of-jail-free card, and I would probably wind up in prison. Trouble filled my mind and spirit.

The negative thoughts were taking over when, in my spirit, like from the pit of my stomach, I heard God speaking to me. He said, **"Tim, you have surrendered to my will. Now you must** commit to me with all of your heart and follow me completely. If you will do this, I will restore everything in your life that sin and the devil have stolen from you." At that point, a visual movie started playing in my head. It was my life and all the mistakes, sins, and perversion that were in it. All my past popped up before me. The countless people that I had hurt, all my broken promises, wasted opportunities, drug dealing, my violent behavior, the sex, the anger, and the bitterness was playing on a giant screen in my mind. **The sense of entitlement and the feeling that God was somehow at fault left immediately, and I began to feel extreme sorrow and regret.**

2 Corinthians 7:10 (KJV) says, "For godly sorrow worketh repentance to salvation not to be repented of: but the sorrow of the world worketh death."

God's gift to every human is the ability to have regret and sorrow. It is what leads us to do the right thing. Sorrow and regret are a part of commitment, and so is the biblical term repentance. The biblical term repentance means to turn or have a change of mind. To turn and go in a completely different direction. Commitment is a decision to turn from your old life and turn to God. Real sorrow from God isn't tormenting, it just gives incentives, or the motive and power to commit, to turn from your old life and commit to your new one in Christ.

I immediately fell to my knees and committed my life to Christ completely. I told God I would live in prison as a Godly man, and I would be a witness for Him as long as He saw fit. At that very moment, the peace of God filled me as I sat in that tiny cell. I was ok. I put it all back in God's hands. My faith became a living reality.

Abraham Lincoln said, "Commitment is what transforms a promise into reality." A surrender will not last very long without a commitment. Soon, your surrender will be tested. You will be tested by adversity, Satan, and human weakness. You must make a choice. Either you will commit, or you will return to your old patterns of self-destruction through addiction and humanistic ideas. The choice was easy for me. What about you? As in my Facebook post above, I didn't stay in jail or go to prison. I was in jail for a total of 17 days. On my fifteenth night, I dreamed I was getting out and being released. I awakened that morning feeling light-headed and excited. I knew God had given me a confirmation that I was going to be released. I thought it would be at any moment. I went through the day waiting with expectation, but it didn't happen. I told the guys in my cell God was going to work a miracle. I went to bed with that same expectation. It just would not go away. I showered and shaved thinking it could be any minute.

The next morning after breakfast, they came and picked me up for court. I appeared before the judge around one o'clock. In shackles, chains, and handcuffs. Just like that, I was standing before the judge hearing him set a future court date for me. Then, I was released on my own recognizance. I did not even have to post bail. I was a free man. My court case lasted about a year and a half. But eventually, after the testing of my faith, God worked several miracles on my behalf, and all my charges were dropped. I am in tears as I write this. The goodness of God is overwhelming. My own story still moves me tremendously. That was the third court battle I had faced. God saved me just in time.

I often think what could have happened to me if I had not committed my life to God that first morning in that jail cell all alone. Maybe you too are being tested. **Why don't you make this day your first day of commitment? Just settle the issue once and for all. I am going to serve God. Just pray with me right here and now. Just tell God you are committing to serve Him with all your heart and have His peace and blessings always and forever!**

Commitment: its meaning and full implications

Commitment is the act of pledging or binding yourself to a person or course of action. Just like in the commitment of marriage, it is becoming a dedicated follower of Christ, an imitator of Christ. A true disciple. Committed to Christ simply means He becomes your priority. Following Him means if He would not go there, you wouldn't. If He would not commit fornication or lie, you would not either, and so on. It is putting God first before all other things in your life. **An unknown writer said that commitment is doing the thing you said you were going to do long after the mood you said it in has left you.** A good comparison of commitment in an average person's life would be their career. Mood has nothing to do with the decision to go to work or not. Most people know what it means to be committed to a job.

Being committed to God works the same way. Except your commitment to God is 24 hours a day. When you are committed to a job, you are there when they need you, and you arrive at the time they need you to be there. Your punctuality matters. It is the same with God. When God needs you, you are a willing candidate. Good employees leave their personal problems at home and keep it professional at work. They make a concentrated effort while at work not to let anything interfere with their productivity. **If we are to be dedicated followers of Christ, we must also put our self-interest secondary to God's.** A dedicated employee makes sure he completes every project on time and follows orders. He also takes the initiative in going the extra mile if a project needs it. It means you are always trying to better your performance, critically analyzing your ability, and always trying to improve. That's exactly how I view my relationship with God. My heart is to do the best I can. **I always give God my best effort. He deserves it.**

Remember, God isn't concerned with the outcome, but the effort. He looks at the heart. He isn't looking for talent, ability, or performance as much as He is looking for someone to show up, and do their best. God has the best reward system ever. He looks inside the heart. While everyone else emphasizes performance, God knows who is giving it their best. Even when other people may seem more qualified or more gifted than you, **God only rewards according to effort and sincerity. That gives every one of us a fair advantage at succeeding.**

1 Samuel 16:7 (KJV) says, "But the LORD said unto Samuel, look not on his countenance, or on the height of his stature; because I have refused him: for the LORD seeth not as man seeth; for man looketh on the outward appearance, but the LORD looketh on the heart."

When God told Samuel to look for the next king of Israel, He told him not to look at outward appearance. God would choose him by what He saw in his heart. And of course, God made the right choice. The youngest son was chosen, the one taking care of his father's sheep, about his father's business. That was King David.

Commitment requires never giving up

Galatians 6:9 (NIV2011) says, "Let us not become weary in doing good, for at the proper time we will reap a harvest if we do not give up."

John 15:7 (NIV2011) says, "If you remain in me and my words remain in you, ask whatever you wish, and it will be done for you."

Jesus said that if you remain in Him, if you stay with Him or be committed, then you can ask what you will. Nowhere in God's word does it say He will reward a lack of dedication and devotion. The requirement for the reward and blessing of God in your life is dedication, devotion, steadfastness, loyalty, faithfulness, and commitment. There will be times when you feel like quitting and giving up. But if you persevere, God will bless you phenomenally. If you do not give up, you will reap a harvest. Reaping a harvest is the same as getting paid for your hard work and effort. The effort required is to have enough faith in God, to be obedient. To keep doing good. You will reap great benefits in the natural as well as the spiritual realm, if you do not give up. A continual commitment to God and His word brings a harvest. So many people quit on the threshold of a miracle harvest. Be careful that you don't give up right before your miracle is manifested, and you lose out with God. Some of you are presently going through circumstances created by your past life in addiction. If you relax, stay committed, and continue doing the right things, the blessing of God will come.

I had all kinds of legal fines, court fines and penalties to pay, and many other things that could have made me give up. But I didn't. I had things that happened between my family and I that bothered me, and said things to people I shouldn't have. These things could have caused me enough anxiety and stress that I would have given up. But I just let go and let God take care of it. I kept doing the right thing, and God handled everything else for me. Fines were paid, I was able to buy a truck, and in time, God reunited me with my family. Jesus said that if you remain, or stay in His word and you keep His word in you, whatever you ask or wish, He will give it to you. It's like God handing you a blank check, signed and authorized by Him, just waiting for you to write the amount that you need in the blank. All you have to do is never quit, just remain in Him, keeping His words in you alive.

Commitment releases heaven's blessings

Psalm 37:4-5 (NLT) says, "Take delight in the LORD, and he will give you your heart's desires. Commit everything you do to the LORD. Trust him, and he will help you."

When you commit everything you do to please God, He

cannot help but feel compassion towards you. He becomes interested in your most sincere desires and longings and fulfills them. All of your dreams become possible. Everything your heart has longed for is now within your reach.

Commitment to God cures conflict

Proverbs 16:7 (KJV) says, "When a man's ways please the LORD, he maketh even his enemies to be at peace with him."

James 1:19-20 (KJV) says, "Wherefore, my beloved brethren, let every man be swift to hear, slow to speak, slow to wrath: For the wrath of man worketh not the righteousness of God."

Being obedient in the words you speak and the emotions you let control you will eliminate conflict completely. When a man is committed to pleasing God, it has a far-reaching impact on those around him, even his enemies. It even affects the way your enemies view you. Even if they don't like you, they will respect you enough to be at peace with you. In my last court case, it seemed like God was in the courtroom with me. I knew the judge did not like me, yet at the last moment, he gave me leniency. By the expression on his face, it seemed like even he was surprised at the words that came out of his own mouth.

Commitment produces good things

Psalm 84:11 (KJV) says, "For the LORD God is a sun and shield: the LORD will give grace and glory: no good thing will he withhold from them that walk uprightly."

All a man or woman must do in this life to become a success is to walk in the ways of God. God wants to provide good things for His children. Everything that you need and more. A lovely home and automobile, money for food and clothing, money to help you with your college education, a wonderful companion in life and any good thing that is missing, God will not withhold it from you.

3

COMMUNICATING RELATIONSHIP

 METHADDICTSHELP, FACEBOOK POST

FEBRUARY 26, 2017

BEHIND EVERY CRAVING TO GET HIGH IS A VERY REAL NEED EXPOSED. I KNEW I WAS AN ADDICT BY THE WAY I FELT WHEN I WAS SOBER. THERE ARE SO MANY UNMET NEEDS IN ALL OF US. MOST OF THEM ARE EXPOSED THROUGH DIFFERENT TYPES OF ADDICTIONS AND PHYSICAL DISORDERS. THE BIBLE SAYS, " MY GOD SHALL SUPPLY ALL YOUR NEED ACCORDING TO HIS RICHES IN GLORY BY CHRIST JESUS." THE NEED FOR LOVE AND COMPANIONSHIP. THE NEED FOR FOOD AND CLOTHING. NEEDS FOR ASSURANCE, STRENGTH, COURAGE, FAITH, JOY, HAPPINESS AND MOST OF ALL FULFILLMENT ARE BLESSINGS THAT COME FROM A RELATIONSHIP WITH GOD. IF YOU NEED PRAYER OR ENCOURAGEMENT, PLEASE MESSAGE US...TPC. (UNEDITED)

221,209 PEOPLE REACHED

11,000 LIKES

2,870 SHARES

881 COMMENTS

*Y*our new life in God satisfies your longing for companionship and fulfillment. God now dwells in you. You now have a source of living water to draw from that reaches into all other human relationships, a completeness and sense of belonging to draw from.

Hebrews 13:5 (KJV) says, "For He hath said, "I will never leave thee, nor forsake thee.""

Your new life of surrender and commitment leads you into a special relationship with God. It is a relationship filled with dialogue and wonderful communication. No relationship can be developed where there is inadequate communication. The most important aspect of surrendering and committing to Christ is that He now becomes your greatest companion and friend. What happened to me was extraordinary. I immediately began talking and having a conversation with Jesus. It started in that tiny jail cell. The greatest surprise and most astonishing aspect of the conversation is that He talked back to me that morning. I heard Him speak in my spirit, and what was astonishing was that I could recognize His voice. In one of the most stressful times in my life, His voice gave me direction and brought peace to my troubled mind and heart.

I know that in the secular world, and in most people's minds, that seems impossible. But if you think about it, you have been hearing Him speak all your life. You have just been deprioritizing it for a long time. It is not that there are no inward voices, but you have just been listening to the wrong voices speaking in your mind and heart. Your human thoughts and Satan's thoughts have been dominating and drowning out the one true compass of your Creator—His voice. God has been speaking to you from the very first day you were born into this world.

John 1:9 (NKJV) says, "That was the true Light which gives light to every man coming into the world."

That light is the voice of your conscience. God has always

talked to you in a very limited way. But you have gone another way, listening and serving yourself and Satan's tempting destructive voice. Satan's voice is one filled with temptation to do things that even you know are wrong. Your voice is a rational one that collects information and decides what appeals to you, and then you do it. Satan's voice comes to you through your intellect and mind. God speaks through your belly, from the very pit of your gut or your spirit. Think about it; would Satan have told you to get this book? Would you have gone out of your way and started reading and studying this book if you had not heard that still, small and gentle voice deep in your gut? It was God who initiated this conversation. It was He urging you to get this book. You see you have been hearing from Him. How wonderful is that?

God tried to prevent you from doing drugs and alcohol before you tried it the first time, but you rationalized the temptation in your head and listened to the wrong voice when you considered it. You rationalized in your mind that it would make you happy or feel good. You justified it by saying, "All my friends are doing this, and they like it; one time won't hurt me; it must be safe, they do it, and none of them have gone to jail, or have had an accident, or have been hospitalized." But deep in your gut, there was a still, small voice telling you not to do it. Every wrong decision we make is a result of listening and choosing the wrong counsel and advice.

I will never forget the day I started a conversation with Jesus. I now wake up every morning and start a conversation with the greatest friend and companion I have ever had—Jesus. I talk to Him all day long. He is a friend that I take with me everywhere. I owe all my success, prosperity, and happiness to talking and listening to Him. Just pray with me as we initiate a conversation with God. Start talking to Him in a personal way from your heart. I believe you will begin to feel His wonderful peace and presence.

Say out loud with me, **"Jesus, I give you my day today and everything in it. Lead me and guide me today in all my decisions. Help me to love the people I meet today and see their** vulnerability. Help me forgive and live in forgiveness. I trust you and want to thank you for loving me so much, and setting me free from myself, addiction, depression, and taking care of me when I make a mistake or need your strength and power. Thank you for watching over me, having my best interest at heart, and having my back. And even when things seem impossible, I thank you for making a way for me financially and restoring my family to a place of health. Thank you, heavenly Father, for sending your Son into my life and forgiving me for all of my mistakes and the sins that I have committed against you, others, and myself. You are so good to me and having you with me is the greatest thing that has ever happened to me. Thank you, Father, in Jesus name, amen."

Don't you feel a load lifted? If you didn't, slow down and meditate on the words of that conversation with God. Then say them again, slower, and with all of your heart. The peace and restful presence of God will come. That is how I speak with God every day, all day long.

Communicating relationship defined

I know the phrase communicating relationship is an unusual combination of words being used here. To be frank with you, I have never heard them being used together like this myself. But that is how I heard these words being used in my spirit. That is why you see them used this way. The word "communicate" means to convey information, to impart and make known, to have an interchange of ideas and be connected with one another. The word relationship is the coming together of two people or parties by the way they are related to each other. By association of blood, kinship, or marriage. It usually implies an emotional bond and connection between people. It could be a romantic involvement or friendship. You may have a weak relationship, or you may have a strong relationship. Relationships are strengthened by good communication and conversation, work, and commitment. When the lines of communication become weakened, the relationship can be in danger.

This idea is about communicating in the new relationship you have with God—a coming together of an exchange of ideas, wants, and needs of each other. God has a desire to talk with you and develop a relationship with you. You have a longing to talk to your heavenly Father. It is the one thing that can complete your existence. This is all accomplished through Christ, as He reconciled us to the Father through shedding His blood on the cross in our place for our transgressions. We are righteous through Him. We are now communicating with God in a relationship with Him and are in His family.

Romans 8:14 (KJV) says, "For as many as are led by the Spirit of God, they are the sons of God."

A communicating relationship is bilateral

Revelation 3:20 (KJV) says, "Behold, I stand at the door, and knock: if any man hear my voice, and open the door, I will come in to him, and will sup with him, and he with me."

Your new relationship with God is not a one-sided affair. It is not just one person doing all the talking and listening. But it is a bilateral relationship. It is two-sided. Jesus said that He is standing at the door of your heart knocking today. If you open that door, He will come in your heart and talk with you. Notice the grammar is present tense. **He is at this moment, right now, and for always, ever present, and ready to talk and listen.** He says we can sit and share a meal together anytime. That's what the word "sup" means. God is talking to you right now, it is like a light bulb, and someone just turned the switch on.

A communicating relationship is residential

John 14:23 (NLT) says, Jesus replied, "All who love me will do what I say. My Father will love them, and we will come and make our home with each of them."

The word "residential" means designed for people to live in. We were designed for God to live within us. That is the most distinguishing and unique aspect of our relationship with God. Jesus said that if we loved God and followed through with our commitment by being obedient, then He and His Father would come and make their home in us. They would permanently stay with us, be our most intimate companions the rest of our lives. We take God with us everywhere we go. Your physical home has a climate, an atmosphere that is set by the occupants. Now your spiritual home's climate and atmosphere are filled with God's love, peace, strength, and power. Just like any home's characteristics take on the owner's and dweller's personality, so does your spiritual one.

A communicating relationship is progressive

2 Peter 3:18 (AMP) says, "But grow in grace (undeserved favor, spiritual strength) and recognition and knowledge and understanding of our Lord and Savior Jesus Christ (the Messiah). To Him [be] glory (honor, majesty, and splendor) both now and to the day of eternity. Amen (so be it)!"

The good news is your relationship has the potential for growing into the supernatural knowledge of God. You are tapped in and seated in heavenly places with God. You have unlimited access to the executive board room of the Creator of the universe.

2 Peter 1:5-8 (NKJV) says, "But also for this very reason, giving all diligence, add to your faith virtue, to virtue knowledge, to knowledge self-control, to self-control perseverance, to perseverance godliness, to godliness brotherly kindness, and to brotherly kindness love. For if these things are yours and abound, you will be neither barren nor unfruitful in the knowledge of our Lord Jesus Christ."

There is so much more that God wants to add to you that will make you strong. If you will talk to Him, He will take you from a place of addiction, helplessness, and vulnerability to a position of faith, courage, productivity, and success. The further you get along in this book the more God is going to reveal His unlimited resources of strength and power to you. Unlimited resources, unlimited accessibility, and unlimited growth are now within your reach. These things come from God's presence within you.

A communicating relationship gives you the power to ask what you will

John 15:7 (KJV) says, "If ye abide in me, and my words abide in you, ye shall ask what ye will, and it shall be done unto you."

When you are involved in any conversation with a devoted friend, it would not seem unusual for you to feel free to ask anything of them. God is a friend that loves you far beyond any other friend you will ever have. He proved that love by sending His Son to die for you before you were ever born just so your relationship with Him could be restored. Certainly, you can ask for whatever you want and anything you need and He will provide it.

Biblical guidelines for prayer

We first come to our heavenly Father through the mighty name of Jesus who is our advocate.

John 14:13 (KJV) says, "And whatsoever ye shall ask in my name, that will I do, that the Father may be glorified in the Son."

It is through that name from which all prayer must come to reach our heavenly Father.

1 Timothy 2:5-6 (KJV) says, "For there is one God, and one mediator between God and men, the man Christ Jesus; Who gave himself a ransom for all, to be testified in due time."

There is one mediator, go-between, or arbitrator between man and God, Jesus.

John 14:6 (KJV) says, "Jesus saith unto him, I am the way, the truth, and the life: no man cometh unto the Father, but by me."

We come to our heavenly Father through the only gate to His pasture: Jesus.

John 10:7 (KJV) says, "Then said Jesus unto them again, Verily, verily, I say unto you, I am the door of the sheep."

Jesus is the path and our advocate with the Father. He is the person that recommends us to the Father. He is the advocate and champion of our cause.

1 John 2:1 (KJV) says, "My little children, these things write I unto you, that ye sin not. And if any man sin, we have an advocate with the Father, Jesus Christ the righteous."

Jesus tells us that if we ask anything of the Father in His name, it guarantees opportunity and success.

John 15:16 (KJV) says, "Ye have not chosen me, but I have chosen you, and ordained you, that ye should go and bring forth fruit, and that your fruit should remain: that whatsoever ye shall ask of the Father in my name, he may give it you."

Our protocol and access to our heavenly Father are through the name of Jesus. There is great authority and power in that name.

Mark 16:17-18 (KJV) says, "And these signs shall follow them that believe; In my name shall they cast out devils; they shall speak with new tongues; They shall take up serpents; and if they drink any deadly thing, it shall not hurt them; they shall lay hands on the sick, and they shall recover."

All salvation and forgiveness of sins comes through that name.

Luke 24:46-47 (KJV) says, "And said unto them, Thus it is written, and thus it behoved Christ to suffer, and to rise from the dead the third day: And that repentance and remission of sins should be preached in his name among all nations, beginning at Jerusalem."

Second, we must come in worship and praise knowing that He is God our Father and our friend. When Jesus taught us to pray, He said our first approach and opening should be one of honor, worship, and praise to God - Hallowed be thy name. We are also called friends of God as faithful Abraham the father of faith. We come to Him with the knowledge of His greatness and honor Him as our Father and respect Him as our closest friend.

Matthew 6:9 (KJV) says, "After this manner therefore pray ye: Our Father which art in heaven, Hallowed be thy name."

James 2:23 (KJV) says, "And the scripture was fulfilled which saith, Abraham believed God, and it was imputed unto him for righteousness: and he was called the Friend of God."

Romans 8:15 (KJV) says, "For ye have not received the spirit of bondage again to fear; but ye have received the Spirit of adoption, whereby we cry, Abba, Father."

Third, He also said that we should come in humility from sincere desire, from the secret place of our heart, and not out of pride and insincere motives. He did not say that we were not to pray publicly, just not publicly to be seen of men. He encourages us to have a place to pray, alone with Him, such as a closet.

Everyone should find such a place to honor God in—one with no distractions.

Matthew 6:5-6 (KJV) says, "And when thou prayest, thou shalt not be as the hypocrites are: for they love to pray standing in the synagogues and in the corners of the streets, that they may be seen of men. Verily I say unto you, They have their reward. But thou, when thou prayest, enter into thy closet, and when thou hast shut thy door, pray to thy Father which is in secret; and thy Father which seeth in secret shall reward thee openly."

Fourth, Jesus told us not to use vain repetitions in our prayers. He did not say we could not repeat certain prayers but used the word "vain" repetitious prayers. Jesus used the word to describe the repetitious chanting of prayers that sound like stuttering or stammering. He taught the disciples to pray instead in clear, concise expressions that communicate worship, submission, supplication, confession, and praise. God wants to hear from our heart, and if we are praying and we do not even understand the words we are using, what good would that accomplish? No one benefits from communication that has no real intent or desire within it. The more intimate we are when talking to God, the stronger your relationship with Him becomes. The mere reciting of prayers, as one kneeling before a statue repeating a thousand memorized prayers, annoys God. Kneeling before statues and idols made with human hands, while reciting repetitious prayers, is not what God desires. It was one of the first laws of recognition found in the Bible and is listed in the Ten Commandments.

Exodus 20:3-5 (KJV) says, "Thou shalt have no other gods before me. Thou shalt not make unto thee any graven image, or any likeness of anything that is in heaven above, or that is in the earth beneath, or that is in the water under the earth: Thou shalt not bow down thyself to them, nor serve them: for I the LORD thy God am a jealous God, visiting the iniquity of the fathers upon the children unto the third and fourth generation of them that hate me."

God desires love and fellowship. Idols do not speak and are not caring, personal, and warming in any way. They are stone, wood, clay, metal, and mortar. They have no mind or heart. Chanting memorized prayers is also a form of penance, not love. Jesus provided our penance; all the penance we will ever need is found in Him and having faith in Him and His name.

Matthew 6:7 (KJV) says, "But when ye pray, use not vain repetitions, as the heathen do: for they think that they shall be heard for their much speaking."

Fifth, Jesus taught us to be specific, to ask about our daily provision and pray that His will be done in our lives, which includes deliverance, healing, prosperity, obedience, and service. He told us to be specific about our temptations and the evil we face. We are to be personal with Him about all our needs. What is your daily bread? Each day we face will have a different set of needs that come with it. We must be specific about our daily needs, humbly bringing them all to God. We also must have a repentant heart, so that we can grow and mature in our relationship with God. Asking God to deliver you from temptation, is a form of remorse and sorrow for getting off the path. It is asking God to keep you from ever walking down that path again or being tempted to.

Matthew 6:11-13 (KJV) says, "Give us this day our daily bread. And forgive us our debts, as we forgive our debtors. And lead us not into temptation, but deliver us from evil: For thine is the kingdom and the power, and the glory, forever. Amen."

Sixth, Jesus also taught us to pray in faith, believing that you will receive of Him, to have confidence and trust in your heavenly Father. Why wouldn't you have faith in someone who loves you, sent His Son to die for you, and is your Father and friend?

Mark 11:24 (KJV) says, "Therefore I say unto you, What things soever ye desire, when ye pray, believe that ye receive them, and ye shall have them."

Seventh, we must converse with God always, talking to him privately within our spirit throughout the day. Many times during my day, my thoughts get an interruption from my spirit with detailed insight and information critical to my assignment and to the welfare of myself and others. This awareness comes from the Holy Spirit. If you are constantly looking upward and listening to God, you will gain the most knowledgeable insight available in the universe.

Ephesians 6:18 (AMP) says, "Pray at all times (on every occasion, in every season) in the Spirit, with all [manner of] prayer and entreaty. To that end keep alert and watch with strong purpose and perseverance, interceding in behalf of all the saints (God's consecrated people)."

Matthew 6:33 (KJV) says, "But seek ye first the kingdom of God, and his righteousness; and all these things shall be added unto you."

Romans 14:17 (KJV) says, "For the kingdom of God is not meat and drink; but righteousness, and peace, and joy in the Holy Ghost."

John 15:7 (KJV) says, "If ye abide in me, and my words abide in you, ye shall ask what ye will, and it shall be done unto you."

John 14:26 (KJV) says, "But the Comforter, which is the Holy Ghost, whom the Father will send in my name, he shall teach you all things, and bring all things to your remembrance, whatsoever I have said unto you."

In the scriptures above, there is a prevailing theme of prayer and communication revealed to us in the most intimate fashion. First, we are to pray at all times. Second, we are to be seeking the kingdom of God first in everything we do. Third, we must recognize that the kingdom of God is spiritual and seek the peace of God in our lives by doing the right thing. Fourth, we do that by abiding and remaining in His presence through an open dialogue and conversation with Him. And fifth, this opens the door for our teacher the Holy Spirit to give us all the comfort and knowledge we need.

In conclusion, we must have disciplined sessions of prayer and time set aside to be spent alone with God without the distractions of other responsibilities and obligations. We must make our relationship with our heavenly Father the most honored, protected, and valued relationship in our lives. We must have intimate private sessions of deep conversation with Him, expressing our deepest desires and concerns, always wanting to please our greatest friend. We need not go to any other example of that kind of dedication other than Christ himself. If the Son of God needed this type of committed and disciplined prayer in His life, we most certainly do.

Morning Devotion: Mark 1:35 (KJV) says, "And in the morning, rising up a great while before day, he went out, and departed into a solitary place, and there prayed."

Evening Prayer: Mark 6:46-47 (KJV) says, "And when he had sent them away, he departed into a mountain to pray. And when even was come, the ship was in the midst of the sea, and he alone on the land."

Solitary Communion: Luke 5:16 (KJV) says, "And he withdrew himself into the wilderness, and prayed."

All-night prayer: Luke 6:12 (KJV) says, "And it came to pass in those days, that he went out into a mountain to pray, and continued all night in prayer to God."

4

MEANING AND PURPOSE

 Methaddictshelp, Facebook Post
November 21, 2016

I was tired of living in a fake reality and waking up in a real world with cold hard facts. The drugs I was using illegally could at any time destroy my freedom or life. I was living on borrowed time. Sure, they felt good, and created a false since of happiness...but even while increasing the dosage those moments of escape began to be shorter and shorter...At the same time it had isolated me from my family, and taken jobs from me. I had always drove a new truck every two years getting another one...now I was sitting in one 30 yrs. old and falling apart. My life as a drug addict began to destroy me as a person and steal my authentic identity. I was so glad to know that God had not forgotten me, and still loved me, and could change, protect, and restore me to a place of healing. We love you, and with every fabric of my being I reach out to you in kindness and *a*t some point in our life, regardless of how successful and prosperous we are, we all come to a fork or pivotal point in our journey where we conclude that life must mean more than just this. More than just supporting our family, building a business, and enjoying the pleasures of family and material possessions. More than entertainment. More than staying busy to keep from boredom. There has to be more meaning to my existence than arriving and then abruptly leaving. Where do we go after that? Will there be any rules in eternity? Will I live on in another form, or will I just cease to exist? Why even be moral or good if this is all there is? What makes me want to be decent and good even when I feel like doing wrong? Why are there people filled with hate? I hate sometimes, but something inside of me constrains me. What is it? We are filled with the possibility of God. Even the atheist starts with the premonition that one does not exist, proving that even he started with the idea of a Creator. So many questions. All of them answered in a fourth-dimensional experience when a man is born of the spirit through the redeeming power of the blood of Jesus Christ.

Before my spiritual awakening, I was completely lost. I awakened that morning (referenced in the post above) and was just a semblance of my old self, a gray shadow of the man I once was. I had become a thief, a fornicator, an adulterer, and was involved deeply in illegal activities. I had no respect for the law. I had my reasons. But at one time I was a good moral man who loved God. The reason so many of us use drugs and lose our way is because we feel emptiness in our lives. We may be going through some painful, hurtful experience, and our lives become meaningless. When the meaning and the reason, or the basis and the motive for living is missing, then a man or woman loses their purpose for living. If your reason for living is wrapped up in a person, place, or thing that will never have the characteristics of permanence, then you are in trouble. People can love you, but they do not live forever and do not always stay with you. If that is all you have in this life, then sooner or later you will lose your will to live.

If pleasure, prosperity, material possessions, friends, your wife or husband, or your children are what you live for, then one day, when that changes, you will lose your will for living, and your purpose will change. That was the case for me. But with so many others, it is just plain boredom. There are some people that will not settle for anything that doesn't offer an exciting, thrilling pace and sense of adventure. They have a zest for life, living on the edge. They were born to be different; they know it and just cannot settle for anything less. They have an identity problem. That zest and daring sense of adventure comes from God. It has to do with your true identity in God. We are born to stretch the limits of human expectation, and explore the realms of spiritual prominence in God. People will search for meaning in every place that appears inviting just to find something they feel inwardly connected to. They just don't know who they are. They will continue to search as long as possible.

Men flounder when they do not have a purpose. When there is no real overwhelming meaning and uniqueness to their individuality, they make huge mistakes. When you have no deep-seated calling to answer to, or great passion existing in your life, you experiment. You are willing to try anything. Without real purpose and meaning, there is no anchor to hold you steady and safe should you face a storm of adversity. People get fidgety, restless, and anxious when there is no real meaning in their lives. No addict will ever be completely free, or made whole again, without becoming who they were meant to be. Becoming their authentic self. If you have not found true meaning, your purpose can change. That is one of the most important statements you will read in this book: **If you have not found true meaning, your purpose can change.**

The addict's purpose for life gradually takes on a destructive pattern. The addict's purpose and goal is to have enough of his drug of choice to stay high and party, or stay high so that he can simply be able to function. He is your friend as long as he is able to get high. The sad thing about it is that he would like to be a good friend, but the quest for his drug of choice is more important. It becomes more important than his children, family, wife, work and everything else. He compromises everything of value in his life to stay high. I know this is true because I lived as an addict for a long time.

Victor Frankl, who survived the Nazi concentration camps, said, "There is nothing in the world, I venture to say, that so effectively helps one to survive even the worst conditions as the knowledge that there is a meaning in one's life." Everyone has a purpose. Someone's purpose might simply be to wake up and find a way to die. Why? Because they have no real meaning for living anymore. How did Frankl survive the Holocaust? Simple. He found real meaning in his existence. Prior to his deportation to Auschwitz, he was developing a new way to treat mental illness in his field of psychiatry. As he was expecting to be deported with his parents, he sat down and wrote a first draft of "The Doctor and the Soul." He thought that at least the essentials of the manuscript should survive him. Later, upon his arrival at Auschwitz, the manuscript was hidden, sewn into the lining of his overcoat. Keeping that manuscript from being destroyed gave him a divine purpose to meet every day with. It gave him a reason to live through the most extreme circumstances of personal pain and torture.

Even though he was a prisoner, he survived to protect a purpose greater than his own. He would survive so that the thousands of others in mental anguish would benefit from his life's work. He had considered his knowledge to be of great value, and at all cost, he must survive. **Abraham Lincoln said, "And in the end, it's not the years in your life that count. It's the life in your years."** In the death camps, camps of torture, deprivation, and human cruelty, God gave him a real sense of purpose and meaning. No one could take his dignity and self-respect from him. God had given him the freedom to be his authentic self. His internal strength and drive were God-given. How he implemented it was unique to him. He realized his eternal purpose. He alone took responsibility for his actions.

After losing the manuscript, he began to write another one using a stolen pencil on the back of pilfered small SS forms at significant risk. He had gained control of his life through meaning and value placed within himself that nothing could take away. He wrote another one in secret, risking his life for it. He lived in the freedom of his mind, even though his body was experiencing great affliction and torture. He would not give up. In this respect, he was still free, although a prisoner in the most notorious prison that has ever existed in the history of the world. His own destiny, self-worth, and meaning for his existence controlled him. It kept him alive during the Holocaust.

What is controlling you? Whatever controls your thoughts controls your destiny. If you have no real purpose for living, then nothing in life really matters. Without true meaning and real purpose, you lose your will to live. If you have no self-worth, then anything can destroy you. You are not living in true freedom. Freedom to grow, to excel, and to choose. When I had nothing to live for, my life became unmanageable. Out of control.

It took God to change that. It took a meaning and purpose greater than myself to give me hope. God spoke to me about my calling, my individuality, and my uniqueness. You do not need to have material possessions and human achievement to validate your existence. Only God can do that. In jail, I felt important and significant. When I got out, while sleeping on someone else's couch without a car and a job, I felt needed and valuable. I would help others find their way. I walked the streets of Houston in search of someone in need. I had no idea what God had in store for me. It didn't matter. Everything I did had a profound meaning. I began to share Christ and win souls. I had a great influence on everyone around me. All of the people in my life began to have hope. They began to accept Christ.

I remembered one of my dad's best friends in the ministry, Rev. Eddie Lebeaux. He had no church. He had no car. He didn't have expensive furniture or clothing. He had one item he used every day: a bicycle. He was a brilliant man with a high IQ. My father used his research and material in his ministry for years. But he was one unique individual. He was vibrant, enthusiastic, and so full of life. He had never been married. He lived alone. He truly was a giant of a man spiritually, yet small in stature. What kept him so happy? He gave me his testimony one day, and I never forgot it. During my way back to God, God reminded me of it.

Eddie was on his way to complete his final bar exam in his quest to become a lawyer. He had the honor of graduating at the top of his class. The previous bar exam results were posted and he had almost perfect scores. The day before his last test he had an experience with God and accepted Christ as his Savior. That night he had a visitation from Jesus in a dream. Jesus stood tall and held one of the most beautiful objects he had ever seen in His hand. He asked Jesus, "What is that? It is the most beautiful intriguing object I have ever seen?" Jesus said, "Eddie that is a miniature world or Earth." As Eddie looked closer, it was remarkable in color, detail, and perfection. He could see rivers, trees, mountains, flowers, and every detail. It was the most intriguing, beautiful object of perfection he had ever seen, and he could not keep his eyes off of it.

Then, all of a sudden, Jesus held out his other hand, and Eddie was almost blinded by the stark, shining brilliance of a diamond

Jesus held in His other hand. It sparkled, and its radiance was magnificent. It possessed the most alluring qualities Eddie had ever seen. Its radiance completely outshone the miniature world Jesus held in His other hand. Eddie could no longer even see what was in Christ's other hand. It took his breath away. He could not get over it and had to ask, "What is that?" Jesus said, "Eddie, that is one soul. The value of one soul far exceeds the value of the entire worth of the world, and so does its beauty." Then Jesus said something that changed Eddie's life forever. He said, "Eddie, he that winneth souls is wise, for what shall a man give in exchange for his soul?"

That changed Eddie's life forever. When he walked in to take his final exam, he lost all desire to become a lawyer. He put his pencil down and walked out. He had a promising career ahead of him as a lawyer, but it no longer was of value to him. He determined within himself that he would win souls the rest of his life. When he told me this story, he was in his seventies. He said every day he rode his bicycle around the city in search of at least one lost soul. He told me he had averaged one soul a day since then. That was over fifty years ago, just think of how many people he has won to Christ.

Luke 12:15 (KJV) says, "for a man's life consisteth not in the abundance of the things which he possesseth."

Without a mission, without purpose, without the true reason for your existence, you will never experience real joy and satisfaction, no matter how many friends you have, how much money you have, or how many drugs you use. There is no replacement of any kind that will give you a sense of accomplishment until you find your true meaning in life, and why God created you.

Meaning and purpose defined and revealed

Meaning answers the question why? Purpose is how you live out meaning. The meaning of life answers the questions of the design and purpose of creation. The meaning of a word provides the intent of the word. It is what is conveyed or intended. It gives a sense of significance. The meaning of a created product came from the idea associated with it and the goal or intent of the product. When you find out its meaning, then you find out its purpose. Meaning reveals and discloses purpose. There are different meanings used for the word purpose. The Collins English Dictionary says, "purpose is the fixed intention of doing something, the reason for doing something, the idea or the thought behind the action."

For instance, an automobile was created for travel. To get somewhere faster and in comfort. But it takes on greater value, meaning, and importance by how it is used. It may be an ambulance, a police vehicle, or an emergency vehicle transporting the "jaws of life." God created us with a specific valuable meaning and purpose. We are all different. But all of us are human beings. DNA proves this. Genetic design proves this. But just for theory, let's say that we are all automobiles. Can you imagine God creating you as an ambulance and then through some hostile environment, your flashing lights are disabled, your paint is removed, and instead of being used as an ambulance you are being used in off-track mud races? How long would you stay a functioning automobile?

Next to the four-wheel drive all-terrain vehicle, how impressive would you be? How misused? What a wasted use of such a valuable vehicle with all of that lifesaving equipment. Just to be demolished in an off-road mud experience for fun. You would be losing so much value and significance from your true meaning or reason for creation by just changing the activity in your life, or the purpose. Not all activity has immense value. Especially if you're being misused. If your purpose for today is just getting high, then, of course, you are going to feel empty and worthless. You were created for so much more. The meaning behind your purpose is the most important aspect of life.

For example, you might say you are going to the store and that is your purpose for leaving the house. But when you say you are going to the store to get baby milk and you hear the baby crying in the background, going to the store takes on a greater meaning. You would definitely feel a greater sense of importance getting milk for your baby than picking up a few things that you might need in the future. All of a sudden you are filled with urgency and your trip to the store becomes one of significant importance. The meaning of your trip has gone from ordinary and uneventful to one of valued importance. Now consider your life trip or journey. When your journey here on this earth takes on that kind of life and death value, your significant value increases giving you a powerful sense of self-worth. That sense of meaning and purpose can only come from your Creator who designed you and has a specific purpose for your existence.

1 John 2:17 (NASB) says, "but the one who does the will of God lives forever."

Can you imagine spending your life wasting it rather than investing it? Being used wrongly will prevent you from reaching your full potential and accomplishing what God intended for you to accomplish. Can you imagine going through life trying to function as an all-terrain vehicle when you are an ambulance? How difficult would that be? Always stuck in the mud, with complicated motor and suspension difficulties. How unsatisfied, unhappy you would be trying to outperform others in the race. Oh, how you would hate your life. And what a wasteful, inadequate, and inefficient existence you would lead.

Now imagine yourself being the ambulance you were designed to be. Just think how important you would feel saving lives and functioning within your design. What a difference you could make doing the right thing. Your self-worth, self-esteem, self-respect, and all-around confidence and sense of accomplishment would soar. It would be hard to be depressed if you were doing what God called you to do. Your sense of value and significance would not allow you to be distracted and unfocused. You would be so busy doing the right thing, and being fulfilled, you would never even think of doing the wrong thing. Now that is real freedom, being set free from the mud and the off-road diversion of Satan to achieve your real purpose and fulfill your true meaning.

Victor Frankl said, "One should not search for an abstract meaning of life. Everyone has his own specific vocation or mission in life to carry out a concrete assignment which demands fulfillment. Therein he cannot be replaced, nor can his life be repeated. Thus, everyone's task is as unique as is his specific opportunity to implement it."

We are all created unique and special. There are no two eyes even identical. Some people have blue eyes, some green, some brown. Some people are right-handed, some left-handed, while some people are ambidextrous. We all have different IQ levels. Different likes and dislikes. Different weights, heights, and body shapes. We have different hair colors, and some of us have thicker hair or thinner hair. We have different skills, talents, and motivations. Some of us are artistically-minded—we draw and paint. Some of us love working with our hands, while others love using other skills. There are no fingerprints identical and have never been any. We are all pre-destined and genetically designed by God to complete a divine assignment. You were engineered to be different for a reason. We all have dissimilar responses to situations and circumstances.

God created us that way; he celebrates our differences. We all have great value, meaning, and a specific purpose in our creation.

Your meaning and purpose are in God's hands, and He is personally presently involved in developing you.

Isaiah 64:8 (KJV) says, "But now, O LORD, thou art our father;

we are the clay, and thou our potter; and we all are the work of thy hand."

You can rest assured in the potter's hands that He will finish and complete you, giving you a life filled with productivity and success and make sure you are given the ability to fulfill your purpose. **If you allow your relationship with Him to grow and allow His mentorship in your life, you can do anything, except fail.**

Philippians 1:6 (KJV) says, "Being confident of this very thing, that he which hath begun a good work in you will perform it until the day of Jesus Christ:"

God chose you for a specific purpose. You are an instrument with a high calling and a priestly work.

1 Peter 2:9 (MSG) says, "But you are the ones chosen by God, chosen for the high calling of priestly work, chosen to be a holy people, God's instruments to do his work and speak out for him, to tell others of the night-and-day difference he made for you."

Your sense of importance and value increases when you see, through the eyes of God, what He sees in you. You have a specific purpose and are not a random creation that just came about by accident. You have an elevated extraordinary calling. **Finally, you are a fine-tuned instrument, designed with the purpose and intention of God, in detail, created to perform greatly.** Your work is of a priestly origin and is divinely inspired.

God has a designed purpose and plan for you, which includes prosperity, hope, and a future.

Jeremiah 29:11 (NIV2011) says, "For I know the plans I have for you," declares the LORD, "plans to prosper you and not to harm you, plans to give you hope and a future."

The greatest comfort I have about my future comes from God's thoughts about it and His intentions concerning it. **God is actively engaged in making your life prosperous, filled with hope, and a viable future. Regardless of where you are in life —whether in prison or homeless—God's plan is not to hurt you, but give you meaning, hope, and a future.**

Your purpose in life was ordained and planned before you were born.

Psalm 139:16 (NLT) says, "You saw me before I was born. Every day of my life was recorded in your book. Every moment was laid out before a single day had passed."

It is also significant to know that your life does not surprise God. He knew in advance all your weaknesses, mistakes, failures, and strengths, **so He designed a path where you would have access to His strength and power through Christ and the Holy Spirit. It is up to you to choose God's prepared path for you.**

Your purpose is unique to your calling, and there are many individual members in the kingdom of God, and we all serve a purpose and have different gifts and talents.

1 Corinthians 12:8-12 (KJV) says, "For to one is given by the Spirit the word of wisdom; to another the word of knowledge by the same Spirit; To another faith by the same Spirit; to another the gifts of healing by the same Spirit; To another the working of miracles; to another prophecy; to another discerning of spirits; to another divers kinds of tongues; to another the interpretation of tongues: But all these worketh that one and the selfsame Spirit, dividing to every man severally as he will. For as the body is one,

and hath many members, and all the members of that one body, being many, are one body: so also is Christ."

The key to your self-worth is the knowledge that you are unique, and there is no one else like you. Another key is that your identity becomes more valuable because you belong to a greater group of special people, and the success of that group requires your expertise. That group is called the body of Christ on earth. You are a member of a highly functional, worldwide organization and global enterprise contributing to the good of humanity.

You were created and purposed for good things, wonderful things.

Ephesians 2:10 (KJV) says, "For we are his workmanship, created in Christ Jesus unto good works, which God hath before ordained that we should walk in them."

After all the strategies, plans, and lies of Satan, it is refreshing and confidence building to know you were purposed for good works, and the bad in your past life was a lie. **You were not born an addict or bad person, and under the care and workmanship of Christ, you can be a facilitator of good works.**

The meaning of life is found in Christ; knowing Christ is knowing God the Father; without knowing God, you can never find your true meaning.

John 14:6-14 (KJV) says, "Jesus saith unto him, I am the way, the truth, and the life: no man cometh unto the Father, but by me. If ye had known me, ye should have known my Father also: and from henceforth ye know him, and have seen him. Philip saith unto him, Lord, shew us the Father, and it sufficeth us. Jesus saith unto him, Have I been so long time with you, and yet hast thou not known me, Philip? he that hath seen me hath seen the Father; and how sayest thou then, Shew us the Father? Believest thou not that I am in the Father, and the Father in me? the words that I speak unto you I speak not of myself: but the Father that dwelleth in me, he doeth the works. Believe me that I am in the Father, and the Father in me: or else believe me for the very works' sake. Verily, verily, I say unto you, He that believeth on me, the works that I do shall he do also; and greater works than these shall he do; because I go unto my Father. And whatsoever ye shall ask in my name, that will I do, that the Father may be glorified in the Son. If ye shall ask any thing in my name, I will do it."

Notice that God talks about your works or your daily activities. God is saying that you now can hear me and receive instructions about your purpose and work here on earth. Jesus says I am the way. Follow me. He lives in you and through you. He guarantees success, and if you need His help, all you have to do is ask. **Anything that has to do with God's original intentions and purpose in your life has all His resources and power backing it.**

Not fulfilling your true meaning and purpose is living a lie

John 8:44 (KJV) says, "Ye are of your father the devil, and the lusts of your father ye will do. He was a murderer from the beginning, and abode not in the truth, because there is no truth in him. When he speaketh a lie, he speaketh of his own: for he is a liar, and the father of it."

It is believing the lie told by the father of all lies. The lie that if you live according to your own will, desires, and lust you will be happy. The lie that fulfilling God's purpose in your life will keep you from experiencing life and missing out on important, meaningful experiences, which is a blatant mistaken fact. Truly the opposite of his lie is true. Just ask those of us who have lived it. **All you have to do is look at your past to know that he is a liar. We know this from our experience of living outside of God and not fulfilling our true purpose. Our past was the most miserable, unrewarding, and unsatisfying way to live.**

Becoming your authentic self, who you were meant to be, and fulfilling your true meaning and purpose is living the dream, living the abundant life.

John 10:10 (KJV) says, "The thief cometh not, but for to steal, and to kill, and to destroy: I am come that they might have life, and that they might have it more abundantly."

It has been Satan that has stolen your life from you. He also came to destroy everything of value around you and used you to do it. Your children, your significant other, your ability, your talents, and your possessions: he will not stop there either. He wants to kill or do away with you altogether. He is a messenger of death. Everything most people are bitter about originates from Satan, not from God. Every time you have blamed God for your circumstances and mistakes it has been Satan's fault and the responsibility has been yours, not God's.

God loves you. Jesus said I came to give you life, and life more abundantly. Until you partner with your original life source, the person who breathed life into your being and created you, you will never experience the life you have dreamed of. You will never become the authentic you. The genuine, original person you were meant to be. Jesus wants to make you strong—full of faith and courage, productive and successful. He wants to fill you with love, kindness, humility, and wisdom, to give you abundant life. He will restore your dignity and self-worth. When I gave my life to Christ, I found true meaning in serving Him. You too can have that connection in life.

Pray with me: "Jesus, I make you my partner and Lord in everything I do. I want to do your will, to be everything you want me to be. Help me say the right words and give to others what you are teaching me. Help me to love and embrace your love in my life. Teach me my true meaning and purpose. Show me my gifts and talents. Put me where I belong. I give you all of my gifting and abilities to be used for your glory in Jesus name, Amen!"

5

SPIRITUAL AWAKENING—A GIFT OF THE HOLY SPIRIT

METHADDICTSHELP, FACEBOOK POST

FEBRUARY 7, 2017

YOUR RECOVERY MUST COME FIRST SO THAT EVERYTHING YOU LOVE IN LIFE DOESN'T HAVE TO COME IN LAST. THERE IS NO CHEMICAL SOLUTION TO A SPIRITUAL PROBLEM. HAVE YOU EVER REALLY THOUGHT ABOUT IT? ANYTHING UNDER GOD'S CONTROL IS NEVER OUT OF CONTROL.... MESSAGE US FOR PRAYER....TPC. (UNEDITED)

167,033 PEOPLE REACHED

9.9K LIKES

2,079 SHARES

617 COMMENTS

It was not like I was asleep having a bad dream and I awakened. It was more like I was in a coffin, embalmed, and my skeleton took on flesh, my heart started pumping, and my lungs started filling up with the best oxygen. I could breathe for the first time. It was like being resurrected from the dead, and becoming alive. I could hear positive, loving words, see things as they really were, and had clarity of thought for the first time in years. I had a view from the top looking down. I could clearly see cause and effect with a wisdom and understanding that had evaded me in times past. God began to show me how much He loved me and had been protecting me throughout my life so that I could finally arrive safely in His kingdom.

I immediately saw that the real root cause of my addiction and pain was Satan. It was clearly a strategy and plan devised by Satan himself. Other people, along with myself, had been hoodwinked by the deceiver. Those who had hurt me and had abandoned me were just as much a victim as I had been. They were totally deceived—although differently—but deceived just as fully as I had been. That is what a real, sober person set free from the bondage of sin, Satan, and addiction is. Categorically and without exceptions, he is new, spiritually alive and instinctively made aware of the truth.

Reflection: If you are not beginning to experience this type of spiritual awakening as fully as you think you should, then don't worry about it. It will come. Keep surrendering, committing, and talking to Jesus. You will keep growing spiritually.

Addiction and the oppression of demonic spirits had controlled me for such a long time that my thinking was messed up. A spirit of anger, rejection, and feeling of not caring had taken over. I had taken on an attitude that nothing would ever change, and it controlled me. When my spirit came alive, those demons were put to rest. Instead of living my life in a continued state of regret and grief, I was living in celebration. It was unmistakable and undeniable—a genuine celebration of being newborn, a birthing of a child of God, a resurrection from death. I went from snorting a line, putting a line in my coffee, smoking a bowl, and eating crystal meth in capsules (literally, refilling giant vitamin capsules with meth) every day—as well as taking pain pills to ease the body aches from being up for days and taking Xanax and Valium for anxiety—to becoming alive again, transformed, and spiritually awakened.

I began to walk in the light after years of stumbling in darkness. I no longer needed to be high. In times past, being sober was not an option unless I wanted to be subjected to depression, anger, and vulnerability. My every thought was ruled by drugs and deception. It was my purpose. I could not live without them and didn't want to. Just before getting arrested, I spent several days in a motel room selling drugs. I was being manipulated by Satan and had no other way out of my personal hell. It was at the end of those several days in a motel that I reached out to God.

I had just kicked my girlfriend's door down and was preparing to kill a guy who was smoking dope with her in her bedroom. When my girlfriend and her mother stood in the way protecting this guy from bodily harm (they understood the danger and knew what I was capable of, having seen me in action many times before), I eventually gave up and left. I picked up a girl, and we were getting high, and hanging out in a casino. Her husband kept calling her even though he knew she wasn't coming home. It aggravated me. I dropped her off somewhere and started driving around in circles for hours. I was trying to find a place to stay for a few days and finally pulled into that car wash.

The insanity of it all came bearing down on me, and it seemed to take my breath from me. The chaos and constant struggle of my life without God hit me. It was then, right there in that car wash that I surrendered to Christ. I was tired and worn out. I'd had enough of the way things were and said to God, "I'm through. I give up. Please help me. I surrender my life to you to do with it as you please. Anything is better than this. I give it all to you!"

Then a peaceful calm entered me, and I fell asleep. The next day, I was sitting in that jail cell, calm, rational and in my right mind. Think about it for a moment. That only could be a miracle. A true spiritual awakening. A real God encounter of deliverance and healing.

I have personally been involved in hundreds of these spiritual transformations through my internet, video, and phone ministries. I have prayed with hundreds of people from all over the world and watched God's miracle power in action. This is your spiritual awakening. Follow through with it. Don't give in or give up until you experience complete healing in your life. Only you can change you. God is now giving you the tools to become a faith-filled, strong, productive and successful man or woman. Use them. These spiritual tools are utilized through a spiritual means in the fourth dimension, outside of time, space, and matter. These tools will last forever, and those who use them will be rewarded eternally for it. Time, space, and matter need not affect your sanity ever again.

A spiritual awakening explained—what it is and what it is not.

The spiritual awakening that is described in this book is a reconnection with God, who is an eternal spirit. A rebirth. A coming alive made possible by the life of the Holy Spirit in you. A spiritual awakening is allowing yourself to be open to the Spirit of God and inviting the living Spirit of God through Christ, and the love of God, to enter your heart. When you Google the term "spiritual awakening," you will pull up all sorts of Google-gobble from mysticism, talking to the dead, crystal power, yoga, and the worship of the life found in trees and flowers. So, I have broken it down to three basic facts that occur within a true and powerful awakening of deliverance, healing, and rebirth through the indwelling power of the Holy Spirit.

First, a spiritual awakening starts to occur when our longing for more, and our search for meaning points to important questions like, "why am I here" and, "is there more to life than this?"

In the addict's life, a spiritual awakening is a real changed state of perception. It is a knowing beyond knowledge. It takes you one step further from the physical world to a spiritual world. It is following through with the longing you have internally and spiritually. A looking from the inside out. Reality has changed for the person who experiences a spiritual awakening. In short, a spiritual awakening is when you come to an awareness that there must be spiritual answers to things we have long tried to answer but could not in the three-dimensional physical world we live in. **It is a coming to the end of ourselves, a place where we hit rock bottom, and as we look inward, all the signs point to a Creator: God.**

Second, a spiritual awakening can only come about through God and His son Christ, and there is no other awakening that can compare to awakening in God's presence. A spiritual awakening is coming to the knowledge of the truth that God has reached out to us through Jesus Christ, the Son of God and Savior of the world, to reconcile man and restore fellowship and communion with God through our spirit and His. Most importantly, a true spiritual resurrection comes about through acceptance of Jesus' work on the cross. We are radically changed, made alive by His presence, in which His blood cleanses us from the death and disease of sin separating us from God. Early A. A. members in the first groups established in Akron and Cleveland simply understood their spiritual awakening as salvation accompanied by the indwelling presence of the Holy Spirit. That God was their source of power and not just some vague idea of a higher power that could range from a radiator, an image of your grandfather, to meditation on your inner-self. Dr. B. in his book *Why Early A. A. Succeeded* stated emphatically that they had a 93% success rate of curing the alcoholic completely, simply by calling it a sinful disease that God can give us the power over through Christ.

Third, a spiritual awakening deals with the new life that occurs and how we are to approach it. We become "born again," and everything becomes new and exciting to us, with wonderful possibilities. We are now alive empowered by the Holy Spirit and filled with revelation knowledge that went unnoticed, or not revealed before. The third stage of a spiritual awakening is about the work of God's Spirit in us, and our personal growth, which is what every word in this book is about. These truths are being revealed in the order that they actually happened in my life, and I am fully convinced that if you will pray, study, and apply these principles, that you will live in total freedom, and experience life to its fullest.

It is from my life of experimentation that none of the "Google-gobble" of crystal power, yoga, trans-meditation, deeper-self meditation, or any "out-of-the-body" experience can create a permanent change of character or deep-seated meaning in a person's life. There is no drug-induced experience that can produce that kind of change in a person either. After using LSD and mind-altering drugs, you just walk away after a while with no lasting assurance. The effect leaves you empty, and you still have no connection with true power and change that comes from the Creator.

What I will describe below is the most powerful existence a man can have: walking in the power of the Holy Spirit, the true and only spiritual awakening. A person trying to solve all of his problems through intelligence or his will and only through the information that his body—the five senses or the conscious mind—will give him, will be at a tremendous disadvantage. It is like trying to run a race with one leg or reading with one eye, thinking it will not affect your peripheral vision.

A spiritual awakening requires the work of the Holy Spirit.

Romans 8:2 (KJV) says, "For the law of the Spirit of life in Christ Jesus hath made me free from the law of sin and death."

2 Corinthians 3:6 (KJV) says, "Who also hath made us able ministers of the new testament; not of the letter, but of the spirit: for the letter killeth, but the spirit giveth life."

It is the work of Christ who sets you free from the law of sin and death, from addiction, and from bondage to fear, anger and hurt. It is the spirit of Christ that makes you alive spiritually. He opens a new window into the fourth dimension outside of time, space, and matter. Christ our advocate then through the Father gives us The Holy Spirit, our comforter.

John 16:7 (KJV) says, "Nevertheless I tell you the truth; It is expedient for you that I go away: for if I go not away, the Comforter will not come unto you; but if I depart, I will send him unto you."

It is the Holy Spirit who is the agent of change. He fills us with the love of God, delivering us from bitterness, unforgiveness, and a dislike of others, giving us a valid, tangible, real spiritual awakening with concrete evidence.

Romans 5:5 (KJV) says, "And hope maketh not ashamed; because the love of God is shed abroad in our hearts by the Holy Ghost which is given unto us."

It is the Holy Spirit who assures us that we are one of God's children, providing the evidence that there has been a true spiritual awakening in our life.

Romans 8:16 (KJV) says, "The Spirit itself beareth witness with our spirit, that we are the children of God:"

A spiritual awakening brings the power and presence of the Holy Spirit

When Jesus ascended into heaven, He didn't leave us to face life and adversity in a hostile environment alone. He told His disciples that it was to their advantage that He go away. It was all part of

God's will and plan for our benefit. He ascended into heaven because if He stayed, mankind would suffer. Christ in His human form could only be at one place at a time. God's desire throughout creation was to restore a relationship with man. He wanted complete access—access to the entire future world, admittance into the hearts of millions of future believers, and to be able to fellowship with all of us individually to unite us in cause and spirit. He desired to have an ongoing conversation and establish a friendship with us. Jesus made that possible by sending us the precious Holy Spirit to live within us. The Holy Spirit's name "Advocate" implies on our behalf or for our support. He is our champion, promoter, supporter, and always backing us up publicly and privately.

John 16:7 (NLT) says, "But in fact, it is best for you that I go away, because if I don't, the Advocate won't come. If I do go away, then I will send him to you."

John 14:16-17 (NLT) says, "And I will ask the Father, and he will give you another Advocate, who will never leave you. He is the Holy Spirit, who leads into all truth. The world cannot receive him, because it isn't looking for him and doesn't recognize him. But you know him, because he lives with you now and later will be in you."

Notice that the Holy Spirit now lives in you, you take Him everywhere. He loves you so much that He has given you complete access to His presence 24 hours a day. You never have to live without assurance, security, or the peace of God again. He is with you always. Anytime your rest is being threatened, and you are troubled, His presence is there to comfort you. His gift to you is His presence. His assistance, leadership, and companionship is a constant source of supply. All we ever have to do is open up a dialogue with our comforter the Holy Spirit and His assurance and peace is accessible to each and every one of us.

The Holy Spirit's company creates fullness of joy.

Psalm 16:11 (KJV) says, "Thou wilt shew me the path of life: in thy presence is fullness of joy; at thy right hand there are pleasures for evermore."

Our lives were empty vessels striving for fulfillment and completeness. Before God was in our lives, there was a dull, empty void. We were incapable of reaching true lasting joy. Now we have an unlimited reservoir within us to draw from. We have fullness of joy and pleasures always to draw from.

John 7:38-39 (KJV) says, "He that believeth on me, as the scripture hath said, out of his belly shall flow rivers of living water; (But this spake he of the Spirit, which they that believe on him should receive: for the Holy Ghost was not yet given; because that Jesus was not yet glorified.)"

Spending time in the presence of the Holy Spirit is the most rewarding and pleasurable source of joy and peace available to man. One of the means of drawing from those living waters is through worship and praise. Spending time listening to worship music and worshipping releases much warmth, comfort, acceptance, security, and joy in your life. Coming before Christ in total abandonment of self in thankfulness is the key to immense joy and ecstasy. **The awakening of life by the indwelling Holy Spirit and all its ramifications are phenomenal. Once you have found the true fountain of life and its meaning in the presence of the Holy Spirit, there is no more need for endless and exhaustive searching. There is no need for experimenting and staggering helplessly through life looking for fulfillment. That struggle has finally come to an end.**

If you exercise your new access to God's power throughout your day, through times of worship, prayer, and reading His word, it will create the atmosphere for the Holy Spirit to work within your spirit or heart. By having a continued conversation with God throughout your day, you can achieve a new and more excellent way to live, free from worry, doubt, and anxiety.

The Holy Spirit is the producer of powerful and wonderful fruit that provides the necessary strength you need to survive life's testing.

Galatians 5:22-23 (NLT) says, "But the Holy Spirit produces this kind of fruit in our lives: love, joy, peace, patience, kindness, goodness, faithfulness, gentleness, and self-control."

The Holy Spirit is an agent of change and transformation of the human spirit. As an addict, I lived in weakness so long that it was astonishing to me that I could live in the strength and power of the Spirit. To know that the strength of self-control is always available to me, and that gentleness, kindness, and the patience of God can be accessible when I am in need, is overwhelming. That a spirit of patience and joy could replace the constant need for instant gratification, indulgence, and fulfillment is what anchors me in trying circumstances. It is my stability and consistency. It brought a transformation in me that was progressive in growth and provided great personal freedom to be my authentic self. I could do things I had a deep desire for, such as loving people again, being productive, and being disciplined in all my affairs. There is no self-help program or type of therapy or drug rehabilitating center available anywhere on earth that can transform a person from the inside-out like that, let alone impart such wonderful attributes and qualities. It is truly a miraculous process. **If you persevere and continue in your commitment to Him, there will be nothing unattainable in your life.**

The Holy Spirit is the person of God in you and can be grieved.

Ephesians 4:30 (KJV) says, "And grieve not the holy Spirit of God, whereby ye are sealed unto the day of redemption."

The Holy Spirit has all the attributes and characteristics of a person. He is the person of God in you. If you offend the Holy Spirit by human responses of anger, bitterness, negative talking, and hateful speech, it is possible to grieve, sadden, and distress Him. When you sadden or grieve the Holy Spirit, He pulls away and leaves you to face the consequences of your behavior. This serves as a blessing and warning from God Himself. Without it, we would continue to make mistakes and suffer from them. So, He gradually distances Himself from you. This leaves you with the spiritual feeling that something is wrong. Because it is identified and singled out by the Holy Spirit, you can now readily correct the wrong, rather than live in the chaos that wrong-doing can create.

John 16:8 (NLT) says, "And when he comes, he will convict the world of its sin, and of God's righteousness, and of the coming judgment."

That is how He convicts of sin in our lives. His gentleness is represented as a gentle dove in the word of God.

Luke 3:22 (KJV) says, "And the Holy Ghost descended in a bodily shape like a dove upon him"

The Holy Spirit is a gentleman and never imposes His will upon us. He doesn't go where He is unwanted. He must be invited and feel wanted if He is to stay. Can you imagine trying to make a dove feel comfortable and welcome in your presence? How easily would a loud movement or unsettling gesture simply cause Him to fly away? He would move to safety as quickly as possible. It is that way when the Holy Spirit senses a disturbance of spiritual purity in your life or the presence of impure, contaminated thoughts of lust or hurt to others. He quickly flees your presence and company. It is impossible to contaminate the Holy Spirit with sin. He will not be a partaker in your sin. **In this way, God establishes boundaries, limits, and guidelines for you to live by. It is a foolproof system, an internal radar that is with you always.** Always pinpointing places of danger, people of danger, and things that are dangerous in your life.

Addicts and hurting people who have had a spiritual awakening become some of the most powerful Christians and people that have ever lived. It is the nature of their deliverance which makes them so powerful. It required complete effort and attention to the leading of the Holy Spirit. Their very lives depended upon it. The gravity of the situation required a soldier's effort. **We have listened to the Holy Spirit because our safety, our very existence, and survival were at stake.** It is not that we take credit to have arrived at this place of recovery but to have simply arrived there by the leadership of the Holy Spirit.

The Holy Spirit is a gift giver.

When a child of God needs special gifting of a supernatural quality, it is available from the Holy Spirit. There are many times in an addict's life when we have felt inadequate, unequipped, or inferior to handle the impossibilities we faced in life. That is precisely when we would medicate more heavily and deepen our involvement and pursuit of a solution. And our situation would worsen. That disparity of balance and a need for enough strength to overcome adversity just increased the desire to use. That is where our new helper and friend in the person of the Holy Spirit becomes invaluable. He is a giver of gifts such as the gift of healing, miracles, wisdom, word of knowledge, and faith.

1 Corinthians 12:4-11 (KJV) says, "Now there are diversities of gifts, but the same Spirit. And there are differences of administra-

tions, but the same Lord. And there are diversities of operations, but it is the same God which worketh all in all. But the manifestation of the Spirit is given to every man to profit withal. For to one is given by the Spirit the word of wisdom; to another the word of knowledge by the same Spirit; To another faith by the same Spirit; to another the gifts of healing by the same Spirit; To another the working of miracles; to another prophecy; to another discerning of spirits; to another divers kinds of tongues; to another the interpretation of tongues: But all these worketh that one and the selfsame Spirit, dividing to every man severally as he will."

So, you now have access to a gift of supernatural faith or another gift of the Spirit under the same set of impossible circumstances that you faced before. With this type of strengthening and empowerment, you can face anything with hope and expect superior results.

The psyche of the former addict is now one that can take on any problem with a sense of assurance and well-being. His words, "severally as He will," means when the Holy Spirit sees a need for gifting, or especially when a person is attempting the perfect will of God in their lives, He responds by giving a spiritual gift designed specifically for that need.

1 Corinthians 12:31 (KJV) says, "But covet earnestly the best gifts: and yet shew I unto you a more excellent way."

As further proof that spiritual gifts belong to you, God urges you to covet or desire these gifts. **He would never tell us to desire something that was unavailable to us.** What a wonderful and loving God, who truly has not left us without the gifting and attributes that create strength.

Also, He says to covet the best gifts, the most advantageous or beneficial gift, the most suitable gift, or the one that is needed the most in your situation. Every problem or need in your life has a gift from the Holy Spirit designed to help you solve the issue or supply the need.

This is an astounding opportunity and tool God has made

available to all of us who are in need. Nowhere has anyone in human history made such an extraordinary opportunity available with the power to back it up with substance. Only our loving heavenly Father who created us and empowered us to fulfill our purpose has done that. The Holy Spirit on many occasions has gifted me with faith when great doubt was present, and granted me wisdom when I had none. Even while writing this book, He has inspired my every thought.

I know that in your life right now, you probably need a special gift for a specific problem you are facing. Why not pick one of these gifts such as a word of wisdom, a word of knowledge, the gift of faith, healing, working of miracles, prophecy, spiritual discernment, tongues, the interpretation of tongues, and covet, desire and pray for it? He tells us to covet these gifts, so we know it is His will for us to have them.

The following verse in the Bible guarantees us access to anything we ask from God when we know it is His will for us to have it.

1 John 5:14-15 (KJV) says, "And this is the confidence that we have in him, that, if we ask any thing according to his will, he heareth us: And if we know that he hear us, whatsoever we ask, we know that we have the petitions that we desired of him."

So, ask in confidence and faith, expecting God to strengthen you.

The Holy Spirit is our teacher.

John 14:26 (KJV) says, "But the Comforter, which is the Holy Ghost, whom the Father will send in my name, he shall teach you all things, and bring all things to your remembrance, whatsoever I have said unto you."

The Holy Spirit is present to talk with, teach, and instruct you. All of life's coping skills that have evaded your abilities to handle and solve difficulties now can be learned from the Holy Spirit. He will also give you the ability to avoid triggers that may cause a relapse and send you spiraling downward into depression. Our teacher will grant you the knowledge that will protect you from wrong thoughts and the lies of Satan that can keep you from making the same mistakes repeatedly. You are now in touch with the unlimited knowledge of your Creator who knows everything about you because He designed you. He knows exactly how your mind and body works. He is all-powerful, all-knowledgeable, and ever-present.

John 14:17 (KJV) says, "Even the Spirit of truth; whom the world cannot receive, because it seeth him not, neither knoweth him: but ye know him; for he dwelleth with you, and shall be in you."

He is also the revealer of truth. The word of God that you might have had a hard time understanding will now be revealed to you by the very person that wrote it: the Holy Spirit.

2 Timothy 3:16 (MSG) says, "Every part of Scripture is God-breathed and useful one way or another—showing us truth, exposing our rebellion, correcting our mistakes, training us to live God's way."

6

BAPTISM OF FIRE

METHADDICTSHELP, FACEBOOK POST

MARCH 23, 2017

GOD THROUGH THE POWER OF THE HOLY SPIRIT AND HIS GIFTS ARE REALLY ALL THAT AN ADDICT NEEDS TO OVERCOME ANYTHING IN LIFE. POWER, WISDOM, FAITH, MIRACLES, A PRAYER LANGUAGE. ETC... THE FRUIT OF THE HOLY SPIRIT IS ALL THAT ANY ADDICT WILL EVER NEED TO SURVIVE AND BE PRODUCTIVE. LOVE, JOY, PEACE, PATIENCE, SELF-CONTROL...THEY ARE SUPERNATURAL AND AVAILABLE... TPC. (UNEDITED)

192,558 PEOPLE REACHED

12,000 LIKES

2,668 shares

1,313 comments

My special helper and wonderful companion, the Holy Spirit, has brought about so much change in my life it is hard to pick one specific area and place of special importance that He has blessed me with above the rest. But there is one phenomenon that rises above everything else when I mention the enabling power of the Holy Spirit, and it is always my first thought. It is most explosive in nature and the most beneficial gifting in its use. That is the baptism or the infilling of the Holy Spirit and the gifting of a prayer language as the initial evidence. **It is estimated that there are approximately 700 million people in the world that have experienced the infilling and baptism of the Holy Spirit.** Throughout the history of God's people from the birth of the early church in a small upstairs room to this very present moment, people have been experiencing the powerful baptism of the Holy Spirit.

With all the achievements of modern science, breakthrough technology, and medical advancements, the Holy Spirit is still our greatest source for personal growth and healing. The Holy Spirit can heal incurable diseases, mental disorders, depression, and addiction and, at the same time, gift you with His presence and fill you with joy. While we are a tremendously blessed generation, like no other before us, with astounding capabilities, none of them are limitless or possess the unlimited power of the Holy Spirit. He is all-powerful and can create something out of nothing. He created you and me. **I would be remiss and negligent in my duty as a fellow traveler in the kingdom of God if I omitted such an important spiritual event and empowerment that has given me such great comfort.** *The Holy Spirit deals in the fourth dimension, outside of time, space, and matter. He is eternal and not limited to travel within our space alone, nor is He limited by time as we know it, and He is not contained by physical matter. He transcends all of man's boundaries. He is the Almighty Spirit of God. He is God.*

God created us in His image. He gave us the ability to speak. Why would He not have a special spiritual language for us to pray and communicate in the spiritual realm that He exists in? Why would He not give us the ability to pray for future events unknown by man but known by God? Why would He withhold knowledge of our weaknesses in such a way that it would be impossible to see them in advance of future trouble that will come when He is completely aware of them? That would be just as damaging as me withholding valuable information from you that could possibly save your life or make it better. If I withheld a bad turn in the road coming up or know of a faulty automobile engine that could cost you your life, you certainly would not view me as a friend.

While still in jail, I faced my own limitations in a special way. I did not know the will of God completely for me. I did not know if I was going to be in jail the rest of my life or whether God would have something different for me. All I really wanted was God's perfect will in my life to be done. I was faced with a dilemma. How do I pray concerning my future? What about special insight relating to my personal growth? I needed supernatural guidance, direction, and leadership.

It was then, in my own inabilities and weakness that God took me back in time, and I was reminded of myself as a little boy at the age of twelve when my mother brought me to church to receive the "baptism of the Holy Ghost." It was an extraordinary event that stayed with me for many years, but through catastrophic events, the attack of Satan, and addiction, I had forgotten completely about it. In the back-slidden capacity that I had lived in for years, I had forgotten about the Holy Spirit and His power. The downward steps of spirituality are common to so many of us former addicts. It was regressive in nature and nothing unusual. I just was not living as close to God as I should have been.

It all started through the divorce and the breaking up of my family. It happened suddenly and completely caught me off-guard. I had been married twenty-three years. I was 43 when she left me. It felt like the deepest part of my soul was gone and there was nothing left but an empty shell. I remember the sensation of feeling like I was falling into some deep black hole, and the darkness was swallowing me up. I couldn't sleep and couldn't think of anything else. It felt like someone had internally raped me and was tearing me apart from the inside out. I had never hurt like that and had never been hurt like that before. I had never experienced that kind of pain before. I was not myself. I was emotionally falling apart from the deepest part of my soul and from the essential core of who I was. In just a few days I had lost my identity, and I was unrecognizable.

She was gone. She didn't love me anymore. I remember the last night we had together. I couldn't sleep as I lay in the bed next to her. I remember stroking her hair and mildly touching her around her face and hair throughout the night. The next morning, she said that I had given her a headache just by softly touching her through the night. It made that morning almost unbearable. I thought I was going crazy. I had never heard her say something like that to me. Right then and there my world fell apart. It would never be the same again. The world as I knew it did not exist anymore. She left and never came back. She was gone in a moment. Satan destroyed my most valued and cherished possession, my family, in just a few brief moments, in a matter of days. It caught me unawares.

But that is the way sin works. The way Satan deceives. She had left me a long time ago. I just hadn't recognized it. I had been vulnerable for a long time and couldn't see it. I didn't know how vulnerable I was until it took me like an unsuspecting, raging storm ripping apart everything in its way. I had been completely out of tune. I felt insecure but didn't understand what was happening until it happened. Nothing drastic happened in the months before, but there had to be little signs that I ignored. She had left me a long time ago little by little, she drifted, and it was secretly done. And then she was just gone. I quickly became a statistic, a casualty, and felt unimportant in this vast empty universe after all I had done. I was alone and had no value, at least not to her, the most important person to me in the world. It seemed like I was easily replaced.

I couldn't work. I couldn't sleep. I had insomnia. She left, moved out of state and in a rush. My life was through. It was done. It was over, and it would never be same again. What do you do when that happens? How do you gather yourself up, every fragmented part, and continue? On top of all of that, she left me with all the mess of explaining everything to our son, my family, and friends. She was so soft spoken, beautiful, kind and pleasant. Everyone just figured it had to be my fault. It made it impossible for me to exist in my own community of friends or church family. I felt like I was in a fishbowl, exposed and in the raw, naked with my weaknesses uncovered for everyone to see. I was being examined by every homegrown psychologist and person I knew.

I could not breathe. I didn't hear from her again until months had gone by. My mother came over to pack my wife's things and get them out of the way. God knows I couldn't do it. I was so bad off, that she couldn't bring herself to leave. She lay in bed beside me and fell asleep. However, I didn't sleep. I couldn't sleep normally for the next two years. The man I once knew that was tough, independent, and resourceful was gone. I couldn't even make it through the night without my mother.

Until that moment in time, I considered myself as a man of God. As a provider and supporter of my family, I had always served a dual purpose as a minister and an employee—a person who worked countless hours to support his family and minister to hurting people. I now became one of those hurting people. I was falling fast and would not be able to recover for years. I had different roles; I was a construction worker, and I was a pastor; I was a welder, an insurance salesman, a shrimp shed worker, clothes salesman, automobile salesman and always a minister. I would work and juggle many jobs at once to support my family and ministry. Every job I had been on I had won a soul for Jesus.

But now I was paralyzed and lost. I tried to go to church and continue my ministry, but the church I had been working with said that it would be unwise to do so while going through a divorce and suspended me indefinitely. I called a pastor friend of mine to see if he could use me. Although I had told him of my wife leaving me, I had left the details out. I did not want to slander my son's mother. He seemed to lay blame and guilt at my door and declined to use me. Everyone was right about one thing: I really and truly could not attend church, much less worship, and surely could not minister.

All I could think about was her. Where was she? What was she doing right then? Why did she leave? The deepest part of my soul had been cut in two. It felt like I had been murdered. I had no ministry left and going to work was the hardest thing to do in the emotional state I was in. That left me with nothing but an absolute failure in every aspect of my life, my family, ministry, and secular work. I had only one thing that seemed to be permanent: insomnia.

The pressure of negative thoughts would come in waves of torment. I would see images and dream the most ungodly dreams about what she would be doing. I was tormented day and night, and it would not stop. I couldn't help myself. I would feel deeply hurt, then deeply in love with her, then get angry and hate her and hate that I had ever met her. I hated that I wasted all those years and then would wish for them again. It seemed like I was a walking dead person, filled with the most uncontrollable passions, desires, and emotions.

I was a walking time bomb. I could explode at any minute. I was the angriest person I ever met. I would have thoughts of murder towards the people involved with my divorce. I would hurt and then the rage and anger would come. I was dangerous. I became a violent person. I vowed no one would ever disrespect me again. No one ever did again without paying a tremendous price for it. I put people who disrespected me in the hospital on several occasions. It was like I was filled with some virus or disease and my flesh was rotting off my body.

I had given it my best, and my best was not good enough. I

was beaten. I was a failure, and I just gave up. I had to get away from that place. I left, moved to Houston, and started a job there. It was on that job I was introduced to meth, and just a few months after my divorce I was hooked—a full-blown meth addict. Shortly after becoming addicted, I became a wholesale distributor of illegal drugs and spent the next twelve years on the run, partying night and day, staying in motel after motel, and vowing to live any way I wanted. After all, I had done it God's way before and where did that get me?

But running began to take its toll on me. My life was spinning out of control. I began to wear down, and the addiction to drugs started threatening my sanity, freedom, and health. I began to remember how peaceful and calm my life used to be. I now lived in a constant state of emptiness. There was a desolate, lonely, hollow feeling that never left me. I began to see the results of living in sin, and addiction.

Several months before I was completely delivered, God started laying the groundwork for my transformation when Jachin Dadar contacted me through the internet. Jachin was trying to get in touch with me and was a true man of God—a pastor and evangelist who had served in leadership positions his whole life. His mother and father were great pioneers in the ministry and were closely knit with my parents in the ministry. For him to reach out like that, after years of being out of touch, was a real sign from God. God had given him a longing in his heart to reach out to me. He had no idea of the life I was leading and my addiction, but even after finding out, he showed me real love and invited me to stay with him and his wife, Cindy. I stayed with them for a couple of weeks. He was the only person from my past that reached out to me. It spoke to my heart.

I had family that would not have invited me to stay with them. There is always a risk involved in helping someone in addiction and sin, but the risk wasn't important to him. It seemed like I was all that mattered. God was talking to me through him and Cindy. I drank coffee, ate tuna fish and crackers and home cooked meals, and wasn't judged. It was a very peaceful moment in time. I felt loved and valued for the first time in over eleven years. It put the desire in me to want to get things right. He reintroduced me to my heavenly Father.

The thing was I couldn't just abandon my girlfriend, Jennifer. When I left Jachin's home, I was worried about her. I also had no safe place to stay and get on my feet. For a couple of weeks, I had given it my best, but the desires of the flesh were more than I could handle. There was much to learn, and I was not willing to give God all of me. Jennifer meant more to me than my freedom from addiction. There is no way that a person who loves to be high and loves the things of the world more than God can walk in deliverance. I loved God but loved her and the world more. I went back to her and fell back into the old lifestyle. I didn't see any other way out. I had tried for a moment, but my love for her and meth overtook me as soon as I left Jachin's. Because of my ties to the world and the cares of life, I was enticed and lured back into addiction.

But it was really different this time around. This time, God's powerful voice and the gentleness of the Holy Spirit would eventually draw me to Christ and Him alone. God began to show me that I was on borrowed time, and I would begin to pay heavy consequences for living in addiction. I was aware that I was breaking God's heart by not coming to Him. The conviction of the Holy Spirit was slowly revealing to me the greatest detrimental choice I was making, that acquiring my identity from someone or something other than God was destroying me. It had destroyed my self-worth and true purpose in life. My life meant nothing without having someone in it to validate my importance, and I realized that if that was someone other than God, I was in trouble. How could any person compete with God, provide spiritual completeness, heal hurt, and give strength to my inward man,

let alone fulfill my deepest desires and longings for eternal meaning?

After years of chaos and confusion, and on the run after avoiding multiple arrests, getting arrested, and now on my third court case, I finally came to a powerful spiritual awakening, a place of surrender, and a re-commitment to God. But this time I was fully aware that Jennifer and everything else would have to be secondary to God's call. Being able to make that commitment is what totally set me free. Even though I was in jail, I was free and had returned home. I was standing in a crowded jail cell but clothed and in my right mind, completely healed and restored.

As I stood there, I began to feel God had much more for me, and I felt like something was missing. My spirit began to ache. So, I asked God, "What is it?" That's when the Holy Spirit allowed me to see a picture of my past that I had misplaced and forgotten. I began to remember a moment in my early childhood, a wonderful moment between my mother and me. I saw us praying at the altar in an old country church in East Texas, and God was baptizing me with the Holy Ghost. As I remembered that glorious transformation at the age of twelve, a deep-seated hunger rose from within me, a ground-swell of spiritual emotions, and I began to call on God. I began to ask God to refill me again with the baptism of fire. No sooner than I began to ask, I began to speak in other tongues. And like a light in a bleak dark world, while standing in the corner of a crowded jail cell, God wonderfully filled me with His presence and gave me a brand new prayer language. A spirit of joy entered my longing soul, and God gave me a new song from that moment on.

My helper, the comforter had returned home. I was never alone again. I used to frequent bars and sit alone in a corner going where only the lonely go, and now I had a resident power with me that emboldened my character. I spoke in an unknown tongue under my breath. God was speaking through me. I was a validated servant and new soldier in the army of the living God. I would continue to pray in my understanding and to pray in my new heavenly language from that moment on. I have never stopped since then. It has been the single most important gift that God has given me. If you let me, I will take you through it, step by step, so that you may comprehend it fully and spiritually. **Hold on to your seat. You are about to embark on the fast track of a miraculous journey. If you are spiritually hungry for all that God has and are committed to making a diligent effort to seek Him first, then as He has promised, "Those that hunger and thirst after righteousness shall be filled." And, "out of your belly shall flow rivers of living water."**

The baptism, its purpose and meaning, and why tongues?

God is an interactive God. He loves to collaborate. He wants and desires to be a partner with you, to work jointly on an activity, especially to produce or to create something with you. He has made you a person like Him with creative desires. He wants to communicate with you. What greater way than having His own language in you, on a spiritual level, where your spirit can communicate with His Spirit unencumbered by the world? Our physical bodies and minds have a limited understanding and view. **He wants to give us His all-knowing, universal knowledge working in us, praying through us, exactly what we need to implement His plan and purpose in our lives. God wants to give us the assurance and the peace of mind we need to reach great achievement.**

Praying in tongues is praying in a language that is unknown to us. It is not familiar, well known, or conversant to us. The Apostle Paul, who wrote thirteen of the books in the New Testament, had a lot to say about praying in tongues.

In 1 Corinthians 14:14 (NLT), Paul says, "For if I pray in

tongues, my spirit is praying, but I don't understand what I am saying."

Paul went on to say that he would pray both ways, from his understanding and without it.

In 1 Corinthians 14:15 (NLT), Paul says, "Well then, what shall I do? I will pray in the spirit, and I will also pray in words I understand. I will sing in the spirit, and I will also sing in words I understand."

We are spirit beings with a body and soul. Through the baptism of the Holy Spirit, we now have an opportunity to communicate in the spirit. A supernatural, paranormal way that frees us from the limitations of our own intellect and reasoning, praying according to the perfect will of God.

In Romans 8:26 (NKJV), Paul says, "Likewise the Spirit also helps in our weaknesses. For we do not know what we should pray for as we ought, but the Spirit Himself makes intercession for us with groanings which cannot be uttered."

When you are experiencing difficult circumstances and your faith has never ventured past a certain level of achievement that a new set of problems requires, the word of God teaches us to pray in our prayer language to build our faith. Men of faith that have extraordinary results pray in the spirit. It becomes highly effective. It strengthens your resolve while strengthening your faith at the same time.

Jude 1:20 (AMP) says, "But you, beloved, build yourselves up [founded] on your most holy faith [make progress, rise like an edifice higher and higher], praying in the Holy Spirit."

Praying in tongues gives the Holy Spirit control to intercede through us. It gives God the opportunity to collaborate with us. So many times, during conflict, stress, and difficulties concerning relationships, decisions, times of change, praying for our children and ourselves, we just don't know what is needed. We sometimes can be praying for the wrong things. With our limited earthly view and understanding, we

get it wrong sometimes. That is where our Helper, the Comforter, the Holy Spirit prays and intercedes for us, guaranteeing success. This gives us the complete assurance and promise of healing, salvation, deliverance, and prosperity of the believer. Hallelujah, glory to God! That is just phenomenal.

Jesus is the baptizer of fire

The most distinguishing factor and characteristic of Christ compared to all other prophets, and spiritual leaders, is the baptism of fire. All others before Him had no beneficial gift or supernatural phenomenon associated with their ministry like this. Jesus offered a baptism of fire available to anyone that would believe. Many Old Testament prophets and leaders had evidence of supernatural happenings and miracles at various times. They all experienced the power of God, but nothing that had a promise like this. And none contained an inclusive invitation to all of humanity. According to biblical prophecy several hundred years before, and John the Baptist, this quality would be only distinctive to the Messiah, the savior of the world. Here is the account of John the Baptist:

Matthew 3:1-12 (KJV) says, "In those days came John the Baptist, preaching in the wilderness of Judaea, And saying, Repent ye: for the kingdom of heaven is at hand. For this is he that was spoken of by the prophet Esaias, saying, The voice of one crying in the wilderness, Prepare ye the way of the Lord, make his paths straight. And the same John had his raiment of camel's hair, and a leather girdle about his loins; and his meat was locusts and wild honey. Then went out to him Jerusalem, and all Judaea, and all the region round about Jordan, And were baptized of him in Jordan, confessing their sins. But when he saw many of the Pharisees and

Sadducees come to his baptism, he said unto them, O generation of vipers, who hath warned you to flee from the wrath to come? Bring forth, therefore, fruits meet for repentance: And think not to say within yourselves, we have Abraham to our father: for I say unto you, that God is able of these stones to raise up children unto Abraham. And now also the axe is laid unto the root of the trees: therefore, every tree which bringeth not forth good fruit is hewn down, and cast into the fire. I indeed baptize you with water unto repentance: but he that cometh after me is mightier than I, whose shoes I am not worthy to bear: he shall baptize you with the Holy Ghost, and with fire: Whose fan is in his hand, and he will thoroughly purge his floor, and gather his wheat into the garner; but he will burn up the chaff with unquenchable fire."

Matthew 3:13-17 (KJV) says, "Then cometh Jesus from Galilee to Jordan unto John, to be baptized of him. But John forbad him, saying, I have need to be baptized of thee, and comest thou to me? And Jesus answering said unto him, Suffer it to be so now: for thus it becometh us to fulfil all righteousness. Then he suffered him. And Jesus, when he was baptized, went up straightway out of the water: and, lo, the heavens were opened unto him, and he saw the Spirit of God descending like a dove, and lighting upon him: And lo a voice from heaven, saying, This is my beloved Son, in whom I am well pleased."

The authenticity of prophecy and the exceptional plan of God are revealed openly, in spectacular fashion, through authenticated dialogue exposed to the world. This is what separates the God of the Bible from all other religions. Our God knows the future.

What makes John the Baptist such an important figure in the history of humanity is the timing of his arrival, the significant high priority of his assignment, and the risk involved in sharing his message. His arrival as the forerunner of Christ the Messiah was the fulfillment of a prophecy given approximately 400 years earlier (Isaiah 40:3). Isaiah the prophet writes about a person in the desert who prepares the way of the Lord. He had the key role of preparing the groundwork for the ministry of Jesus Christ.

John, with bold, unrelenting preaching, appears suddenly on the scene in the Judean desert clothed in coarse camel's hair, wearing a rugged leather belt, eating locusts and wild honey and proclaims Jesus to be the Son of God and the Lamb of God who takes away the sin of the world. John also sees Jesus as the Lord over humanity, separating those who refused to believe, casting them into never-ending fire and baptizing His followers with the Holy Ghost and fire.

So, let me lay down the facts as I see them, as the Holy Spirit laid this out in my mind at the same time I am writing this strictly from inspiration. I'll give you six important facts that shed light on the uniqueness of this meeting between John and Jesus.

John is a robust, strong, hearty man coming from the desert area prophesied by Isaiah.

He obtains fame and a huge following.

His message is the same message prophesied in Isaiah.

As it appears in scripture, he sees Jesus for the first time while baptizing his followers. It catches him by complete surprise, and he shouts, "Behold the Messiah, the Christ, the lamb of God," which recognizes His identity and describes His ministry and crucifixion.

Jesus had not even started His ministry yet and was completely unknown to the public. He was part of the crowd who came to be baptized, with no distinguishing outward qualities.

It was political and religious suicide to make this announcement.

John and Christ would mean nothing to me if the circumstances of any of this changed. First, if John was a man who had no following or fame (which took time to build, and a special type of man), it would have been between two unknown people commenting to each other, although a true statement, it would not be important. It is the witnesses, and the future expectation of the witnesses, that makes it important. It makes John liable and his followers judges. Just mere preaching without fame and followers would not have risk involved in John making the statement. No one would have cared, but at the same meeting he called out religious leaders to repent, and he publicly placed his approval on an obscure man called Jesus. Validation becomes more credible through the risk involved. Without risk, no one would have even cared what John said.

Second, if Jesus had been famous at the time, then it would not seem spiritually inspired, and it would not have required supernatural prophetic insight. Any normal person could have said it otherwise. But at the time, Jesus was an unknown figure. If Jesus would not have gone on to be the greatest of spiritual advisers, the most influential man in the history of mankind, and had Jesus not died as the lamb of God, then none of this would have meant anything to anyone then, now, or tomorrow. **For all of that to come about from 400-year-old prophecy is mind-boggling to me. It validates the Holy Spirit's knowledge of the future and His importance in finding our true purpose, which He has planned for us.**

Most astonishing when talking about Jesus, you are talking about the most unique and unusual extraordinary life in the annals of time. He was a man who did not travel very far and traveled on foot. He was never married and did not even own a home. He taught on hillsides and by lakefronts with no amplified speaker system. He also taught without the use of a digital recorder, camera, video, or digital film recorder. Without a printing press, or copy machine. In a time when there were no televisions, the internet, cell phones, or radio signals. The common people loved him. The religious, the political, and the famous didn't. He made public appearances for only three years. He was persecuted and narrowly escaped with his life many times through some stealth-like maneuvers.

He healed the sick, raised the dead, cast out devils, and taught a revolutionary way to live. He taught us to love our enemies, and that meekness is real strength. He died the death of a criminal and was buried in a borrowed tomb. He was the only one to have been resurrected from the dead and appeared to over five hundred people after his death and resurrection. More books have been written about Him than any other man that has ever lived. Time stopped at His birth and started after His death (B.C., A.D.) Nothing has ever been the same since. People are still willing to die for their belief in Him, and no one has yet been able to live 100% as He lived, yet millions are trying. This book is a testimony of Christ living in me and saving my life. **When John says that Jesus baptizes in fire, I believe him. It is my testimony and my personal, profound experience that the baptism of fire is real and powerful. Not only because I experienced it as a little boy, but because when I became a man and so desperately needed that fire, He gave it to me.**

The promise is to all believers

Not only does God want to give you this great blessing in your life, He has given us specific orders that explicitly command us to do nothing else but seek, desire, and receive it. In the Great Commission, Jesus' final words to His closest followers, He promised that supernatural signs would follow those that believe.

Mark 16:15-20 (NLT) says, "And then he told them, "Go into all the world and preach the good news to everyone. Anyone who believes and is baptized will be saved. But anyone who refuses to believe will be condemned. These miraculous signs will accompany those who believe: They will cast out demons in my name, and they will speak in new languages. They will be able to handle snakes with safety, and if they drink anything poisonous, it won't hurt them. They will be able to place their hands on the sick, and they will be healed. When the Lord Jesus had finished talking with them, he was taken up into heaven and sat down in the place of honor at God's right hand. The disciples went everywhere and preached, and the Lord worked through them, confirming what they said by many miraculous signs."

These are the signs listed:

1. They will cast out demons.
2. They will speak in new languages.
3. They will be able to handle snakes with safety (accidental contact, such as Paul on the island of Malta in Acts 28:3).
4. If they drink anything poisonous, it won't hurt them (again accidentally).
5. They will be able to place their hands on the sick, and they will be healed.

Notice these signs are promised to anyone. The only qualification is to believe. Notice that all the signs are unique to abilities beyond the laws of scientific understanding. They also defy laws of nature and physics. They are miraculous. At no time in the chronicles of our history has God not been there for us. He has always been a valuable source of healing and miracles. He is a very present help to those who call upon Him. He has conditions that we sometimes must meet, but they are not laborious or grievous. The promise of a prayer language or "tongues" is on the same order of supernatural quality as the other signs. He is not talking about a learned language in this text. A learned language would not need to be listed in this passage simply because it does not require a miracle to learn how to speak in a known language; human effort can do that. These signs are evidence of faith in our lives. What is important to understand is Jesus did not instruct His followers to do anything but believe. He didn't order us to pick a certain language and learn it naturally. It is a gift, and all we have to do is receive it.

Jesus commanded the disciples to wait for the baptism of the Holy Spirit

Acts 1:4-5 (KJV) says, "And, being assembled together with them, commanded them that they should not depart from Jerusalem, but wait for the promise of the Father, which, saith he, ye have heard of me. For John truly baptized with water; but ye shall be baptized with the Holy Ghost not many days hence."

Ephesians 5:18 (KJV) says, "And be not drunk with wine, wherein is excess; but be filled with the Spirit;"

That same command applies to every disciple of Christ in this generation also. The Holy Spirit reaches globally and interdenominationally, to every born-again believer and crosses all ethnic and cultural barriers.

Romans 2:11 (KJV) says, "For there is no respect of persons with God."

Acts 2:39 (KJV) says, "For the promise is unto you, and to your children, and to all that are afar off, even as many as the Lord our God shall call."

God does not show favoritism. The purpose for them to do nothing until they were baptized in the Holy Spirit is because they needed power to become witnesses or overcomers.

Acts 1:8 (KJV) says, "But ye shall receive power, after that the Holy Ghost is come upon you: and ye shall be witnesses unto me both in Jerusalem, and in all Judaea, and in Samaria, and unto the uttermost part of the earth."

If the disciples who walked with Jesus—lived with Him, knew Him in the flesh, and witnessed His death and resurrection—needed power, how much more do you think you, and I need it? If they needed it in their day, how much more do we need the baptism today? We live in a far more wicked generation and period of history than the disciples. We are faced with temptation 24 hours a day, and the pressure to do wrong is before us constantly in the form of smart phones, tablets, and computers. Wicked advertising and other forms of evil constantly bombard us with thoughts of temptation. God would not leave us in a vulnerable and weak position lacking power. Certainly, God who empowered them will empower us.

Psalm 84:11 (NIV2011) says, "For the LORD God is a sun and shield; the LORD bestows favor and honor; no good thing does he withhold from those whose walk is blameless."

The Apostle Paul, the human expert on the Holy Spirit and His baptism, says, "be filled with the Spirit" (Ephesians 5:18 KJV), "forbid not to speak with tongues" (1 Corinthians 14:39 KJV), and "I thank God that I speak in tongues more than all of you" (1 Corinthians 14:18 NIV2011). Throughout the history of the early church in the New Testament, it was the customary practice after salvation for the believer to experience the baptism of the Holy Spirit. Acts 2 records the birth of speaking in tongues among the disciples and the 120 gathered in the upper room, the baptism of the Samaritan believers in Acts 8, of Saul of Tarsus in Acts 9, of the Roman centurion and his entire house ten years after the Day of Pentecost in Acts 10, and also of the Ephesians in Acts 19.

Twenty years after the upper room experience, the early church was still receiving the baptism of the Holy Spirit, and the disciples were still laying hands on common everyday believers to receive this phenomenal experience. We can clearly see it was a customary experience the disciples encouraged all believers to experience. They also preached it to all believers, in various geographical locations, and times. We see the doctrine of the laying on of hands and prayer of faith as the primary means of receiving the baptism and the customary practice in the early church's history. Nowhere in scripture is the baptism of fire denied to any believer with proper motives and intentions. The very dynamics of holy scriptures teach us to move on, continue and grow in spiritual knowledge and experience. Throughout God's instructions, it is taught that there is always more God has to offer us and never less. Everywhere in scripture, we see a God who is encouraging us to receive everything available to us.

How to receive the Holy Spirit

All you have to do is ask and receive. In Luke 11:9-13 (NLT), Jesus says, "And so I tell you, keep on asking, and you will receive what you ask for. Keep on seeking, and you will find. Keep on knocking, and the door will be opened to you. For everyone who asks receives. Everyone who seeks finds. And to everyone who knocks, the door will be opened. You fathers—if your children ask for a fish, do you give them a snake instead? Or if they ask for an egg, do you give them a scorpion? Of course not! So, if you sinful people know how to give good gifts to your children, how much more will your heavenly Father give the Holy Spirit to those who ask him."

Jesus said that all you have to do is ask expecting to receive. He also said that you do not have to be afraid. God will not give you something you didn't ask for. God knew the human mind and how it works. He knew that we were prone to resist change, and could be afraid of something new to us. So, He made guarantees and promises. He said nothing evil would come upon you. So, ask. It will come upon you as it did to me and the countless millions before me.

Mark 11:24 (KJV) says, "Therefore I say unto you, What things soever ye desire, when ye pray, believe that ye receive them, and ye shall have them."

Jesus says it again—if you desire something when you pray, just believe you receive it and you will have it. Another essential key is thanksgiving and praise.

Philippians 4:6 (NKJV) says, "Be anxious for nothing, but in everything by prayer and supplication, with thanksgiving, let your requests be made known to God"

Most people get filled with the Holy Spirit after asking God for it during worship. They ask God to fill them, and begin to thank Him for it, and worship Him, and love Him for all He has done for them. As they begin to feel His warmth, they have a spiritual encounter, and begin to utter, and speak in other tongues. Just begin to worship the giver of all gifts, the baptizer of the supernatural in your life, the Lord of Lords, the King of Kings, the Champion of Champions, the lover of your soul, our Savior, Jesus Christ of Nazareth. Humbly and modestly come before Him, by whom the worlds were made, and the universe was formed. Submit to His command to receive, and thank Him in advance. Continue to pray, waiting in faith, opening your mouth wide so He can fill it with words you do not understand, talk, and let it flow without the slightest doubt, and the well of water will become rivers of anointing and power.

Psalm 81:10 (NLT) says, "For it was I, the LORD your God, who rescued you from the land of Egypt. Open your mouth wide, and I will fill it with good things."

7

THE ESSENTIAL, INDISPENSABLE, CRUCIAL ATTITUDE OF FAITH

METHADDICTSHELP, FACEBOOK POST
DECEMBER 26, 2015

GOD WILL NEVER STOP LOVING YOU, NEVER GIVE UP ON YOU, AND NEVER LEAVE EVEN IF YOU FAIL TIME AND TIME AGAIN.... SO, DON'T TORMENT YOURSELF OVER CONSTANT FAILURE...RATHER REPLACE IT WITH THE CONSTANT GRACE, LOVE AND FORGIVENESS OF GOD. HIS PLAN HAD ROOM FOR ALL OF YOUR MISTAKES OR YOU WOULDN'T BE HERE. IF YOU KEEP TRYING AND NEVER GIVE UP BELIEVING IN YOURSELF AND THE LOVE OF YOUR HEAVENLY FATHER, THEN YOU CAN BEAT THE ODDS. THE ONLY DIFFERENCE IN MY LIFE AND THE ADDICTS IS NOT THAT I DIDN'T FAIL IN MY FIGHT TO OVERCOME ADDICTION BUT THAT I DIDN'T QUIT, ALTHOUGH I HAD MANY OPPORTUNITIES TO BE OVERCOME WITH GUILT, CHAOS, CONFUSION AND DEPRESSION THAT COMES WITH RELAPSE....I JUST REFUSED TO ACCEPT IT AND KEPT BELIEVING IN MYSELF AND GOD'S GRACE....AND HERE I AM PRAYING AND ENCOURAGING HUNDREDS OF OTHERS WHO ARE IN THE SAME BATTLE I WAS...JUST A SHORT FEW YEARS AGO THIS WAS UNTHINKABLE..........TPC. (UNEDITED)

*H*ow far you go in your life will depend on what you believe about God and yourself; it is the one crucial and indispensable quality that you need to recover everything in life that belongs to you. Your full recovery depends upon it. It is the critical and essential element required for your future success. Even when all else fails, and everything around you is falling apart, if you still have a solemn resolve to believe in yourself, and that God is still with you, you will eventually become a winner. Faith guarantees a rebound.

What you believe is the motivation behind everything you do in life. It has been said that a man will go as far as his faith will take him. For a long time, I didn't believe that my life would ever be a success again. I just couldn't see it. My dad could see it, but I had given up. My dad would tell me that I was going to come out of this, and God was going to bless me. He had faith. He was a praying man. He would talk about my calling and just love me. He never said one negative thing to me. He never pleaded or begged me to change. I would come home to visit with him and mom periodically. I stayed there off and on. I know I would not be in the position I am in today if it were not for Dad's prayers. In the end, I had his example to look to. God had taken care of my parents. My dad had unshakable faith. He led a simple life. He was not flashy, or egotistical. He had a modest home paid for and always had a reliable automobile.

When hurricane Rita ravaged the small town he lived in, his house was not touched. Every house around him had been damaged but his. I remember asking Dad if he had insurance. He said he didn't have the conventional kind. His insurance was in his faith that God would protect his home. My parents were in their late seventies and waited until the last minute to evacuate. The only reason they did is because my sister would not have it any other way. Then, they were the first to return to their home after the hurricane. The conditions were so bad that the city officials were not allowing anyone back. That lasted for a couple of weeks. But not for them. My sister could not stop them. Even the city ordinance couldn't stop them from returning. My sister said it was too dangerous. There was no electricity, power lines were down, and trees had fallen. The streets were blocked with debris and trees. But Dad and Mom just got in their car the day after and drove through and around it all. They got home to see those huge walnut trees in their yard still standing and not even a shingle had been misplaced on their roof. They didn't mind not having electricity. They lit oil lanterns and rested quietly in their home undisturbed. Had they stayed, they would have been better off. We would have worried and been the worse for it, but not them.

Dad didn't have a lot of money, but what he did have was worth more than what money could buy. He had faith. He knew that God would make up the difference. If he didn't have the money for a need in his life, he knew God would come through. My father was always up hours before everyone else. He would pray and read the Bible several hours every morning. He knew I was using drugs and living badly. He knew I had lost my faith. But he always acted like it would turn out ok in the end. He said, "God is going to take all of that hurt, and pain that you feel and turn it into a good thing." He said, "God is going to use what you have been through to prosper you, God is not through with you yet." I would call him every day. I would be partying, high, and out of state somewhere, but would always stop long enough to talk to Dad. I loved hearing his voice, and he would always say, "I'm praying for you, Tim." I wanted what he had. I just didn't think God cared about me that much. My parents loved me. They were good parents and had raised me in church. I loved them, but I was a broken man.

My faith was destroyed. I felt like a failure. More than that, I was angry with God. I didn't think that God cared about me. I had lived for Him, and my life ended up in a mess. He didn't protect my home or family. My work for God was unrewarded. When Satan steals your hope, you have nothing left to live for. If Satan can rob you of your trust and faith in God, then your life becomes meaningless and purposeless.

During this recovery process, there will be many moments when you might feel like this isn't working. Time might seem to stand still. While looking for a job and getting back on your feet, things could look impossible. You might feel like you are facing insurmountable odds and there is no way you will be able to reconcile with your wife or husband, or maybe get your kids back. Your court cases could be overwhelming, and you might not have anyone left in this life who believes in you but God.

Remember God loves you and He sent His Son to die for you before you were born. He has invested His best in you. During those times of testing, if you will just trust God and continue being faithful, God will come through for you. God honors faith. As normal human beings made in God's image, His DNA is in us. We gravitate toward people who have a favorable opinion of us, who respect us, enjoy our company, and most of all believe in us. We couldn't hang around someone who didn't. We couldn't bear it.

It is the same with God, except more severe. He sees what we really think in our hearts. That is where He communicates with us, in our spirit. It is impossible for Him to ignore an unbelieving heart. It saddens Him and grieves His Spirit. Like you and I, God is attracted to someone who believes in Him. He knows it's difficult to have faith, so when He finds faith, He cannot deny His presence from you. He offers Himself wholeheartedly to you. He enjoys your company. Because of the respect, honor, and faith you have in God, your door becomes open for God's love and companionship. Faith is the one thing that touches God's heart. It moves

God more than anything else. It is not a wonder to me why Jesus said,

Mark 11:22 (KJV) "Have faith in God."

Mark 11:24 (KJV) "Therefore I say unto you, What things soever ye desire, when ye pray, believe that ye receive them, and ye shall have them."

So, when you pray with the right attitude, you can write your own ticket with God. God desires faith and confidence in Him. That's what matters the most with God. He doesn't care about how talented and strong you are, just whether you believe in Him, want Him, need Him, and trust in His love for you.

A person will never put himself in the position of obedience if they do not believe in the person who gives the charge. God's commandments are what He uses to protect us from the hurt and the results of bad decisions. But it takes faith to be able to receive God's wisdom and counsel. When I hurt so bad I thought, "How could God love me?" **When your image of God becomes distorted, your faith is threatened.** The reason I am writing this book is to restore your faith. So many people have lost hope in life. **Hal Lindsey said, "Man can live about forty days without food, about three days without water, about eight minutes without air, but only for one second without hope."** I can testify to that.

My hope and faith were in my wife, family, ministry, and work. My view of God was connected to the way my wife felt about me, and my performance at work or in the ministry. When my wife left, my family was destroyed, my ministry taken from me, and I was no longer able to work or walk around in a sane fashion, it destroyed me and my image of God. All of those things were connected to my faith in God, and I felt God had let me down. **Emil Brunner said, "What oxygen is to the lungs, such is hope to the meaning of life."** When the things in your life are your hope, just like oxygen, when they are gone, your meaning for living is also gone. **If your faith in God is connected to those** things, then when they leave you, your faith in Him is also gone. More importantly, you lose faith in yourself. If all those things are representative of who you are and your abilities, the next thing that goes is self-respect and self-worth, and you begin to feel inferior to other people. You begin to doubt everything you have ever done.

It is then that depression sets in and nothing has importance anymore. For many of us, that is where drug use starts or gets worse. If a man has nothing to lose, he is game for anything. A man that has nothing to lose is a dangerous man. He no longer cares about his life. His life is not that important to him any longer. The more you lose of yourself, the worse you become. **That is why our faith must be in something that is permanent.**

Malachi 3:6 (KJV) says, "For I am the LORD, I change not;"

Hebrews 1:10-12 (KJV) says, "And, Thou, Lord, in the beginning hast laid the foundation of the earth; and the heavens are the works of thine hands: They shall perish; but thou remainest; and they all shall wax old as doth a garment; And as a vesture shalt thou fold them up, and they shall be changed: but thou art the same, and thy years shall not fail."

God never changes. Your faith must be grounded in a purpose for your life that nothing in life can affect or touch. It was when the revelation came to me that God was not in all the terrible things that had happened to me, that I began to heal. In reality, Satan, people, and I had caused them. What caused my catastrophic failure was my faith was never completely in the God of this universe, and that I could not find happiness in Him, and Him alone. Jesus said that a person's life does not consist of his possessions and property. When your possessions disappear, what do you have left? When people disappear and leave you holding the bag, where do you put your trust?

Luke 12:15 (KJV) says, "And he said unto them, Take heed, and beware of covetousness: for a man's life consisteth not in the abundance of the things which he possesseth."

If your happiness depends on your success, achievements, or relationships, then you are in trouble. None of those things are permanent. **When I surrendered my life to Christ, I found out that the very thing I had been running from was the only thing that could save me. Once I had God's acceptance, I was free to fail, and at the same time, free to believe that if I did fall, God would see me through. I finally experienced true freedom—freedom to live again.** The wonderful thing about having faith in God is that it is a personal thing and permanent. No one can take that away from you. It is between you and Him. **How ironic that I was on the run with nowhere to go, and that I found the freedom a person can only dream of, in a lonely jail cell.** It was where I caught up with myself, where there was no place to go but one, to my Creator, and I was set free. When my faith was restored, my life was restored. If you can hold on to your faith, you can achieve everything you have ever dreamed of.

What is an attitude of faith?

What is faith? Faith is belief with a strong inward conviction that something is true and real even though there might not be any tangible, visible, proof. Faith is complete trust, confidence, reliance or devotion. Faith is being convinced of the truth—willing to die for it and act on it even if it is only partially manifested or not manifested at all. Faith is knowing that if you live as though it will come to pass in your life, it will. Faith is that awesome inner assurance that everything is going to be fine. **When Jesus took me in as the little, lost boy that I was, I felt His warmth, presence, acceptance, and reassurance, removing all my fears and** doubts. I had an attitude of faith that from that moment on, all my needs would be taken care of for the rest of my life here on this earth. Even though I had great needs in the natural world I lived in, my faith was not based on that, it was based on my spiritual condition.

What is an attitude? It is a noun—a person, place or thing. All nouns have certain qualities about them. A noun is something you can keep, hold, protect, and call your own. **The definition of attitude is a settled way of thinking about someone or something, typically one that is reflected in a person's behavior.** So, an attitude is a way of thinking you keep with you that determines your behavior beforehand.

That is where my faith is. I have thoughts of faith that remain in me and determine my behavior before I act or think. My attitude is that God will work a miracle, do the impossible, or change the order of things, all on my behalf if necessary. **It is based on my knowledge of the character of God. The more I know about my heavenly Father, the more faith I have.** Just like my Dad's attitude. It appeared to him that nothing I had done would affect his view of how I would end up. He had taken me to rehab once. My body was filled with every drug you could think of—cocaine, meth, heroin, marijuana, opiates, and only God knows what else. I was a mess. They were talking about putting me in the hospital and getting a room available for me immediately. I had an elevated temperature, and the guy was scaring me. Not my Dad. Nope. No fear. I have never seen fear in my Dad's eyes, ever. He said, "Son, what do you want to do?" At that moment, I knew, as I looked into my Dad's eyes of faith, all fear left, and I said, "Dad I think I'll just come home where I'm safe." I never brought drugs to my Dad's home. I always respected him and mom. I stayed there for a couple of weeks, sleeping long hours. After a few days of eating home-cooked meals, I got better physically, but I was still a bag of bones.

The spirits of oppression took over again, and I was gone. I regret that my Dad and Mom went through that with me. I wish I could have been stronger, I just wasn't. I would play the guitar, mom would sing and play the piano, and for a few days, I had peace. **But through all of that, my Dad's attitude, before any event or troubled situation I was in, was an attitude that God was going to take care of me. I could hear it in the tone of his voice. The lack of urgency on his part, and the calmness that his presence ushered in the room.** My greatest example of faith came from my own precious father. I miss him so much.

I still look at his picture sitting on my desk—a picture I took from the window of my truck as I was leaving, just a brief moment, during that dreadful time in my life—and feel that deep assurance that God is with me. He walked up to my truck's open window, holding a cup of coffee in his hand, smiling to tell me bye. As I am writing this special love story of a man and his wayward son, it speaks volumes of the love of our heavenly Father. The rush of warmth and the presence of the Holy Spirit is in this room with me, tears are flowing and I am praying in tongues, emboldened with the power of love. I just want to say to you that I believe in you. I believe that God has a special plan for you, just like He sent me to write these words, my testimony of His love. He has not forgotten you. It doesn't matter how lonely you might feel, or unworthy you might think you are, God is crossing the lines and barriers, penetrating the very walls of your heart, to emphatically say, "I love you."

I now have that attitude of faith that my Dad had. I am his legacy and the next generation of faith. I take it with me everywhere. I have walked into rooms and changed the entire landscape of spirituality. There is no fear in my life. Where there is hopelessness, sickness, addiction, and the oppression of demonic spirits, my attitude of faith changes the very dynamics of the room from death to life. I always know that God is going to set someone free because I take God with me. My attitude carries His presence. I have prayed with hundreds of people from all over the world via phone and video from my Methaddictshelp page, and miracle after miracle of the same transforming power of God has changed their lives. I am just one man, doing things that I thought were impossible, no different than you except maybe one thing, an attitude of faith. You too, as I have described in the fourth chapter of this book, have that same calling and uniqueness from God. Whatever that calling may be, you can walk in it with confidence, trust, and with an attitude of faith in God that He will accomplish it.

Philippians 1:6 (NKJV) says, "being confident of this very thing, that He who has begun a good work in you will complete it until the day of Jesus Christ;"

Faith's foundation is the character of God

You can only have faith in what you know. If you do not know God intimately, how could you trust Him or believe in Him? It takes years for even married couples sometimes to be able to trust their partners with everything. There are some secrets of the past that a wife or husband may never tell each other until time has passed, and he has proven to be trustworthy, and she has proven to be faithful. Fear of the consequences prevented it from happening before. It is the same with God. You must open the line of communications with Him so that your relationship can grow. Growth comes from studying His written word (the Bible), prayer, and discipline. We will talk about some of that later on in this book. Right now, I just want to lay the groundwork of God's character for you, so that you can learn to walk in faith.

It is the character of God to actively pursue you when something is wrong

To give you concrete evidence of this fact, all you need to do is remember some things –like after you have failed at some point or disobeyed God and walked into a church service while people are worshipping, and immediately you felt the warmth and inviting presence of the Holy Spirit, pursuing you in love, reconciling you; or, remembering a time when you heard a message on the goodness of God, when all hope was lost in your situation, and immediately you felt His assurance. All you need to do is remember all the time you spent away from God and seeing there was never a time when He abandoned you completely. Every time you ever did something that was dangerous, or maybe thought of suicide or hurting someone, it was God pursuing you that stopped you.

In the garden of Eden when Adam sinned, he hid from God's presence. God pursued him and initiated the conversation, not the other way around. Adam was hiding cowardly trying to cover himself inadequately. It was God whose love and desire for fellowship pursued Adam behind those flimsy leaves. It is God pursuing you behind those layers of leaves covering your hurt and pain. It was God that provided the first sacrifice needed to restore their relationship. Can you remember those words? Adam, where are you? In reality, God was saying, "I need you. It's time for our visit. Come meet with me." God longed for fellowship with Adam. He has longed for fellowship with you also. Adam was walking in his own garden filled with fear, naked and vulnerable to Satan's attack, just as you might be. God is calling your name also. Desiring to protect you, cover your nakedness and have fellowship with you. Adam sinned, we all have sinned, but that hasn't stopped God. The word of God tells us, "while we were yet sinners, Christ died." God is always pursuing you.

Genesis 3:8-10 (NLT) says, "When the cool evening breezes were blowing, the man and his wife heard the LORD God walking about in the garden. So they hid from the LORD God among the trees. Then the LORD God called to the man, "Where are you?" He replied, "I heard you walking in the garden, so I hid. I was afraid because I was naked."

Genesis 3:21 (NLT) says, "And the LORD God made clothing from animal skins for Adam and his wife."

The thought of God pursuing us is revealed in the three parables of Christ in Luke 15.

In the parable of the lost sheep, Jesus left the 99 to find the one sheep that had lost its way. God is always concerned with those who become disenfranchised, alienated, and alone.

In the parable of the lost coin, although the woman had nine left, it had once been a set of ten. With God, nine is not good enough. It is within the fabric of who He is not to leave someone behind. The woman sweeps the entire house and searches until it is recovered. God will sweep the entire earth to locate any one that is missing from His valuable creation.

In the parable of the lost son, when the prodigal son returns home after wasting all his inheritance on sinful living, his father sees him from afar, and he is so glad to see him, he takes off in a run to meet him. He clothes him, restores his position as his heir, kills the fatted calf and celebrates because his son, who once was lost, has come home.

I just want you to know that God has taken off in a run to meet you as you are reading this book. He is overwhelmed with joy that you are pursuing Him. We see in this parable that God is not just interested in not leaving you behind, but much more. He loves us and celebrates our homecoming. He also acts as though we had never left, restoring our lives back to sanity, giving us full privileges, and our inheritance, with complete access to everything that belongs to us as His children.

So, when you feel like you have failed Him, know that He hurts as much as you do and is pursuing you, not willing to let you go. You can have the faith to always look to God when you see His unwillingness to let you go.

His character is revealed in the person and works of Jesus

John 10:30 (KJV) says, "I and *my* Father are one."

Many times, in the human mind, we wonder and mutter to ourselves, "If God was here right now, what would He do?" Jesus answered that question as He walked the earth's dirt floor, and entered man's dwelling. When He became a man, and dwelt among us, Jesus was God manifested in the flesh, God, Logos, or the Word. To be the Word of God, Jesus' life had to reveal the intentions of God in His words and actions. Jesus revealed the character of God to humanity. He illustrated the character of God in many ways.

Here is what Jesus did while on earth that will reveal the character of God. **In the volume of miracles listed below, the very expression of God's intentions and desires are revealed in a dynamic way. His love and compassion for humanity are self-evident. He felt compassion for everyone's needs. It is expressed in a variety of situations.**

Jesus never turned away anyone who needed healing. He healed them all.

Matthew 12:15 (MSG) says, "Jesus, knowing they were out to get him, moved on. A lot of people followed him, and he healed them all."

Jesus healed the nobleman's son (John 4:46), Peter's mother-in-law (Matthew 8:15), the centurion's servant (Matthew 8:13), lepers (Matthew 8:3, Mark 1:42, Luke 17:14), paralytics (Matthew 9:7, Mark 2:12, Luke 5:25), the impotent man at the pool of Bethesda (John 5:9), withered hands (Matthew 12:13), the woman with the issue of blood (Matthew 9:22), blindness (Matthew 9:30, Mark 8:25, John 9:7, Matthew 20:34, Mark 10:52), deaf and mute person (Mark 8:35), the woman with the spirit of infirmity (Luke

13:13), dropsy (Luke 14:4), and the soldier's ear when Peter had cut it off (Luke 22:51).

He set free everyone oppressed by demons and unclean spirits, including the man in the synagogue (Mark 1:26), the man possessed by the dumb demon (Matthew 9:33) and the blind and dumb demon (Matthew 12:22), the Gergesene demoniacs (Matthew 8:32), the Gadarene demoniac (Mark 5:13, Luke 8:33), the daughter of the Syrophoenician woman (Mark 7:30) and the lunatic child (Mark 9:26).

He hated to see people grieve so He raised the dead, including the son of the widow of Nain (Luke 7:15), Jairus' daughter (Matthew 9:25, Mark 5:42, Luke 8:55), and Lazarus (John 11:44).

He felt the need to help fishermen catch fish (Luke 5:6, John 21:6), to help Peter pay his taxes (Matthew 17:27), He relieved stress and embarrassment of the wedding party by turning the water into wine (John 2:9), He fed the hungry, including the 4,000 (Matthew 15:32, Mark 8:8) and the 5,000 (Matthew 14:15, Mark 6:41, Luke 9:12, John 6:5).

He rose from the dead and instead of returning to heaven immediately, was more concerned with His followers and appeared unto them first, and spent time with them consoling and instructing them (Matthew 28:17, Mark 16:14, Luke 24:36, John 20:19).

He also showed his mastery over creation by calming the storm (Matthew 8:26, Mark 4:39, Luke 8:24), **walking on water** (Matthew 14:25, Mark 6:49, John 6:19), **and cursing the fig tree** (Matthew 21:19).

Jesus met every need that man presented to him with compassion and love. He provided His miracle power to everyone that needed it. To anyone who believed on Him He was there for them. It is God's character to do the same for you.

It is in God's character to forgive

Hebrews 8:12 (NIV2011) says, "For I will forgive their wickedness and will remember their sins no more."

1 John 1:8-9 (KJV) says, "If we say that we have no sin, we deceive ourselves, and the truth is not in us. If we confess our sins, he is faithful and just to forgive us our sins, and to cleanse us from all unrighteousness."

As a former addict who has committed grotesque acts of perversion, and lived in the most inexcusable way, to know that God forgives, forgets, and continually forgives those that make mistakes, gives me the greatest foundation for faith in God. It also gives me a love for Him that I have for no other. I live in a total attitude of gratitude that shatters all unbelief and doubt.

It is the character of God to love, for God is love

1 John 4:8 (NKJV) says, "He who does not love does not know God, for God is love."

1 Corinthians 13:4-7 (NIV2011) says, "Love is patient, love is kind. It does not envy, it does not boast, it is not proud. It does not dishonor others, it is not self-seeking, it is not easily angered, it keeps no record of wrongs. Love does not delight in evil but rejoices with the truth. It always protects, always trusts, always hopes, always perseveres."

The word of God explains who God is. God is Love. The attributes of God as expressed in love are:

1. God is patient with you.
2. God is kind towards you.
3. God isn't envious or jealous of you.
4. God is not too proud to be your friend.

5. God will never be rude to you.

6. God has your interest at heart and is not thinking of Himself.

7. God is not easily provoked or angry toward you.

8. He is not thinking evil thoughts about you.

9. God doesn't rejoice when you fail and do wrong.

10. God rejoices when you live in truth.

11. God always protects, will never give up on you, and bears all things.

12. God never loses hope, gives up, but endures all things.

So, if you knew God's character, it would be impossible not to have an attitude of faith. When God's word reveals His nature to us, we come to the full understanding that God is not thinking evil of us, and He is patiently enduring, forgiving, and desiring to show us His kindness and love. Having knowledge of our heavenly Father destroys all doubt. When I am tempted to be discouraged, I just remember that God is watching over me to do good in my life and that I can expect Him to do good things for me.

James 1:17 (NIV2011) says, "Every good and perfect gift is from above, coming down from the Father of the heavenly lights, who does not change like shifting shadows."

When I pray, I come before God with an attitude of faith in His character that is attractive and inviting to God. This is the type of faith that God rewards.

Hebrews 11:6 (KJV) says, "But without faith *it is* impossible to please him: for he that cometh to God must believe that he is, and *that* he is a rewarder of them that diligently seek him."

Finally, here's my advice regarding the things that can distract you from maintaining an attitude of faith, and the way my faith is activated.

First, I am never confused when I focus on the outcome and not the details. The details of every battle may become complicated, and difficulties may come. But I take it in stride knowing it will pass and the outcome is in God's hands. Anything in His hands will prosper, and any battle fought with His power will be won. Because I know God intimately and have experienced who He is, His character has become beyond reproach. I have 100% trust in the outcome.

Jeremiah 29:11 (KJV) says, "For I know the thoughts that I think toward you, saith the LORD, thoughts of peace, and not of evil, to give you an expected end."

Second, I do not have an unreasonable expectation of people. Sometimes even when they try it is not good enough, they are just like me, and have limitations. My expectation is in God through the people that God will send.

Psalm 62:5 (NKJV) says, "My soul, wait silently for God alone, for my expectation is from Him."

Third, I never rely on my own efforts and abilities. I do give a 100% effort. I believe God deserves it. I use the abilities God has given me for His glory. But my effort alone without His miracle power will not heal the sick, and raise the dead, or might not be good enough to even find me a job. Even when I give 100% effort, my best, it will still require humility and God to perfect the outcome. Our works are not the basis of mountain moving faith. The works of Christ are the basis and foundation for salvation and answered prayer. Good deeds do not align you with the promises of God. The blood of Jesus does. The cross does. Faith justifies us. Faith in Christ.

Romans 5:1 (KJV) says, "Therefore being justified by faith, we have peace with God through our Lord Jesus Christ:"

Faith then is a position that grants us God's favor in all our prayers.

Romans 5:2 (AMP) says, "Through Him also we have [our] access (entrance, introduction) by faith into this grace (state of God's favor) in which we [firmly and safely] stand. And let us rejoice and exult in our hope of experiencing and enjoying the glory of God."

Life teaches us this. It is the same way with my abilities,

particularly so. If it were not for the inspiration of the Holy Spirit, I would not be writing this book. I couldn't. When God began to deal with me about telling my story, I felt like it was definitely a reach in my abilities, but as I grew in this same knowledge I am sharing with you, faith was birthed in my heart and gave me the motivation I needed to do it. Faith was birthed by a direct word from God that I heard in my spirit. It produced motivation and favor, in which I began to receive inspiration and wisdom to accomplish the writing.

Philippians 4:13 (NKJV) says, "I can do all things through Christ who strengthens me."

And fourth, anytime, I am facing a specific need in my life, I immediately meditate on God's character. I think, if Jesus were here, He would forgive my sins, He would heal my body if I were sick, and if I am in need, I think of Him being concerned about my needs, and actively engaged in acquiring whatever I need. When anything is bothering me, I know I can take it to my heavenly Father, and He will handle it. If I need instructions to get it done, He will reveal knowledge to me. All I must do is spend time with Him. If it is beyond my abilities and man's strength, I'll just believe a miracle is on the way. Why? Because it is who He is. God's character is my shield of faith. It is a permanent attitude that protects my mind and heart from the lies of Satan and unbelief. My intimate knowledge of how God really feels about me becomes an impenetrable shield that guards my heart.

Ephesians 6:16 (NKJV) says, "above all, taking the shield of faith with which you will be able to quench all the fiery darts of the wicked one."

8

A FAITH THAT WORKS

METHADDICTSHELP, FACEBOOK POST
MAY 5, 2017

Having faith in Christ is the answer. If you lose faith, you lose hope, and if you lose hope you die. God believes in you. I believe in you. Believe in yourself. You can do this. God invested his breathe in you, and gave you ability, inspiration, intelligence, and a strong will. You are God's answer to a hurting world. We need you, and are not complete without you. Addiction has destroyed your influence in this life. But, praying, and believing will rebuild what addiction has destroyed. The word of God says that the "prayer of faith shall save the sick". Keep praying, keep believing, if you are going to doubt, doubt your doubts. Jesus said, "nothing shall be impossible to them that believe." .... TPC. (unedited)

214,783 PEOPLE REACHED

13,000 LIKES

3,843 SHARES

1,691 COMMENTS

*T*his post represents a faith that actually works in a person's life. I have heard a lot of people tell me over the years, "Just have faith, it will work out." Have faith in what? Nothing in my life was normal, average, and easy. I was either staying in a 5-star hotel or sleeping on someone's couch. I was having a good day, or so blitzed out of my mind, that I didn't care. The only thing I had faith in was maintaining a good supply of drugs. If I could do that, I could stay high, keep a good supply of girls and friends around me, and have money to spend. That's all I cared about and lived for. It was exciting, adventurous, and dangerous. Early on in my addiction, I had a new truck, a condo, modern furniture, artwork on my walls, and a job. I lived right on the bay and had bought a lot of fishing equipment. But, I hurt inside, and was angry, bitter, and couldn't sleep. If material things could have provided happiness, I should have had it. I had money and an excellent job, but I was miserable. I was tired, depressed, and lonely. It wasn't long, after I started using meth that I never spent time at my condo. I was so alone and needy.

I quickly met so many people in the partying world, that everything began to spin out of control, and in a different direction. I was partying and using every day. I was going to strip clubs, spending nights at girl's homes, and going through vast sums of money. But, when I was coming down, the pain, and emptiness would be worse than it was before I started using drugs. The only answer to that was just to stay high. I started buying massive quantities and then was recruited to distribute them. I refused at first, thinking that it was too dangerous, and it was something I was very unfamiliar with. But, the temptation was too much for me to overcome. As far as quality, I had one of the best connections in the United States. I quit my job and started selling drugs. I was constantly entangled with groups of people partying. The people in the group changed from day to day and were much younger than I was. Random girls would stay with me and I was never alone at the condo anymore. One day I left the condo, and never went back. It was months before I even remembered I had one.

I was partying every night, meeting new people, and never staying anywhere more than a couple of days. I stayed in motels mostly. I was kicked out of them with a police escort several times. I have a lifetime ban from the largest casino in Louisiana, and a couple of motels. I was threatened that if I returned I would go to jail. I was arrested and booked at that casino for returning. I had to go to court. Those people meant business. Of course, the reason I was not allowed to be on the property was that I had been arrested there for distribution. While staying in a $3,000 per night room, the State Narcotics Division busted my door down and arrested me. I was later released and no charges were filed. That was a pretty scary situation. During the twelve years I spent in addiction, I was arrested several times.

Not long after that, in another casino, a much smaller one, I was surrounded by the FBI swat team in their parking lot and arrested. I was also released and no charges were filed, but still under investigation, and advised to stay close to home while under investigation. I was very fortunate because their information wasn't that reliable. I had a brand-new Lincoln, and someone was transporting drugs in my vehicle just a few days before. I had five pounds of meth in my car just prior to my arrest. Five pounds of meth at a $120 a gram has a street value of $268,800. I would have been convicted, and been in prison serving time if their timing had been on track.

I quickly went to work and left the state. Needless to say, I wasn't sticking around for someone to investigate me. I went to Chicago, then to Oklahoma, and from there to California. I went back on the road working construction again. I would repeat this cycle of distribution and working periodically from then on. I would pick the jobs I wanted and looked interesting. I stayed out in California, spent a long time in Salt Lake City, and Hawaii. I was using drugs and partying continually. But, nothing worked for me. It wasn't like I wasn't game for anything, I tried everything. I tried every drug and combination of drugs out there, and I stayed in resorts, played and played, I wrote a lot of poetry and started painting on canvas, but the anger didn't leave, and the struggle to overcome my emptiness was always present. I had tried to medicate. But medication or drug use was not the answer for brokenness. Female companionship was not enough either. I had been with a lot of young women, and it just seemed to make it worse. Sin just leads to more brokenness and complete spiritual bankruptcy.

It eventually took me to a place at the end of the road, and there was no hope left, but God. **So, when I say that the only thing that really worked is the faith that I now have in my heavenly Father, it is not coming from someone who has not experienced the other side. It is not that I haven't lived any other way because I had lived every way a man could live without God, but faith in God is the only thing that worked. It is the only thing that brought me to a place of sanity, prosperity, and happiness. This is my testimony. It is one of having a faith in God that works.**

Approximately 18 months after God had set me free, I was married and had a good paying job. God began to speak to me about my calling and spiritual assignment. The assignment He had given me from the very beginning, a supernatural calling, and I lived with a sense of being on that fast track of excellence. It was unique and special. I knew I had a call to minister, a burden for the addict, the mentally oppressed, and the people that are living with extreme emotional and psychological pain. Those are my people, people just like I once was. I understand them and have unbelievable compassion for them. They are my every thought. But I didn't know where to begin. I just had an overwhelming desire to help people. I already had won everyone I knew to Christ, my wife, my best friend, my wife's mother and many others. But, that is all I knew, plus I had a family to support, a wife and two step-children. I just couldn't wrap my finger around what God wanted me to do exactly. God was dealing with me every day about helping people in addiction and pain. It was getting stronger and stronger. I would wake up hours before work to pray, and talk to God about it.

Then one day at work I heard God say in the deepest part of my gut, "I want you to quit your job today." I was startled and completely surprised. I immediately began to question God. I asked, "God what do you want me to do? If I quit my job, how will I support my family, tell me your plan for all of that." I began to think about it. It was placed in my heart, and now I was trying to make sense of it in my mind logically. I will never forget that day as long as I live. The voice kept getting stronger and stronger. Finally, I heard the voice say, "Tim, I said, quit and leave now, don't waste any more time about it!" It had such urgency. It scared me. So, I started to gather all my expensive tools, my grinders, my Heliarc welding torch, and gauges. Then God spoke to me very strongly and said, "Tim, I want you to leave your tools, and exit this job location now, and never look back!" **The fear of the Lord was in that place.** It reminds me of when God told Moses at the burning bush, "Take off your shoes Moses, you're on holy ground!"

I looked at Joe, my fellow worker, and close friend, "Joe, I have to leave right now! God just told me to quit my job." I left my tools, and on my way out shouted to Joe, "Could you please let them know that I quit!" I couldn't leave that job fast enough. I had some worries in my mind about things like my next meal and money. **But deep inside of me I knew, I knew that I knew, that God would not ever tell me to do something without providing the resources to do it. He was my provider.** I had been living daily on my understanding of God's character. God had spoken to me about the job I was on. He told me not to look for a job, just to continue my daily routine, praying, reading the word, and God said, "Tim in a couple of days, someone is going to call you about a job, and that is the one that I want you to take!"

When God spoke to me to marry Jennifer, I was working a high-paying, non-standard, critical welding job for General Electric in Houston. When I married Jennifer, she was living in an economically depressed area, where most welders were making less than half of what I was making in Houston. But, God said to do it, move, marry her, the timing is right, and I will take care of you. I am preparing the way. So, in a few days Jennifer's uncle, Joe called, and said, "Tim, G.E. has contracted a job to one of our construction companies down here at the port, and they cannot find qualified welders to do the job, and they are hiring. You want to come to work?" It was the very position I had just left in Houston. So, God provided, and I knew how God worked. Just obey His voice, and leave everything else up to him. He is the provider.

Immediately after leaving my job, on the way home I called Jachin. I wanted a witness, someone who could authenticate my experience later. Every time God speaks to me, I always incorporate witnesses. So that God can be attested as true in His dealings with me. I am adamant about it, I believe in leaving a validated and undeniable trail of evidence for the unbeliever that will authenticate my testimony. Immediately God spoke to my heart to drop in and see a friend of mine from my drug days. He was one of my closest friends and was there from the beginning. He had even been arrested with me. He had been on my heart for some time now. But it was hard to get a hold of him and see him at the right time. My work would get in the way.

The only problem with just showing up at his house was that I was unwelcome. I risked going to jail. His mother did not want me around him. I don't blame her at all. We definitely were out there at one time. But, I knew that the only way for me to see him would be to catch him at his mom's, he would periodically go there to get rest and sleep for a few days. Otherwise, he could be anywhere. After listening to the Holy Spirit, I just went over there. It definitely was God's timing. He was home, and I was able to pray with him and later get reacquainted with his mom, the right way, sane and sober. It was a good meeting, and I knew God had opened a door of opportunity.

From that moment on I would follow God's leading. **I found out that God is in the details, the moments, and I should only plan my life in such a way that God could change my plans at any time.** This was truly becoming a remarkable journey. I was excited but concerned. When God told me to leave my job, He wasn't just saying He wanted me to quit my job, but He was saying He didn't want me to ever hold a secular job again. He said, "leave your tools, and never pick them up again!" Welding was my career, I had become a very high skilled welder, and welded all over the world, making top wages, in some cases, more than project managers, and engineers. I was a Lead Double-A, Mirror Welder, trained in all types of metal, and alloys, and had been certified in all welding processes. It was my primary way to earn a living. We were living in a rented trailer and had electricity to pay, water, cable, automobile insurance, the internet, household supplies, groceries, gas, auto-maintenance, clothing, and a storage bill. I said, "God I am not going to worry about it, I am going to leave it up to you, you told me to do this, I guess you know what you're doing."

The following morning, I awoke hours before daylight as I was accustomed to doing, and started praying. I was having some second thoughts and began to worry and get anxious. The doubts began to come rolling in. I began to talk to my heavenly Father, read the word, worship, and listen for His voice. The Holy Spirit began to draw me to YouTube, which was basically my church at the time. My routine was to search for what God would say search for. I do not know how I found this particular minister on there this morning, but, as usual, God was leading me again. I had never heard of him before. But, while I was scrolling down the page viewing different ministers preaching, God said, "This is it, listen to this Man of God."

His name was Bill Winston. I was watching his message, "Speak the Word Only!" The message was uploaded in 2011. He was saying, "If God said it, just believe on it, act on it, don't have a mentality of begging God for something that He has already promised you." Of course, I hadn't got down to begging God yet, I was just loving on my heavenly Father, but it was like God was saying, don't worry about your needs, don't even pray about them, other than in praise and gratefulness for what I am about to do for you. Pastor Bill went on to say that my destiny was in God's hands, that God even knew about the car I had wanted, the house, and all my needs were in the mind of God before I could ask, and that God was on it before I could even think about it. The house Jennifer needed, the automobiles, money we were going to need, and all my needs had nothing to do with my ability. If I was relying on my ability, I was setting myself up for failure.

Pastor Bill said, "If I rely on my own ability, I have just cut out my source, I have just negated the very provision that has been given here for me to dominate in this earth, I have just cut Him (God) out, because bringing it down to where I can figure it out, where, hopefully with my strength, be able to pull it off, wasn't where God wanted me. He said, "No, God doesn't want it there, He wants it so far out there, that if God doesn't come through, you are really going to fail." I said, "God is this really for me? Will you do what you have done in his life for me?" Boy, was I out there. With my spiritual eyes of understanding, I understood that God was going to have to supernaturally work finances in my life for this to work. I had no promises of any sort of financial support from anyone or anywhere.

Then under a heavy anointing Pastor Winston quoted:

Isaiah 54:17 (KJV) "No weapon that is formed against thee shall prosper; and every tongue that shall rise against thee in judgment thou shalt condemn. This is the heritage of the servants of the LORD, and their righteousness is of me, saith the LORD."

Then God spoke to me deep down within my spirit, and said, "Yes son, this is directly for you, every word, and it is your heritage also, you and pastor Winston are brothers on the same journey." That verse was forever etched in my memory. Immediately faith was born in my spirit. My ability would have nothing to do with it. I would never weld again. I would spend my days working for Jesus. I was employed by God. I was God's man. The message completely changed the atmosphere and landscape of my spiritual being. Faith was born, and I knew I must be completely obedient. I am so thankful that God connected me to Pastor Bill. I will forever be connected to him, and his ministry.

Then at that moment, I saw a vision of a beautiful house. Jennifer and the kids were in it, I saw vacations, and joy coming into her life, and I began to weep. God then spoke to me and said, "Go wake her up and tell her what I just showed you, I want her to know about this." So, I went to the back bedroom in that tiny, crowded trailer, and gently woke her up, and said, "Jenn, God told me to tell you that everything you have ever dreamed of is going to come true, the house that you have wanted, everything. You will never have to worry about anything again, never, you and the kids are going to be happy, don't worry about anything, everything is going to be great." I never again asked God about money.

A few days after that, while I was praying God spoke to me again, He said, "Tim, in a few days a person you introduced to me and is now serving me is going to give you $100,000. Then he is going to try to give you more than that, but just take the $100,000, do not take less, or more, even if it is offered to you." God even showed me who it was. But, those were unusual instructions, and I was puzzled. He said, "I do not want you asking anyone for anything you need, that's my business. Do not mention this to anyone, or even bring your needs up to him.

Again, that's my business." In a few days, God told me to visit the man. He needed prayer and encouragement. So, I went and spent a few days with him. We prayed, listened to hours of sermons, and discussed the word of God. I was to disciple him.

Then one morning, he came into his office where I had been sleeping, and said, "Tim, God spoke to me to give you $75,000." I said, "I don't think I can take that from you." He began to insist. I repeated the statement. "I don't think I can take it." He left the room, and then it hit me. "God, just what did I do?" He said, "You did what I told you to do." The man returned a few minutes later and came into the room. He handed me a check for $100,000. While handing me the check, he said, "Well, God had originally told me to give you $100,000, but I got scared and changed it, but then when I went to my room, God said it again to me, so, I said, 'Ok, God, I'm sorry. I will write him a check for $100,000 right now!'" I quickly said, "Now, that I can take, God is in that, that's true obedience."

Soon after, I walked outside, praising God. My heart was filled with gratitude and thankfulness. Nothing like this had ever happened to me before. It was an extraordinary event. A few minutes later, the man walked outside and said, "Tim, I have never paid tithe my whole life, and I feel like I owe more than $100,000. I should give you more." Then, I remembered God's instructions. I said, "God doesn't want more, your past is no longer remembered, and in Malachi, God says, when you start paying tithe, He counts it as though you are already caught up. God is a God of the present, He is forgiving, and when He forgives He forgets. You are a free man, free from the mistakes of the past, and free to live without any guilt from it."

Hebrews 8:12 (KJV) says, "For I will be merciful to their unrighteousness, and their sins and their iniquities will I remember no more."

That is one of the reasons why our faith in Christ works. It is because it sets us free from our past. There are so many people that feel unworthy to come to God. They feel they have committed too many horrible things. John Newton, the writer of "Amazing Grace," was the captain of a slave-running ship. At one point when the British were after him, he tied 150 slaves to an anchor chain so he would not be caught with them. Needless to say, he murdered all of them. He too felt unworthy and was tortured with guilt, until he was miraculously saved and forgiven. No wonder, when God saved him, those beautiful words, "amazing grace," came to him. God's grace is enough. Jesus paid the price for our sins on that cross.

Ephesians 2:8 (KJV) says, "For by grace are ye saved through faith; and that not of yourselves: it is the gift of God:"

Keys to making your faith work, hearing first, then acting

Romans 10:17 (KJV) says, "So then faith cometh by hearing, and hearing by the word of God."

Certainly, my faith was producing results. I meet so many people of God that are not producing results through their faith. I am thoroughly convinced that it is because they fail to do what God says. They do not act on what they believe. If I would not have listened to God or obeyed Him, I would not be where I am today. As a new Christian, I believed, acted, and received from God the truth He was giving me. I knew Him to be true to His character and acted like it. I quit my job. I spoke faith to my wife, and I revealed God's words He spoke to me to others. I spoke it and lived by His word in my life. When God confirmed what He was saying to me through Pastor Bill Winston, I readily took note of its importance and began to act it out in my life. My faith involved human risks, but I never tempted God. I do not act on anything without a strong conviction from the Holy Spirit, and confirmation from God's word. I wait before God daily. In mostly praise and worship. I talk to Him about what concerns me on a very real personal level. I am talking not only to my God, but I am talking to Him as my loving Father. When I get instructions, then I act.

Isaiah 30:21 (NKJV) says, "Your ears shall hear a word behind you, saying, "This is the way, walk in it," Whenever you turn to the right hand or whenever you turn to the left."

I talk, I listen, I worship, I honor, I hear, then I act. The results come from my actions. If you do not act, then what good can you get out of hearing from God. I do not even pray for anyone unless I hear God telling me to pray for them, and then I don't even open my mouth until I hear what God wants me to say. I honor His voice and His written word above everything else in my life. I refuse to make any decisions without hearing from God. Everyone in my life knows this.

Another key to hearing a word of faith, and having faith is relationship and intimacy

John 6:63 (KJV) says, "It is the spirit that quickeneth; the flesh profiteth nothing: the words that I speak unto you, they are spirit, and they are life."

Being close to Jesus, abiding in Him, talking, praying, and listening to Him, is where faith is. I might have key information to give you, but if you are never in my presence, then I cannot speak to you about it. Logistics is keeping you from receiving that information. If we do meet, and we meet in a noisy room, filled with loud music, shouting, or noisy equipment, chances are, you still won't be able to hear it. The words "the spirit quickeneth," means to be made alive, or real. How can a word be made real, or give you faith if you cannot hear it? When God created man, the word says that He breathed His life into us.

Genesis 2:7 (KJV) says, "And the LORD God formed man of the dust of the ground, and breathed into his nostrils the breath of life; and man became a living soul."

How intimate is that? Can you get more personally involved than that? God personally and physically gave us mouth to mouth, or literally speaking, His breath. We became connected and part of Him when he created us. We have His life and are an extension of God Himself. We are made in God's image, and from the very beginning were meant to have a close relationship with Him. Without that closeness, we lose in every area of our lives, and we cannot be enriched spiritually with life and faith. **We must be so intimate with God that we can feel His very breath upon us. That is the first clue to God's plan for man.** He desired fellowship in the most intimate way, and for man to walk in confidence and faith without God's breath is impossible. Just try any action without the presence of God or His anointing, and you will find out that you will fail.

John 15:5 (KJV) says, "I am the vine, ye are the branches: He that abideth in me, and I in him, the same bringeth forth much fruit: for without me ye can do nothing."

Jesus reiterated this thought and principle throughout scripture. He says, "Without me, ye can do nothing." He is telling us to rely on Him, talk to Him, and lean on Him and His voice. To have me, you must abide in me. To have strength and power you must be intimately connected and engaged with Him, the source of faith and life.

John 15:7 (KJV) says, "If ye abide in me, and my words abide in you, ye shall ask what ye will, and it shall be done unto you."

If you are abiding, living close enough, remaining connected to Him and His words are in you, then you can ask whatever you will, and it will be done. **Anyone who wants to live in the power of faith must live in God's presence and close enough to feel the very breath of God upon their lips.** We must start a conversation with Him, listen for His voice, and humbly never leave His side in practice daily. It must be your habit, and customary lifestyle to remain in His presence throughout the day. It is the only way to hear a word of faith. This requires intimacy with your heavenly Father. Enoch was so intimate and close to God that his faith physically translated his body from this earth into the kingdom of heaven. The word says that Enoch's testimony was that he walked with God. Now that is intimacy and power!

You must add action to what you believe; action is the purest form of faith, commitment, and surrender

The devils believe in Jesus, but they do not follow, it is not good enough to just believe in God. If your religion has no risk in it, then you have no religion **Everything in life involves risk. However, it is a fleshly risk, a human risk, carnal and logical risk, but never a risk within your heart or your spirit. God's word has peace in it, love in it, and assurance in it. You must train your mind to follow the only voice in this life that has that kind of reward, God's voice.**

James 2:17 (KJV) says, "Even so faith, if it hath not works, is dead, being alone."

Psalm 29:11 (KJV) says, "The LORD will give strength unto his people; the LORD will bless his people with peace."

Galatians 5:22 (KJV) says, "But the fruit of the Spirit is love, joy, peace, longsuffering, gentleness, goodness, faith,"

John 6:63 (KJV) says, "It is the spirit that quickeneth; the flesh profiteth nothing: the words that I speak unto you, they are spirit, and they are life."

Faith will activate the holiness of God in your life, develop fruit and character. The word of God demands a response of action.

Faith says, this is the truth, and the right way to live, if I live and act on the truth I will have good success.

Joshua 1:7 (KJV) says, "Only be thou strong and very courageous, that thou mayest observe to do according to all the law, which Moses my servant commanded thee: turn not from it to the right hand or to the left, that thou mayest prosper whithersoever thou goest."

God is all about action. When God speaks to us we must act on what He says. We must act like it will happen, or as though it has already happened, and casually just go about our business unworried, and thankful. A person who knows his God does not live in panic, and in an emotional upheaval of chaos. He just believes God when He speaks. God told Joshua that if he trusted enough in God to act on all that is in the law, observe them, and practice them, he would be prosperous and successful. He went on to tell him to meditate on the words of God day and night.

Fear, the contaminator of faith

The thing that destroys faith the most in your life is fear. **I heard Kenneth Copeland say, "Fear tolerated is faith contaminated."** Fear of what others will think, fear of failing, fear of embarrassment, fear of the unknown, fear of dying, fear of losing material possessions, fear of losing face and honor from men, fear of losing respect, fear of being laughed at, criticized, mocked, and ridiculed, fear of the consequences, fear of the future, fear of the cost, fear of being inconvenienced, fear of suffering, and all kinds of fear can control you if you let it. **But if you just look at it in the right way, all those fears do not mean anything, because if you do not obey God you will suffer much more than any of those things you fear.** You will suffer from losing your peace, joy, and happiness that comes as a result of abandoning all else and relying on God. All those things are temporary. God's peace isn't.

When you honor your fear, you destroy your commitment to God. This life is temporary. Our life just begins in eternity. Most all your fears are based on what others will think, not what God thinks. I have been set free from the approval of man. It was living for the approval and acceptance of man that helped destroy me. When my wife left me, I felt devalued, inferior. It was God who restored my sanity, healed me, and gave me value, meaning, and purpose. **Fear is a diversion and distraction from your true eternal value, meaning, and purpose.**

Hebrews 13:6 (KJV) says, "So that we may boldly say, The Lord is my helper, and I will not fear what man shall do unto me."

Jesus set me free from all my anxieties and worries. I am never going back and living in that trap again, it is the ultimate trap of Satan. Satan cannot threaten a man that has lost it all, had nothing and found peace and joy in his "nothing experience." Ambition, honor from men, and acceptance of men are all carnal attributes of the flesh and pride. People can distract you from you seeking the approval of God, de-value your authenticity, and destroy your unique identity, and calling of God. When the cares of life and the approval of men mean nothing and the word of God takes precedence in everything you do, then there is nothing left to fear.

Failure is not an option, failure is basically losing faith before God comes through with a miracle or special knowledge that solves the situational circumstances. **Fear destroys your self-worth, not failure. Failure mixed with faith in God creates success.** All great men and women before us who have made a difference in our world, such as scientists, doctors, mathematicians, writers, leaders, and other world figures have failed many times. Faith in God keeps you in the battle, remember you might have some testing or setback, but God is in the final results. **The words "fear not" appear 74 times in the King James Version** of the Bible, 29 more times it uses the phrase, "be not afraid."

In Luke 12:4 (KJV), Jesus says, "And I say unto you my friends, be not afraid of them that kill the body, and after that have no more that they can do."

Even Jesus said not to fear other people in your life. They can only do things that have no eternal effect upon your life. I counted eight more times Jesus said personally to someone "be not afraid!" Jesus commanded us never to be afraid or troubled.

John 14:27 (KJV) says, "Peace I leave with you, my peace I give unto you: not as the world giveth, give I unto you. Let not your heart be troubled, neither let it be afraid."

We might feel little and insignificant but Jesus says in Luke 12:32 (KJV), "Fear not little flock, for it is your Father's good pleasure to give you the kingdom!"

Fear comes from Satan, and it leads to insanity, repeating the same mistakes, expecting a different result. Afraid to do it God's way and continuing down your own path leaves behind a journey filled with heartache. The only way to change any bad situation in life is to conquer fear and act on faith. **All doubt starts with fear of the consequences or results.**

2 Timothy 1:7 (KJV) says, "For God hath not given us the spirit of fear; but of power, and of love, and of a sound mind."

God gives us power, love, and sanity, or a sound thinking mind. Fear is not from God, anytime you are afraid, if you listen closely, you can hear Jesus say, "fear not, be not afraid."

The foundation of faith, the Word of God

When God breathes life upon His written word, the Bible, or He speaks in your heart, faith comes. If you have no faith, it is because you either have not studied His written word or have not been living close enough to Him to hear His voice when He is speaking to you directly. Sometimes God uses a minister or someone else to speak through, but you will always know it, because **when God speaks, it is inspired, made alive, and it leaves a deposit of faith. After all, if God speaks, wouldn't it be special, it is God speaking.** Jesus makes this very distinction concerning His voice in the book of John.

John 6:63 (KJV) says, "It is the spirit that quickeneth; the flesh profiteth nothing: the words that I speak unto you, they are spirit, and they are life."

The words of God are spirit and life. They are energy. They are faith. They are life to your dying dreams. The word of God leaves a spiritual deposit of warmth, love, and assurance. It is different from all other voices. It is like instantly knowing something new and profound. Jesus also says that the spiritual man's faith depends on eating or feeding on the word of God.

Matthew 4:4 (KJV) says, "But he answered and said, it is written, Man shall not live by bread alone, but by every word that proceedeth out of the mouth of God."

Faith comes by hearing a word from God.

Romans 10:17 (KJV) says, "So then faith cometh by hearing, and hearing by the word of God."

The word "hearing" is a present tense word. Not every word you read will be made alive, powerful, and real. Not everything you read will speak to you the same way. It is like in your kitchen, there are all kinds and different types of food, but only the food you cook or prepare is ready to eat. It is just like this with the word of God, not everything in it is prepared by God to supply your needs for today, but if you are storing them in your memory, God at any time can breathe on them, prepare them as a meal for your spiritual man, this is how our spiritual man grows, and dominates, by what God inspires, only a fresh (manna, or bread) meal prepared daily will have the proper safe ingredients for you to act on. Or be a word of faith. We must go daily to His written word and listen or wait for His breath to be felt in our life. Again, this requires effort and a close intimate relationship with God.

Matthew 6:11 (KJV) says, "Give us this day our daily bread."

Jesus is not only talking about our physical needs but our spiritual needs also. He tells us to pray for whatever it will take to survive the day. Hope and faith are just as valuable to your survival as food on your table. If you are weak in faith, then spend more time talking to God the way I have described in this book and start reading the Bible. It's not complicated. It is accessible and applicable.

The battle of faith is won from the source of knowledge that controls your mind, sense knowledge of the flesh and emotional feelings of doubt are Satan's tools and his greatest weapon

You must debunk, deflate and expose the failures of the past and feelings of doubt that oppose the word of faith God has given you. Memories are the primary strongholds of Satan that he uses to create doubt and fear in your life. So many people have given up on their assignment and calling in life because of past failures. Soulish information always opposes the miraculous supernatural life of God in you. Soulish (fleshly) information comes from the workings of your soul, which is broken down into its three distinct parts, your mind, emotions, and your will. You can will what feeds your mind and emotions. Or choose what to believe. Also, our sense knowledge can be opposed to faith and create doubt. Our five senses feed what we see, touch, taste, hear, and smell to our mind. Sometimes they give us factual information that contradicts the final outcome of faith. We must never let our own intellect be the final authority when doing God's will.

2 Corinthians 5:7 (KJV) says, "(For we walk by faith, not by sight:)"

Romans 8:7-9 (ASV) says, "because the mind of the flesh is enmity against God; for it is not subject to the law of God, neither indeed can it be: and they that are in the flesh cannot please God. But ye are not in the flesh but in the Spirit, if so be that the Spirit of God dwelleth in you. But if any man hath not the Spirit of Christ, he is none of his."

So, the mind of the flesh is hostile to God, the supernatural, and the fourth dimension. It lives in a natural world filled with reason and human logic, Satan's web. Anything that supersedes the natural laws of time, matter, and space, it rejects, and cannot understand.

1 Corinthians 2:14 (KJV) says, "But the natural man receiveth not the things of the Spirit of God: for they are foolishness unto him: neither can he know them, because they are spiritually discerned."

That's why God never commanded us to understand Him in that way, just believe Him. We don't know how a black cow eats green grass, makes white milk, and yellow butter, yet we drink the milk, and use the butter. A lot of us really do not know how a lot of things work, but we use them, put our trust in them every day. So, this is not a foreign concept to us, to just believe in something. **In the scripture above it says that we do not walk by sight, or the knowledge obtained through our five senses, based upon sense knowledge. It says we walk by faith.**

What we feel, touch, see, taste or hear naturally should not be our only source of knowledge. Although the knowledge of our senses is important, the word of God makes a distinction in how we are to use these senses. They are never to be used as a source of determining spiritual matters, or faith choices that the word of God gives us. When determining your destiny, and spiritual matters, the five senses can often oppose the truth. Even facts that exist can oppose the truth that exists. The facts might be that you are sick, and are in need financially. The facts may be that you are in addiction, and may have failed many times.

But, when you insert the truth within the facts, God says in His word that we are healed and delivered through Christ and that God will supply all of your needs through Christ. **To be a successful believer, productive and accomplishing your goals you must incorporate the Holy Spirit and the word of God in analyzing every situation you face.** You must rightly give authority and preeminence to God's voice and His word above all else. Not listening to your feelings, five senses, or memories of past failure. To be carnally minded is death. **We most certainly do not want our carnal mind filled with Satan's web of reason and logic to negate the miracle power of God in our life.**

Not long ago I was waiting for a minister to come pick up some tithe I had for him. I was worshiping God and full of thankfulness in my heart. I was standing in my home that God had promised me, it was beautiful, I looked outside and saw two brand new cars in my driveway, and I was taking a mental note of all the beautiful furniture my wife picked out that was in our home, the computers, and new appliances, all top of the line, we had no needs, everything was paid for, God had fulfilled every promise he made to her and I. As I stood there I began to long for my brother and the needs in his life. I knew his home was not paid for, and he had been in the ministry for 45 years. He had been a key factor in my growth and maturity in the spirit. He had become like an older brother to me, his friendship was worth everything to me.

I began to weep, I said, "God why isn't my tithe at least the $75,000 mortgage that he has in his house?" and I immediately heard God say, "Is there anything too hard for me?" I chuckled in my spirit and was kind of taken aback for a minute, then God said in a real authoritative tone to me, "I said, Tim, is there anything too hard for me!?" I began to weep again, and again, I said, "No God, there is nothing too hard for you!" I told him what God had said, and we went about our business, and I handed him his tithe.

I knew that it wouldn't be long and God was going to make that possible. Every time I would look at the facts in my life, they contradicted the truth, and the word of faith that God had spoken to me, I would always rehearse the moment God spoke to me, and just trust in God's timing. I knew God had something in mind, and how it was going to happen was His business. I didn't know how God was going to do it, and in the soulish realm, it would be impossible.

But with God all things are possible. A couple of months later someone handed me a check for $750,000. The exact amount of tithe needed to pay his mortgage off. When you hear the voice of God, it is a guarantee that great things are about to happen. I put all that money in my ministry account and took care of his mortgage. We were able to support an entire ministry group in India, with three orphanages, and hundreds of ministers. We clothed hundreds of people, provided thousands of meals, and paved a local church's parking lot. Not a penny of that money was spent on anything but the glory of God. God doesn't lie. It is impossible for God to lie. I am testifying to you from personal experience, that you can have a faith from hearing God's voice that will transform your life. If you are in need, just commit to Him, become intimate with your heavenly Father, and get close enough to His written word to hear Him. You will never in a million years regret knowing your heavenly Father.

It just so happens while I am writing this portion of the book, I have a testimony of the miracle power of God happening today. Just about eight blocks from my home was the American Legion Hospital. They had recently moved and were selling the facility. Ravi, a ministry board member and close friend, and I were walking around looking at it one day when the Holy Spirit sovereignly fell upon us. We simultaneously had a vision of faith birthed into our hearts to buy the hospital, and provide a place for addicts to be loved back into the kingdom. A place where they can receive deliverance through Christ. We knew it required thousands of dollars, but God had spoken to us. We obeyed His voice and pursued the vision through prayer, fasting, and waiting before God. After waiting before God, we began negotiations. In miracle fashion, as always, God worked behind the scenes. We purchased the building for a fraction of what it is worth. There will be much work involved, and we will need the support of God's people, but we have no fear, and there is no weapon that will be able to stop us. We plan on providing inpatient care, free of charge. There is much work to be done. The world we live in is crying out for help. It is our vision to be able to help other men and women who have no place to stay, no money, and feel so trapped, to find help and love. Men who are a mirror image of my past. I am so proud of my heavenly Father, and ever so confident in Him keeping His word, that it has become my all-consuming desire to brag about Him, compliment Him, and expose His greatness to the world, and everyone I meet. I am dedicated to using whatever method I can find for this cause. For I have a God who cannot lie and stands behind His word to fulfill it.

Numbers 23:19 (KJV) says, "God is not a man, that he should lie; neither the son of man, that he should repent: hath he said, and shall he not do it? or hath he spoken, and shall he not make it good?"

9

SATAN THE DECEIVER, THE DECEPTION OF THE MIND, AND THE DELIVERANCE OF STRONGHOLDS

METHADDICTSHELP, FACEBOOK POST
APRIL 3, 2017

MENTAL HEALTH ISSUES PLAY A BIG PART IN DRUG ADDICTION. YOUR MIND IS A BATTLEFIELD OF THOUGHTS WARRING AGAINST EACH OTHER. SO MANY PEOPLE FEEL TRAPPED, HOPELESS, AND SO DESPERATELY ALONE. THEIR ATTEMPTS AT FREEDOM ARE OVERCOME BY THOUGHTS OF DEFEAT, INFERIORITY, AND MEMORIES OF FAILURE. A LOT OF MEN AND WOMEN HAVE BEEN FALSELY DIAGNOSED WITH MENTAL DISORDERS, SIMPLY BECAUSE THEY HAVE NOT COMPLETED THE CYCLE OF WITHDRAWAL, AND HAVE NOT BEEN SOBER LONG ENOUGH TO RETURN TO NORMAL. SOMETIMES A DIAGNOSIS OF SCHIZOPHRENIA, BIPOLAR DISORDER, OBSESSIVE COMPULSIVE DISORDER, AND MAJOR DEPRESSION CAN BE LINKED TO JUST THE THOUGHTS THAT FEED THE MIND, AND STEM FROM EXPOSURE TO EXCESSIVE DRUG USE. IF YOU CAN CHANGE OR TRANSFORM THE MIND, AND WHAT FEEDS THE MIND, YOU COULD CURE MOST ALL MENTAL PROBLEMS...GOD CAN TRANSFORM YOUR MIND,

THERE IS A SPIRITUAL SOLUTION TO YOUR SITUATION....
MESSAGE US FOR PRAYER, TPC. (*UNEDITED*)

116,868 PEOPLE REACHED

4,200 LIKES

1,835 SHARES

414 COMMENTS

*T*hey say that what controls the mind controls the man. If that which controls the thoughts is deception and untruthful, then it serves to reason the man is living in deception also. I was such a man. The deception was real. The deceiver was real. The battle for my sanity was at stake. Some of the lies were created from logical conclusions. Some had a slight factual basis, but they still were lies. All lies have a portion of the truth misstated in them, or they would be unbelievable. A lie can control your destiny and change your purpose. Your mind is a battlefield of conflicting thoughts and ideas. What feeds the mind determines what you perceive as truth. How you think and gather information is important. The more credible the source, the more reliable the information will be. A rational mind should always check the source. In the political, social, and personal arena, everything has to do with the credibility of the source. Is it responsible, can it be fact-checked, and does the source have a history of trustworthiness? Just where are you getting your information?

Most addicts and emotionally depressed people believe they have no way out. **Their mind has gathered intelligence from their past experiences and knowledge obtained through other information, which leads them to believe they are helpless, are trapped, and have no way out. A person who believes their situation is permanent and that nothing can be done about it lives like it.** Their entire purpose and direction are controlled by their reasoning. People start accepting things that they ordinarily would not accept. If they feel they will never find a good job, they stop looking. If they conclude that they will be poor the rest of their lives, they settle for less, and their drive to succeed is altered.

There is a war raging in your mind between good and evil. **There is also a war raging externally for the attention of your mind, to gain access. There is trickery going on all around you to increase the probability of gaining that access.** All you have to do is look up from driving your car on any busy highway, and there is a billboard full of imagery to get your attention, just so that they can access the thoughts of your mind.

In the world of addiction, some of these are called triggers. A trigger that solicits a decision to use. There are things that have a spiritual connotation attached to them. Whether you recognize them are not, they are there. Habits are formed from our thoughts. Thoughts are very powerful, and within the seed of a thought is desire. Thoughts are like links in a chain, they link together to reinforce an idea or decision, you keep thinking a certain way long enough, and the links to those thoughts will form a chain that strengthens a decision. **You act on those thoughts enough they become a habit. A habit becomes your identity. Your character is formed by your habits.**

You can lie, or steal enough until it becomes a habit and your normal behavior. It is then within your character to steal when you get the chance. It all started with rational thought, one thought that led to another. In the final result, you might have some truth in the thought from the beginning, but everything else could be a distortion of the truth because one thought in the chain changed the whole pattern of rationalization. Our thoughts are who we are. They develop our character and influence all of our actions. How you think is really who you are. **Who you allow to educate your mind controls your personality, character traits, and environment. The atmosphere around you adds to this process of development.**

The development of the mind can also be controlled

emotionally and physically. **Physically through your five senses and emotionally through your memories and imagination.** Our mind is wonderfully created and creates the atmosphere in which we live. It is our primary source of stimulation to our spirit and feelings. It can create great contentment through imagery, and our memories. It stores our past. It also can be the primary cause of discontentment or feelings of panic and depression. Our thoughts can be stimulated even by touch and smell. Smelling a pot of coffee, or perfume can stimulate thoughts of desire. Touching certain things like a hammer, a steering wheel, fishing rod, or a gun, can give one a sense of control, pleasure or power. Our mind can be stimulated through visual images that create thoughts that arouse emotions that inspire other thoughts. This process becomes the deciding factor of our actions and decisions. **So, what we view, listen to, read, hear, taste, touch, and smell become a guiding resource of our thoughts, and how our character is formed, which determines the direction our lives will ultimately follow.**

That is why you must choose who educates your mind, and it becomes very important to set boundaries and certain criteria that determine what you think. You must have standards of truth, and the source of your thoughts must have proper values that your moral judgment agrees with. What you value may be different from others. Your values determine how you view life, and what is important. Someone else's thoughts of you attending a family event could be very different from yours, they might not consider their family very important and might have been raised in a toxic environment, giving them a negative view of the importance of family relationships. Our children could be going to school with other children like this. The influence of these other children in their lives could produce a similar view, and create difficulties between you and your child. Because their thoughts are coming from a source of influence that has different values than yours. We are triune beings, Body (five senses), Soul (mind), and Spirit.

Our mind gathers information from various sources. Our mind and thoughts are stimulated by what we see. We can choose how our mind thinks by the standard of truth we use to interpret the information. Satan is a liar, and he misinterprets the truth, takes it out of context, and slanders the author, God. He systematically will destroy your self-worth, and the image you have of yourself. We are created in the image of God and are wonderfully made. Satan hates God's image and anything that has the potential to attribute to the glory of God. We can set the atmosphere for failure or defeat in our lives, by what we choose to believe in our mind. Just as we set the table to feed our body, we can set the "table" for what we think. What we eat determines the condition of health our physical body will be in. The type of food we eat either gives us the proper nutrition and vitamins, it takes for our bodies to survive, or we can starve from malnutrition.

To have a healthy mind, we must provide it with accurate, reliable, positive information. **Satan's strategy is to destroy you through the thoughts of your mind.** He has a complete set of values different than yours. You cherish your life. He despises your life. Satan is a spirit being. **He is jockeying, and maneuvering into position to compete against God for the truth that enters your mind. He is the major distraction from truthful information. I have listed below many scriptures in God's word that reveals the character of Satan.**

1 Peter 5:8 (NKJV) says, "Be sober, be vigilant; because your adversary the devil walks about like a roaring lion, seeking whom he may devour."

James 4:7 (NKJV) says, "Therefore submit to God. Resist the devil and he will flee from you."

Revelation 20:1-3 (ASV) says, "And I saw an angel coming down out of heaven, having the key of the abyss and a great chain in his hand. And he laid hold on the dragon, the old serpent, which is the Devil and Satan, and bound him for a thousand years, and cast him into the abyss, and shut it, and sealed it over him, that he should deceive the nations no more, until the thousand years should be finished: after this he must be loosed for a little time."

John 8:44 (ASV) says, "Ye are of your father the devil, and the lusts of your father it is your will to do. He was a murderer from the beginning, and standeth not in the truth, because there is no truth in him. When he speaketh a lie, he speaketh of his own: for he is a liar, and the father thereof."

Revelation 12:10 (NKJV) says, "Then I heard a loud voice saying in heaven, "Now salvation, and strength, and the kingdom of our God, and the power of His Christ have come, for the accuser of our brethren, who accused them before our God day and night, has been cast down."

1 Corinthians 7:5 (NKJV) says, "Do not deprive one another except with consent for a time that you may give yourselves to fasting and prayer; and come together again so that Satan does not tempt you because of your lack of self-control."

2 Corinthians 11:3 (NKJV) says, "But I fear, lest somehow, as the serpent deceived Eve by his craftiness, so your minds may be corrupted from the simplicity that is in Christ."

2 Corinthians 2:11 (NKJV) says, "lest Satan should take advantage of us; for we are not ignorant of his devices."

2 Corinthians 11:14 (NKJV) says, "And no wonder! For Satan himself transforms himself into an angel of light."

John 10:9-10 (NKJV) says, "I am the door. If anyone enters by Me, he will be saved, and will go in and out and find pasture. The thief does not come except to steal, and to kill, and to destroy. I have come that they may have life, and that they may have it more abundantly."

2 Corinthians 4:4 (KJV) says, "In whom the god of this world hath blinded the minds of them which believe not, lest the light of the glorious gospel of Christ, who is the image of God, should shine unto them."

2 Timothy 2:26 (KJV) says, "And that they may recover them-

selves out of the snare of the devil, who are taken captive by him at his will."

Acts 10:38 (KJV) says, "How God anointed Jesus of Nazareth with the Holy Ghost and with power: who went about doing good, and healing all that were oppressed of the devil; for God was with him."

The devil is your enemy, and would like nothing more than to destroy you. In the verses above he is described and identified as:

Your adversary (enemy), seeks to destroy, destroyer of human lives, oppresses, deceiver, liar, father of lies, accuser of man, tempter, crafty (sneaky, devious, cunning, shrewd), uses devices to take advantage of us, will appear in complete disguise to trick you, thief, kills, destroys, blinds your mind, sets snares, takes you captive.

Satan is a deceiver and his primary target is your mind, his weapon is deception, trickery, devices, and lies

Life is hard enough without having this guy after you. We face hardship, distress, and conflict on our very own, without ever dealing with Satan. We face the weight of gravity bearing down upon our bodies every day. Accidents and human error plague us. But, Satan takes it to a different level of intent. Intent to completely steal, and seek to destroy all those vulnerable to his devices.

His primary target is your mind, and his primary weapon used is deception or a lie. The word of God says he is the inventor or originator of lies and the truth is not in him. His attack on man began as early as the first man and woman in the garden of Eden. It was a distortion of the truth then, and he has not changed and is still using a distortion of truth to destroy anyone vulnerable to it. He blinds your spiritual eyes and keeps them from the truth. We see the Apostle Paul's fear that as Eve's mind was deceived, tricked, hoodwinked and misled through the crafty design of Satan's lie, we could also be led astray from our sincere and pure devotion to Christ.

2 Corinthians 11:3 (NIV2011) says, "But I am afraid that just as Eve was deceived by the serpent's cunning, your minds may somehow be led astray from your sincere and pure devotion to Christ."

Paul also warns us not to be ignorant of Satan's devices, which could be a strategy or something in your life that is used as a source of temptation.

2 Corinthians 2:11 (NKJV) says, "lest Satan should take advantage of us; for we are not ignorant of his devices."

So, Satan uses stimulation through imagery and information received through your five senses that build a case for a lie to destroy your confidence in God. He makes sin appealing and makes it appear like it is the right thing to do, knowing that it will destroy you. Like a mirage in the desert, its oasis of palm trees and water that will quench your thirst turns into the hot and dry sand of the desert. Satan uses the power of suggestion through advertisements, internet images, magazine covers, certain smells, and music to distort the real with the fake mirage.

Why would Satan attack your mind and start there? Because that is where the battle is. The battle for control starts in the mind. It is because that is where God communicates the knowledge of His will and plan for our lives. Most Christians are living defeated lives because they have minimized the significance and importance of what they think. But God tells us to transform our minds, and not to walk in the uselessness of the darkened mind contaminated with untruth. Our mind has been programmed through human experience and is in standard default mode before we are saved. We must not walk and chose our actions in our default mode, or the futility of our mind.

Ephesians 4:17 (NKJV) says, "This I say, therefore, and testify in the Lord, that you should no longer walk as the rest of the Gentiles walk, in the futility of their mind"

Notice that people live or walk by the way they think. If their thoughts are based on lies, they live the lies. The Bible says that we are to not be conformed to this world, or the things around us, the devices and trickery of Satan, or the misrepresentation of the truth, but we are to be transformed and changed by renewing of our minds by the word of God.

Romans 12:2 (NKJV) says, "And do not be conformed to this world, but be transformed by the renewing of your mind, that you may prove what is that good and acceptable and perfect will of God."

John 17:17 (NKJV) says, "Sanctify them by Your truth. Your word is truth"

1 Peter 1:13 (KJV) says, "Wherefore gird up the loins of your mind, be sober, and hope to the end for the grace that is to be brought unto you at the revelation of Jesus Christ;"

Romans 7:23 (KJV) says, "But I see another law in my members, warring against the law of my mind, and bringing me into captivity to the law of sin which is in my members."

Ephesians 4:23 (KJV) says, "And be renewed in the spirit of your mind;"

Philippians 2:5 (KJV) says, "Let this mind be in you, which was also in Christ Jesus:"

Just like any computer, to change the way the mind works, it must be reprogrammed, and no longer operated in the basic default pattern, but a new one programmed by the living word of God. The spirit of the mind must be reprogrammed, renewed, and take upon itself the mind of Christ. Think like Him. That is the battle that you face in this life, in its simplest form, it is a battle-field in the mind. A war raging between a lie and the truth. A battle of conflicting powers fighting for the control of your mind.

My deliverance, and how Satan destroyed my life

My life was destroyed through deception of the truth, accusations, and an assault on the character of God. Satan destroyed my self-image. He de-valued my individual significance. Satan also used my hurt to created bitterness toward God, my wife, family, friends, and church. During this process, it caused so much damage that I lost every bit of self-worth and respect I once had. How did this happen to a man of God? To someone who at one time had given all to God. There are a lot of people out there that believe it is impossible to walk away from God once you are born again. But I did. I didn't want to have anything to do with God. I began to dislike Him. To those people that believe that is impossible, all I can say is that they did not go through what I did. And they are very ignorant of the power of the lies of Satan, even a small distortion of the truth, and where it will lead.

Satan began to systematically attack the truth in the images and thoughts of my mind. Here is how it unfolded. See if you can identify with any of these thoughts that Satan proposed to me.

1. He began to cast doubt on God's protection and divine power. "How could God let this happen, was He not protecting your wife, while you were out preaching His word?"

2. How could God love you and let this happen? God must not really love me.

3. Good definitely does not overpower evil, and after all the good things you have done, God rewards you by letting Satan steal your wife, and destroy the most important thing in your life, after all of the sacrifices you have made for the gospel, and hardships, to put you through that, and then your wife leaves you, that's your payback.

4. Just look at God's family and servants. All of them have abandoned you and discarded your ministry as worthless, and you cannot even do what you once loved to do.
5. How could God not heal all of this hurt, and pain in you? He heals others, or maybe He really doesn't heal, maybe you have been preaching a lie all these years.
6. Why would you want to go to heaven with all of these judgmental people of God, and the people involved in your divorce, they all profess to be Christian, can you imagine spending time with these hypocrites?
7. God doesn't even care about your son, and he is innocent in all of this.
8. Look at yourself. You can't even hold a secular job, you're a mess. Where is the compassion of all those ministers and so-called friends you once had? What about God's compassion? People have more compassion for their pets than for you. God even feeds the animals. They don't go through this.
9. You do not have anything left in your life of any value, no job, ministry, family, or friends.
10. See, I told you that no one cared about you, you are not important at all. Not even to God. I must not be important at all to God, my son isn't either.
11. Life is just that way. God has no power to change it. You have no power to change it, these things happen. Why waste your time doing good?
12. Why live for God, or other people? Live for yourself, do what you want to do. 23 years of providing for other people, loving other people, spending all your time like a slave providing for your wife, for what?
13. Your family members doubt your ability, self-control, intelligence, just like your wife, you have heard the accusations, and the complete assassination of your

personality by your wife, and others as proof she did the right thing, you know you did not deserve her, you are worthless. I should just die, I would be better off. I wish I was dead.

14. Even your wife knows the truth, she left you for a man with stability, a career, a law enforcement officer who serves with honor, and has the support of others behind him, the same people who judge you as unstable. All of that work you did for God just created the atmosphere and platform for instability.

15. She got out, don't you think you should? I should abandon my beliefs, after all they did not prevent any of this.

16. Why don't you just enjoy life for a while, you deserve it. That is what she is doing, and everyone else. You are the only fool who isn't.

17. Remember you said you would pray and wait for her. How big of a fool could you be? She was enjoying herself, while you were worried, praying and hurting.

18. Don't you hate her? Don't you hate him?

19. Shouldn't they be punished? You should kill him. Why not, he certainly doesn't care about you. I really should kill him.

20. You should never trust anyone again, including God. Who needs a family? No one stays married anymore. It doesn't work. All that is a lie from God.

21. You should never let anyone disrespect you again or hurt you that way again, especially without paying for it. That is the only way people will stop hurting you if they pay for it. Only you can stand up for yourself. God will not. I vow to you God, that I will never let any man disrespect me again without being hurt, crippled, or dead for doing it. I promise, I am willing to die hurting them, and fight to the death.

22. You cannot even sleep, function, hold a job, be loved, stop hurting, stop being angry, or even stop loving her. You are an idiot. You are worthless, unimportant, helpless, and it looks like this is going to stay that way. You should kill yourself. Life isn't worth living. Yes, I should.

23. Don't you regret how you handled this? You wouldn't have been able to even stay with yourself. How can you blame her for leaving? You should blame yourself. You are stupid.

24. You had no sexual experience before you were married. How do you know if you were even sexually adequate to meet her needs? She was a virgin when you guys married, maybe she found herself sexually aroused by someone else, and found them more satisfying. Maybe, there is something wrong with you. You are just inferior like you always supposed you were.

25. God couldn't keep you happy, He can't now, and never could, how stupid are you? You should do whatever it takes to make yourself happy, anything you want, God couldn't, it is left up to you now. It is left up to me, that God thing doesn't work.

26. You should be free to drink and do any drug you want to, after all, God cannot heal your sadness.

27. If drugs can help you feel better, help you sleep, and save your life, then you should use them.

28. There are people using a prescription medication that call themselves Christians and criticize others and are using, addicted, and in the same shape. What hypocrites.

29. It might be illegal, but it is the only thing that helps. No one should tell me what to put in my own body. That is my decision, and no one else's.

30. A person in law enforcement was involved with my wife, how right is that.
31. The law did not protect me and caused more damage to me than any law that is already established. Why respect the law?
32. People are phonies, liars, cheats, and hypocrites. Why should I respect them?
33. I should do whatever makes me happy, others do. They have no right to judge.

I could keep writing, and that list would grow. I wrote these down just to show you how fast your mind works. That's a long demoralizing progressive thought pattern that would run through my mind at record speeds, during a typical day. That list takes a while to read, but it is short in comparison to what a person thinks in just a few moments of time. Our mind is powerful and works like a computer with unlimited storage ability. The astounding capabilities of the computer, and as wonderful as it is, its creation comes from someone's mind. These thoughts evolved into strongholds. There are hundreds of thousands of people who think thoughts very similar to these. It is no wonder that so many people live the way they do. These people become addicts looking for relief. They become suicidal and lose all hope. Our hospitals and mental wards are filled with people diagnosed with clinical depression, and all sorts of mental disease as a result of these voices heard in the recesses of their minds.

These thoughts began to affect everything about me. They changed my purpose for living and led me down a life filled with destruction. I was game for anything. I had nothing to lose, I had lost it all. I could see a picture in a photo album and the thoughts would just come in waves, they would be accompanied by all kinds of regret, and emotions. I quickly became depressed, angry, and hopeless. Why, because I believed the lies of Satan. Every addict and person experiencing abnormal pain in their lives will never be free from it unless they learn how to deal with conflict and hear the truth.

After my surrender to Christ, I was a different man. Just the presence of the Holy Spirit brought about a feeling of worth and acceptance. The demonic spirits of depression left when the presence of God came into my life. But periodically something would happen that would threaten my freedom. A thought or a memory triggered by an image, or something someone would say would bring back negativity and a slight feeling of guilt. Then a pattern of progressive thoughts would start to occur. But because I had been praying and reading God's word, I knew exactly how to handle it.

Romans 12:2 (KJV) says, "And be not conformed to this world: but be ye transformed by the renewing of your mind, that ye may prove what is that good, and acceptable, and perfect, will of God."

Proverbs 4:23 (KJV) says, "Keep thy heart with all diligence; for out of it are the issues of life."

2 Corinthians 10:4-5 (KJV) says, "(For the weapons of our warfare are not carnal, but mighty through God to the pulling down of strong holds;) Casting down imaginations, and every high thing that exalteth itself against the knowledge of God and bringing into captivity every thought to the obedience of Christ"

I still had strongholds in my life. A stronghold is a memory that produces a predetermined thought pattern that has become a practiced line of thinking, well-rehearsed, and habit-forming in your life. It is associated with the pain of a memory or traumatic event. Or it could be based on your pleasure sensors. Every time a feeling or a certain mood presents itself, it could create a desire to use again or drink. It could be just a sin that Satan tempts you with on a daily basis. Satan eggs you on, and a spirit of lust, envy or jealousy is attached to it. That thought process and memory become what the Bible calls a stronghold, something that has become a weakness and place of vulnerability for you, yet a stronghold of Satan.

It has a hold on your life. It can control your decisions, your mood, and emotions. It is an area where Satan still has some control in your life and will not relinquish it easily. He is relentless. You must guard your heart against the lies of Satan. The above verses say to guard and cast down these imaginations and thoughts, bringing them into captivity of the knowledge and obedience of Christ. He is illegally controlling your life because you have allowed him to do it. Jesus has given us the power to overcome Satan. He has no authority over us. You must also renew your mind with the word of God. Memorize it, meditate upon it, write it down, put it in your heart, think it, study it, and know it.

Joshua 1:8 (KJV) says, "This book of the law shall not depart out of thy mouth; but thou shalt meditate therein day and night, that thou mayest observe to do according to all that is written therein: for then thou shalt make thy way prosperous, and then thou shalt have good success."

Psalm 1:2-3 (KJV) says, "But his delight is in the law of the LORD; and in his law doth he meditate day and night. And he shall be like a tree planted by the rivers of water, that bringeth forth his fruit in his season; his leaf also shall not wither; and whatsoever he doeth shall prosper."

The following scriptures were written in the precious blood, and life Jesus gave on the cross, are permanently recorded in the eternal word of God and discloses our delegated authority over Satan.

Luke 10:19-20 (NKJV) says, "Behold, I give you the authority to trample on serpents and scorpions, and over all the power of the enemy, and nothing shall by any means hurt you. Nevertheless do not rejoice in this, that the spirits are subject to you, but rather rejoice because your names are written in heaven."

Mark 16:17 (NKJV) says, "And these signs will follow those who believe: In My name they will cast out demons; they will speak with new tongues;"

Revelation 12:11 (NKJV) says, "And they overcame him by the blood of the Lamb and by the word of their testimony, and they did not love their lives to the death."

James 4:7 (NKJV) says, "Therefore submit to God. Resist the devil and he will flee from you."

1 Peter 5:9 (NKJV) says, "Resist him, steadfast in the faith, knowing that the same sufferings are experienced by your brotherhood in the world."

1 John 2:13 (NKJV) says, "I write to you, fathers, Because you have known Him who is from the beginning. I write to you, young men, Because you have overcome the wicked one. I write to you, little children, Because you have known the Father."

In the scriptures above, Jesus has given us authority to walk on the devil, and the power in His name to cast him out of our presence, and life. It says that we have overcome him by the blood of Jesus and by reminding him and others around you that God has delivered you. We can resist him in faith and he leaves. Anytime you feel negative emotions, feelings of depression, and negativity, it is part of the spirit of this world. All you have to do is not accept it in Jesus name, cast it out of your life and it has to leave. Jesus didn't even allow the devil to speak.

Mark 1:34 (KJV) says, "And he healed many that were sick of divers diseases, and cast out many devils; and suffered not the devils to speak, because they knew him."

You don't even have to allow the devil to speak, because Jesus gave you that same power. He delegated that same authority to you in Luke 10:19 and Mark 16:17. Because the devil recognized His authority and knew Jesus, they know, and recognize the power of His name and His spirit in you also.

The road to freedom... Free. Free at last!

Freedom has nothing to do with physical restraints and limited accessibility. Freedom is the ability to have unrestrained liberal thoughts of a productive mind. Free to think without negative, hurtful imagery that controls your emotions, and desires in such a way that you cannot be inspired to create, laugh, and produce in a sane, free-flowing pattern, unrestricted by doubts of inferiority, and incapableness. The seed of the lies of Satan destroys the productive fruit of positive thoughts that empower a person's value and ability to achieve. If you destroy the lies of Satan, you create the atmosphere for freedom.

I was crippled by depression and hurt. The hurt in my life created doubt, and Satan systematically began to destroy everything I believed in. I was a man that once had faith and confidence. But I was vulnerable, worn down, hurt, and Satan attacked me in the arena where he performs at his best, the battlefield of the mind, in my thought life, and through the imagery of trauma. He attacked my value system. They say that when a religious man falls, he has nowhere to go. That was me. Contrary to that, when a non-religious man falls he turns to religion to save him, and not Christ in many situations. Finding emptiness in ritual. Satan reinforces untruth in a different more viable way to the non-religious. But in the same way, by deception. In both cases, personal freedom is lost. To think freely is lost. The lie paralyzes the mind and its patterns of thought. A man can be living on his own, have a new vehicle, and lovely home filled with luxurious furniture, fishing equipment, and next to the beach. But have no freedom in his spirit or mind to utilize anything he owns. He can be a living, walking prisoner. I was that man living next to the beach, and could not enjoy a single moment in life unless I was blitzed out of my mind, steeped in addiction, to drown out the thoughts of my mind. A prisoner of my own mind.

On the other hand, you can be a prisoner in a solitary jail cell filled with spiritual freedom and mental productivity. The Apostle Paul was freer in prison than when he was living on the outside, unrestricted by a jail cell. In jail, he had no one to answer to, no responsibilities to perform, no secular obligations, and he was free to devote all of his time for Jesus in prayer and study that would eventually shape the entire world. He became an unrestricted free agent of God. There he found the time to write half of the New Testament, 13 epistles. He was able, with unrestrained, unprejudiced and liberal thought aided by the Holy Spirit with truth to correct, encourage, build faith, foretell the future, restore ethics, install procedures, and laid the foundation for the church, influencing entire generations for ages to come.

The road to freedom has a beginning in Christ

It began when I surrendered to God and accepted Christ. His presence displaced feelings of unacceptance, unrest, and agitation. The depressive spirit that had oppressed me for so long was gone. Instead, the presence of God brought relief, healing, value, acceptance, rest, and peace. I began to be able to reason clearly and see things differently for the first time.

Mark 3:27 (KJV) says, "No man can enter into a strong man's house, and spoil his goods, except he will first bind the strong man; and then he will spoil his house." Jesus tied the hands of Satan and spoiled his activity in my spirit.

John 8:36 (KJV) says, "If the Son therefore shall make you free, ye shall be free indeed."

Only Jesus can do that. You cannot overcome a spiritual problem with human intervention, but it must come only from our spiritual champion, our Savior. He came to save us from ourselves and Satan. In His presence is the fullness of joy, and pleasures for evermore.

Matthew 1:21 (KJV) says, "And she shall bring forth a son, and thou shalt call his name JESUS: for he shall save his people from their sins."

The Greek word for sin "harmatia" is used for the Hebrew word "awon" which means harm, trouble, injustice, and deceit. Jesus came to set us free from the harm, injustice, trouble and the deception of sin in its fullest revelation, also the lawlessness and anarchy of disobedience. The word saved, in its purest Greek form, in the original text, has a wonderful meaning. It comes from the Greek word, "sōzō", *a* verb, which means to save, keep safe, preserve, rescue, make well. So, Jesus is my Savior. He saved me from those depressive spirits of Satan, He keeps me safe, preserves my life, mind, spirit, and body, He rescued me, and made me sane and well again.

The foundation of freedom, the precedence for spiritual truth is an experience with God

I now experienced through Christ feelings of relief and acceptance. Through Christ's personal involvement, and through the knowledge of the great price He paid to achieve personal contact with me intimately, which was the revelation of His death on the cross. I now felt significant, important and valued. I felt wanted and needed. Purposely created to be productive, loved, cherished, and significantly needed in the world I was born in. I was important enough for God to have died for. It is from that precedent that I gained my freedom. **Satan had no control over me, for God had gifted to me a standard of His spirit and presence that removed all doubt and every lie Satan had told me. The strongholds of Satan began to tumble in the imagery of my mind, and deep recesses of deception were falling. The strong powerful force of the loving Holy Spirit and the truth of God's word began to systematically destroy the lies of Satan.**

Implementing truth

When Satan would speak a lie, or through some trigger of

emotion, imagery or thought, I now would instinctively insert my new spiritual freedom and thoughts of value and acceptance which annihilated the lie of Satan. He had no more foundation to deceive me from any longer. When a feeling of hopelessness would come, instead of building upon that in my thought life, I now built a case for hope, trust, and prosperity based on God's character. My attitude had changed. Faith based on spiritual knowledge and the word of God systematically would destroy untruth and replace it with truth, the basis of human liberties. The basis for all civil liberty and freedom can only come from the truth, that we were all created with a divine destiny, and have an equal uniqueness of purpose. We are all valuable and equally have something to bring to the table. Satan could no longer destroy that truth with memories of failure or trauma. God began to use His word to insert truth in trauma and personal tragedy. Such as my calling to help others with the healing in which I have been made well with, and the insight to give it to others. The source from which this book came is a primary example.

The results of freedom

The practical application of truth produces fruit. It is the leading of the Holy Spirit who is our teacher and guide that points us to the truth, and reminds us of truth, as He said, "He would bring all things to our remembrance." One of my patterns of deception was to blame God for the actions of myself, my former wife, and the others involved in my divorce. I was occupied with guilt, and low self-esteem because of internal blame. I was filled with hate and bitterness from blaming others for the pain they afflicted. These thoughts of blame then centered in on God and destroyed my belief in Him.

But when I started inserting the truth in those memories, I was completely set free from the trauma of the past. When blame and responsibility were placed where it belonged, I no longer blamed myself, my former wife, other people, or God. I laid the blame at Satan's door, his deception. We had all believed a lie. A mirage and distortion of the truth. That sin, or the apple in the garden was better than the life God had planned for us. The responsibility of that lie was at Satan's feet, our adversary the devil. He was the enemy and all of us were victims of this miscarriage of justice.

I was, through the truth revealed to me by the Holy Spirit, and God's word, able to see each one of us as victims. All of us had been trapped and overtaken through Satan's craftiness. Seeing each of us as victims, it became easy to forgive, and trust God again. I could love again. I could identify myself and others as one and the same, a victim. Seeing the victim in them freed me to love them. It resulted in a release of love toward God, her, others, and most of all, I could love myself. There is a victim in all of us. There is tragedy, trauma, and deception found in everyone. When you see the victim in the source of your conflict or pain, it becomes easy to forgive and to love them. Looking at a person, and seeing past the exterior, seeing a trapped, vulnerable target of Satan inspires sympathy and compassion, all fruits of the spirit.

John 8:32 (KJV) says, "And ye shall know the truth, and the truth shall make you free."

2 Corinthians 10:5 (KJV) says, "Casting down imaginations, and every high thing that exalteth itself against the knowledge of God, and bringing into captivity every thought to the obedience of Christ;"

The battle is in the mind. The opposing force is Satan. His weapons are imaginations, things that are not real, and thoughts that destroy the knowledge of God. Our duty is to bring every thought into the obedience of Christ. Our defense is the truth which comes from the word of God.

Hebrews 4:12 (KJV) says, "For the word of God is quick, and

powerful, and sharper than any two-edged sword, piercing even to the dividing asunder of soul and spirit, and of the joints and marrow, and is a discerner of the thoughts and intents of the heart."

One day, I was walking in mid-town Houston, not long after I had been saved. I was witnessing to people and thinking, where are all the church people, the Christians? We need their help here on the streets where it counts. Satan said, "Tim, what about those Christians, all of those hypocrites, you know the ones that judged you, and the ones that never even reached out in love? They sure do not deserve your loyalty and trust." I had heard these words before. They were hurtful and I felt a shriek of pain when I heard them again. I began to become disheartened when I heard my comforter ever so gently speak, "Tim let me guide you, there is a path of truth that will free you from the hurts that you think were afflicted by your brothers in Christ. Although there is some truth in what Satan is saying, once again he is grossly distorting the facts. You must be careful."

2 Thessalonians 2:9-10 (KJV) says, "Even him, whose coming is after the working of Satan with all power and signs and lying wonders, and with all deceivableness of unrighteousness in them, that perish; because they received not the love of the truth, that they might be saved."

The Holy Spirit continued, "First, you must always look inward when you judge, the only individuals who can see the real you are God and yourself. That's why it is pointless for you to judge others and their motives. They might be in the wrong, but have good intentions and motives, just mistaken or deceived. Just because you do not see them here on this street doesn't mean that I do not have a mighty army doing it somewhere else. They are not needed here because I have an expert already on location, and that's you. You have lived these streets and understand these people. You and I make a majority, wherever we are."

And then the precious Holy Spirit brought me down memory

lane, this time, the imagery came from Him, not Satan. For reasons of love, the Holy Spirit reminded me of my Dad. I remembered my Dad, and all the kind words, prayers, love, gentleness, and dedicated loyalty he had for me. I could hear my heavenly Father speak in a voice behind me saying, "Tim walk this way as my servant your father did, he was the first example of Christian service that was sent specifically for you. I used him to get you through life's journey, he not only lived his life for me but he lived his life for you, his son, and never, not even once, betrayed you, or not believed in you, but valued you like I have." Tears began to flood my soul.

Then I began to see just a couple of years back, about a year before I was completely delivered, Jachin Dardar, a minister and childhood friend was trying to get a hold of me. I hadn't seen him in years, and he had no idea of the shape I was in. At that moment, when he called, I was trying to get clean and needed a place to stay. He invited me to stay with him and his wife. God was reaching out to me. I went and stayed a couple of weeks at his home, and he helped me complete the DISA drug program, so I could go back to work. I stayed clean for those couple of weeks, and while I was there, I felt love and acceptance and genuine concern. God began to speak to me while I was there, and I'd seen firsthand, what the real people of God were about. I left to go back to work, but never forgot their act of kindness and help. They truly displayed selfless love. It was a witness of Christian love in practice.

But I just couldn't stay clean once I left. I had too much on my mind. I loved my girlfriend and wanted to see her. I was alone again still facing the demons. I fell back into addiction, but this time it wasn't the same, it was harder to use, and I felt guilty about it. It was the beginning of God so gently speaking to me again, and calling me home. God said, "See I did have Christians reaching out to you, some of them risked everything for you, some of them, you didn't know anything about, but they were on their knees praying for you." He said, "What about J.E., he took you in for a couple of weeks also." And more tears began to fall. "What about your sweet Aunt Rita, who through blind faith in you, sent you money for a room, and a phone when you were fresh out of jail, think honestly about your sister, even though you have had disagreements, she was worried about you, praying for you, and even loaned you money." Tears again. I had a new-found respect for the children of God, and love started pouring out of my spirit for them. Again, God had exposed the half-truth of Satan, and another stronghold and place of Satan's control had been overcome through the healing power of the Holy Spirit.

Like a stack of dominoes, they all began to fall, one by one. The Holy Spirit and I would deal with them all, and I was gloriously set free. Each memory would now be inserted with truth and laced with traces of God's love. I was constantly being reminded of God's miracle saving power and protection. I would see mixed in with all my failures God's protection, how He kept me from prison, and on multiple occasions even saved my life. Many times, while dealing with criminals, and gang members, it would get violent and threats were made against my life. Some of these people were cold-blooded killers who had killed before. Yet, I came through all of that without losing my life. I couldn't help but think of Mom and Dad's prayers. There would be many more times Satan would attack me, with the temptation to use, get angry, or lose faith, and there were times I would make a mistake. But through it all, I would insert the truth in every thought, build the case for faith, and the fruit of the Spirit would clothe me with patience and humility.

The stronghold of drug use and its lifestyle was completely obliterated

From day one, it was finally broken. I was through. I didn't want anything more to do with drug use and everything that went with it. Every memory I had of drug use ended with chaos, confusion, and conflict. I had lost valuable time and wasted it on sinful unproductive living. My memories were full of bad decisions, and financial loss, thousands of dollars. I had lost a home, automobiles, friends, family and all respect. Just the thought of addiction would create waves of disgust. God did this. It was the way he protected me, by opening my eyes to the devastating consequences of addiction. I had memories of being stranded, broke, sleeping in parking lots, being arrested, fighting, and awakening after spending nights or days with women feeling disgusted and dirty from the things we had done while high.

But in time, after several months, I had some tempting moments. I would remember some of the closeness felt with others, and their friendship while in addiction. Then a few times, Satan would remind me of the pleasure of using, the actual pleasure of the drug itself. Sin is pleasurable for a season, that's biblical. If it wasn't, no one would do it. Those moments would only last a few seconds. Because, every time they came, my mind would automatically construct the impenetrable wall of truth. As pleasurable as drug use is, nothing compares to the peace of God, the baptism of the Holy Spirit, and the fruits of the Spirit. I had lived both lives. I knew the truth. I was set free. I cannot even remember when the last time that happened.

My testimony

It is my testimony that if you are hearing voices of unbelief in yourself, others, and God, if there is paranoia, fear, suicidal thoughts, anger, bitterness, images of trauma, guilt, apathy, hopelessness, helplessness, or extreme mood swings, that the God I serve can set you free. I have experienced all these thoughts and lived in depression, hurt, pain, and addiction. It has been part of my experience. But it is now part of my experience to have witnessed the power of God in my life and the voices of Satan to be defeated. There is hope for you. There is a blessed hope for everyone who will call upon God for help. There is a "balm in Gilead," a place where all healing waters flow and that is from our eternal heavenly Father, the ministry of His dear Son, and the comforting presence of the Holy Spirit.

These are the tools I used which completely delivered me from the deception of Satan

Salvation, a continued surrender, commitment, living with value, meaning, and purpose, communication with God, use of my prayer language, an attitude of faith, renewing my mind with the truth of the word of God, inserting that truth in my thought life, worship, praise, and there is much more to come in this book that will thoroughly equip you for your journey, we are merely touching the surface of God's glorious transforming power.

10

THINGS

 METHADDICTSHELP, FACEBOOK POST
JANUARY 17, 2017

YOU SHOULD NEVER PLACE BEFORE YOU WHAT DOES NOT BELONG IN YOU, AND WHAT YOU ABSORB OR TAKE IN IS WHAT YOU BECOME AND EXITS YOU. IT BECOMES WHO YOU ARE AND WHAT YOU IMPART TO OTHERS. YOU MUST GUARD THE GATES OF THE MIND, YOUR PHYSICAL RECEPTORS, WHICH ARE OUR FIVE SENSES FROM PEOPLE, PLACES, AND THINGS THAT TRIGGER A RELAPSE. DRUGS AND ALCOHOL CREATE ABNORMAL RATIONAL THINKING, BECAUSE IT FEELS GOOD WE JUSTIFY IT. OUR BODY UNDER THE INFLUENCE OF DRUGS CREATES ABNORMAL CHEMICAL CHANGES AND WE BECOME A WEAKER SELF WITH LESS CAPABILITIES AND BODY FUNCTIONS—THAT USUALLY DESTROY US. SO, YOU START OUT NORMAL AND TAKE IN ABNORMAL AND EXPECT TO BE BETTER? IF YOU NEED PRAYER OR ENCOURAGEMENT MESSAGE US ...WE REALLY CARE...TPC. (UNEDITED)

102,050 PEOPLE REACHED
4.5K LIKES

*T*hings have the ability to control your life. You can control things, or they can control you. They also can set the atmosphere or mood in your life. They possess an unseen or unrecognized power.

I learned quickly the need to discard and replace some of the things in my life that were having a negative effect. Living can become a stressful adventure simply by certain things of choice we allow in our lives. What is important to remember is that we can regain control of our lives when we utilize our power of choice. **Through this process, we can alter our perceptions and dramatically reduce experiences of ongoing stress.** If we reduce a problem area and source of stress, we can dramatically improve our lives. Every postcard, photo, and keepsake possess powerful memories and suggestive thoughts. Address books, your phone, and its contacts give you access to choices of persuasion, and possible stress or temptation. Cell phones, televisions, and computers are objects of unbelievable control in some people's lives.

Objects can hold incredible mysteries of our past. Things can become more than an indulgence or a necessity. They can be an object that can trigger negative thoughts and decisions. The smell and feel of a closet, room or piece of clothing could remind you of a person, or moment in your life of happiness or tragedy. Things can create sadness and joy. The passing by a store, bar, school, or place you once lived will often produce a nostalgic feeling or emotion. Some of these are a source of powerful suggestions of alluring temptation, depression, or of a happier time. Things play a big role in the recovery of an addict, and the healing of someone who is experiencing emotional pain. Books, magazines, advertising, commercials are a way in which others access your mind.

Satan, the enemy of a healthy soul, will use everything he can to gain control of your mind and create an environment for failure

People tend to keep mementos, souvenirs, keepsakes, and reminders of important memories and events in their lives. **Music can hold a very vivid memory of your past, and flood your heart with emotions and feelings. Feelings that create desire, regret, loneliness, and fleshly needs.** You must be very careful what you listen to, and the type of music of your past that you keep. It is a sure and fast way to set an atmosphere to use again. Music can also be a source of depression, accompanied by feelings of nostalgic longings of past destructive behaviors. Things like shot glasses, a tee shirt, postcard, or even a towel or cup taken from a motel can remind you of a historic party, or special intimate moment from your past life in addiction or mental anguish. Possessions can have a powerful pull on one's emotions and desires. These objects tend to glorify the past and distort reality. **Most of these events are a blur of the truth at best.** Most of the chaos and confusion of the moments are conveniently left out. It is a way that we try to find worth and meaning in our former lives, an attempt to salvage something of the past, so that all may not be lost. We should see our past as what it was, filled with hurt and bad decisions. We deliberately leave out the lies we believed, and the fools that we once were, in order to salvage our dignity. Our fleshly identity, living independent from God, is a contradiction to living humbly and relying upon our Creator for guidance. It is human arrogance and fleshly pride that destroyed us, and is creeping through a back door for entrance once again.

In our regenerated mind, God reveals the truth so that we may accurately view the past and move on to create a new life filled with memories of strength, love, and power. Satan and human nature cannot sneak around in our present lives because we are wise to his craftiness, but in these areas, there are moments of nostalgia that become very emotional, tempting us to maybe compromise some of our new-found freedom and values. We might casually see certain objects around our homes that have these memories attached to them, or we may get a call from a friend and be convinced for "old times' sake" to meet them for a few minutes, at a place we usually would consider off limits. And just like that, we have aided in the possibility of a relapse, or a sinful encounter with an old friend. **All because we refused to clean house.**

I made a moral inventory of the things in my life and cleaned house

I took a personal moral inventory of the things in my life shortly after my conversion to Christ. This inventory was taken in consideration with the teachings found in the Bible to reveal what things would be important to keep and those that must be discarded. **Cleaning house is taking an inventory of your life, getting honest, removing defects, making amends and continuing to clean the house daily. It means that our spirits must be clean, and we must readily correct the record, and make amends. We must simply insert the full truth, and reveal the lie in all our memories. We must be honest about the old life and see it in the reality of chaos, hurt, loss, and the danger that it was.** Upon my surrendering my will to Christ and submitting it to His word, I immediately began to clean house. I viewed many things that I had kept in my belongings as points of pain and temptation to glorify something that I was no longer willing to glorify.

When I returned to my impounded BMW about 2:00 a.m. in the morning after getting out of jail, I immediately found the pipe, the leftover meth, and paraphernalia and threw them away. They were a source of my greatest weakness and destruction. I did not want them around anymore, not even for a second. That was my first test. I know people who have kept a bottle of whiskey, or some other leftover vice as a reminder of their victory over it, and their addiction. Only at some other point and time to return to it again as the "dog that has returned to its vomit." Not me, that had happened to me before, but not this time. Cleaning house really means cleaning house. I packed things tightly away and began to throw things away. I remembered Jesus' warning about looking back, and James telling us to clean house.

James 4:8 (KJV) says, "Draw nigh to God, and he will draw nigh to you. Cleanse your hands, ye sinners; and purify your hearts, ye double minded."

Luke 9:62 (KJV) says, "And Jesus said unto him, No man, having put his hand to the plough, and looking back, is fit for the kingdom of God."

James says, clean your hands or the things that are within your reach. Clean up your life from sinful things, or things that are ungodly. Clean house.

Having plowed in my grandmother's garden, I know what that means. There is no way you can keep a row straight if you do not focus on where you are going. Crooked rows make it hard to harvest, not finding the plants to weed and take care of, losing your seed, and a painstaking harvesting when your rows are running together. No one who is blinded by the past can be productive in the present. You can either bury your past or it will bury you.

Hebrews 11:15 (KJV) says, "And truly, if they had been mindful of that country from whence they came out, they might have had opportunity to have returned."

Certainly, Satan the great deceiver would like to create in your mind a devil's workshop with the intention to get you to return to a place of defeat and moral bankruptcy. There will be opportunities for you to lose heart when things are not working as fast as you think they should, and you are not communicating as you should in your relationship with your heavenly Father. It is during these moments you surely do not need any reminders of your past hanging around conveniently alluring you back to the old unproductive, dangerous ways of coping that produce death, sickness, and pain. **We must clean house, remove inventory, reveal the lie, and unveil the truth daily if we are to stay walking in freedom and not be entangled in sin again.**

1 Timothy 4:1 (KJV) says, "Now the Spirit speaketh expressly, that in the latter times some shall depart from the faith, giving heed to seducing spirits, and doctrines of devils;"

The world in which we live is the last days, as prophesied in Biblical prophecy. The word of God talks about "seducing spirits," specifically about them enticing, persuading, and seducing people in the doctrine of devils. I want you to look at the title that the Holy Spirit gives them. He calls them "seducing." In the original, the word just simply means to deceive, or persuade someone to abandon their duty, and what they believe. They are the spirits behind temptation.

Like a powerful seductress, they make sin inviting and use many things to do it with. They are what fuels false doctrine, the occult, political correctness, and all types of sexual immorality that we face. They are the counterfeit of the truth. The source of this apostasy is demonic. It is supernatural. Drugs are openings for demonic spiritual activity. We know this to be true by what they persuade people to do under the influence. They are not themselves, and can even feel suicidal after participating in things under the influence of these powerful drugs. They become ashamed and tormented with guilt. But Satan has many more tools than just drugs.

Ephesians 6:12 (KJV) says, "For we wrestle not against flesh and blood, but against principalities, against powers, against the rulers of the darkness of this world, against spiritual wickedness in high *places*."

As you see, we are in a spiritual battle, and we are wrestling against rulers of darkness, and spiritual wickedness in high places (the fourth dimension, outside of time, space, and matter). These are spirit beings that can accompany objects of worship found in the occult. They can be an invisible, powerful, lustful spirit attached to pornography. A spirit of hate, jealousy, rage, and anger attached to a movie or book. That is why we must test the spirit, to see the type of spirit behind the things we keep around us and before us. If a publication, program, or person promotes anything other than the Lordship of Christ and His death, burial and resurrection, then you know that it is not from God, it could be of the occult, or propaganda promoting ungodliness. You must stay away from it. It is part of a foreign spirit's dominion, and control, demonic in origin.

The blood of Jesus protects us, and the Holy Spirit will warn you with a strong conviction in your spirit or conscience. We all have alarm clocks. They may be annoying, but without them, we might not be on time for work or an important appointment. We have smoke alarms, and alarms that come with every car in the form of a check engine light. They might be annoying also, but they could save our lives. **The Holy Spirit is your internal alarm system in the spiritual realm. He will signal a disruption of peace or rest, sounding an alert that something is wrong.** Very much like an intuition that a mother has when she feels like her children are in danger. **You must always follow the "gut checking" power of the Holy Spirit, and test everything, or examine everything in your life under the light of the written word of God.**

John 16:8 (NKJV) says, "And when He has come, He will convict the world of sin, and of righteousness, and of judgment:"

1 Thessalonians 5:19 (AMP) says, "Do not quench (suppress or subdue) the [Holy] Spirit;"

Ephesians 4:30 (KJV) says, "And grieve not the holy Spirit of God, whereby ye are sealed unto the day of redemption."

Idolatry

Exodus 20:4-5 (KJV) says, "Thou shalt not make unto thee any graven image or any likeness *of any thing* that *is* in heaven above, or that *is* in the earth beneath, or that *is* in the water under the earth: Thou shalt not bow down thyself to them, nor serve them: for I the LORD thy God *am* a jealous God, visiting the iniquity of the fathers upon the children unto the third and fourth *generation* of them that hate me;"

Idolatry is selfish. It is a way foolish men and women try to control or manipulate God. The purpose for their creation comes from the idea of God serving us, rather than us serving Him. People will put their idol on display, or a special place signifying where it must serve them. In their car, or their bedroom thinking that they are actually placing God's presence there. Saying to a piece of wood or stone, serve me. Creating an image, and burning candles, are ideas from Satan. They are born from a master manipulator of deception. He would like nothing more than to deperson-alize God and take away the intimate conversation that forms a heart filled relationship with your heavenly Father.

Isaiah 66:1-2 (KJV) says, "Thus saith the LORD, The heaven *is* my throne, and the earth *is* my footstool: where *is* the house that ye build unto me? and where *is* the place of my rest? For all those *things* hath mine hand made, and all those *things* have been, saith the LORD: but to this *man* will I look, *even to him that is* poor and of a contrite spirit, and trembleth at my word."

God is not impressed with your creation. What impresses God is your worship and humility. Your sincerity is what God desires. Talking to idols is easy, and requires no commitment or compliance on your part. If you made an image of your husband or wife and spent time with it, never becoming intimate with them personally, that behavior would probably get you locked away in an insane asylum. What makes you think that God is any different than we are? You certainly would not enjoy someone you love, who is more involved with an idol of you than of you personally. Idolatry and the involvement of inanimate objects are from the occult and seducing spirits. They attach themselves to these idols, at times inhabit them, and draw attention to them to distract you from the true and living God. The true and living God answers the prayers of our hearts and gives us power over Satan through the name of Jesus. That power is found in God in us. Our words have power and authority, not wood, stone, and fire. God says you are my temple, I will dwell in no house made with human hands. What makes places of worship special is that the people of God are there. They usher in God's presence.

Ephesians 2:22 (KJV) says, "In whom ye also are builded together for an habitation of God through the Spirit."

Not all material possessions in your life are spiritual and demonic.

Things are tools and can be necessary to provide for different needs and desires. Things can cost you a lot of money, and take up a majority of your time. A true Christian is free from the bondage of all things. When Christ healed my brokenness, I was no longer a slave to material possessions. Status quo meant nothing to me. What others thought of me, and what the secular world thinks of prosperity was completely rooted out. **Jesus was my everything. I had no needs. I had no wants. That is a type of freedom and liberty that money cannot buy.** I had lived at times with lots of cash, partied in the best of clubs, stayed in the best of hotels, done the best of drugs, had nice things, and sex with numerous women, none of that took away my pain. Only Christ and His power did that. I had lived both lives and returned to life's only hope.

I would not be a slave to material possessions ever again, or a slave to other men's acceptance. Acceptance from my Lord, my Savior, and my greatest friend was all I needed, and would ever want. **Still, to this day, I would rather live on a borrowed couch, with no material possessions, except the clothes on my back with Jesus than all of the accumulated wealth of the world.** Things can become idols. They can steal from your devotion to God, steal time from real quality moments with your children, or your significant other. Before you know it, a thing can become more valuable than your family, or your real assignment in life, from which you acquire meaning and purpose from your Creator. It can quickly be classified as an idol.

1 Corinthians 10:6-7 (KJV) says, "Now these things were our examples, to the intent we should not lust after evil things, as they also lusted. Neither be ye idolaters, as were some of them; as it is written, The people sat down to eat and drink, and rose up to play."

Hebrews 13:5 (KJV) says, "Let your conversation be without covetousness; and be content with such things as ye have: for he hath said, I will never leave thee, nor forsake thee."

1 Timothy 5:6 (KJV) says, "But she that liveth in pleasure is dead while she liveth."

You cannot let things become more important than the very God who rescued you from them. Worshipping the created rather than the Creator. A part of those things are the drugs that almost destroyed us if it was not for the grace of God. Things have a tendency to take over our lives and destroy what is valuable to us. **Things break down, do not perform as promised, do not last as long as they should, they do not comfort you when you are hurting, they cannot bring healing to your sick body, they cannot add true meaning or real value to your existence, they** cannot give you a gentle touch, a warm hug, and good advice, after all, it is just a thing. God warns us of men with different values and talks about contentment, a value that only God can give.

1 Timothy 6:5-6 (KJV) says, "Perverse disputings of men of corrupt minds, and destitute of the truth, supposing that gain is godliness: from such withdraw thyself. But godliness with contentment is great gain."

I had learned the hard way that material gain does not bring happiness. That only godliness with contentment is truly a gain of self-worth and value, a value found in one's own self as a created being with a destiny, filled with meaning and purpose.

Romans 14:17 (KJV) says, "For the kingdom of God is not meat and drink; but righteousness, and peace, and joy in the Holy Ghost."

Luke 12:15 (KJV) says, "And he said unto them, Take heed, and beware of covetousness: for a man's life consisteth not in the abundance of the things which he possesseth."

Truly, things do not represent the kingdom of God. Some things are dangerous and can destroy you such as drugs, alcohol, fast cars, motorcycles, and other toys. They could be a source of tempting God. We cannot throw ourselves at the foot of the mountain saying God's angels will take care of us, as we see in Jesus' response to Satan tempting Him in the wilderness. Christ said, "It is written, thou shalt not tempt the Lord thy God!" Things come and go. They get broken, stolen, and lost. **But the kingdom of God is within you, and it is joy and right standing with God. God is the only permanent source of contentment.**

I have one more final thought on the subject of things, and material possessions. Today as I sit here at my double screen computer thinking of my life now, and taking a personal inventory of my life, I must confess that I am truly a blessed man. I have many things in my life and have no debts. Many of them bring me pleasure, and many of them fulfill a need. But none of them are more important to me than my relationship with God.

God is not concerned about how many things you own, but He is concerned about the things that own you. Nowhere in scripture is poverty associated with godliness. The truth is poverty is a result of disobedience and a lack of wisdom in most cases. God gives us many scriptures with the promise of him supplying our needs and blessing us. Being poor is not a sign of humility. It is a sign of need. God wants to supply your needs, and much more. God requires us to help others in need. How could you do that, if you did not have more than enough for yourself? Humility can be expressed more out of abundance than need. If you have an abundance of contentment, and an abundance of supply, you can truly express a lack of pride and of self-importance by bringing glory to your true source of supply, God.

Even sacrifice is a form of giving. Everything that you remove in your life to help others or to promote the kingdom of God through sacrifice is giving. Anything you sacrifice upon God's altar brings reward and blessing. But we are never told to choose poverty. Poverty is not the same as sacrifice and living in need. You can sacrifice many things in your life, but all it will ever bring is wealth and blessing if it is sacrificed to God out of obedience. You simply cannot out give the greatest giver, God the Father of all good gifts, and not be rewarded for it. There will never be a time when you sacrifice something for God that it will go unnoticed or unrewarded. God is a gift giver.

James 1:17 (KJV) says, "Every good gift and every perfect gift is from above, and cometh down from the Father of lights, with whom is no variableness, neither shadow of turning."

Psalm 37:4 (KJV) says, "Delight thyself also in the LORD; and he shall give thee the desires of thine heart."

If you call my personal phone and you get my message, you will find it is somewhat different than most messages you will normally hear. It will say that I am praying, helping someone in need, or riding my motorcycle. That sounds so contradictory to some. But it describes to me the perfect life, one where God has set the priorities of my life in such a way as to make it enjoyable. I always wanted a motorcycle. But in my mind, I was concerned about it taking away from my responsibilities and priorities in life. I also made a lot of excuses for not spending money on a bike. Besides, I could use the money helping others.

But God spoke to me through one of the members on our ministry board of directors. He said, "Tim, I have never met anyone that has given more of their income away as you, not in my life, and never have seen it done in any other ministry either." He said, "I think God wants you to get that motorcycle. You need a place to relax and have time to yourself. It is probably something God is trying to give you. For the explicit reason of making you happy, and prolonging your life and ministry. I have my boat, it works that way with me, it is where God speaks to me, and it is another form of communication I have with God, your motorcycle is my boat! I think you need to get it!"

So, yes, I have a motorcycle, and I ride off into some of the most beautiful sunsets with my friend and comforter the Holy Spirit. Sometimes the presence of God is so strong that I must pull over on the side of some country road and worship. It has been a blessing to have. I am so thankful for having a heavenly Father who knows what makes me tick and takes joy in pleasing those He loves. Just like any other father. God feels the same way about you too. He loves you and wants to supply every need in your life, and the very desires of your heart. But, there are many days that I don't ride, or even think of my motorcycle. I am too busy, enjoying the work of God. The bike doesn't own me.

I could give up anything I own because I am complete. I am in want of nothing. In Mike Murdock's book about the Holy Spirit, he describes an encounter with the Holy Spirit that way. An experience of absolute no need. I can identify with that because I too have had many encounters with the Holy Spirit, and it always leaves me breathless, with no need of men's approval, material things, or any other need at all, just complete. God wants to bless you with self-worth, value, meaning, and completeness. **Even to a man who has everything, it is God's good pleasure to give gifts that have life in them. He enjoys giving you the kingdom.**

Luke 12:32 (KJV) says, "Fear not, little flock; for it is your Father's good pleasure to give you the kingdom."

Here are a few things I have listed that could give you problems in your new life of freedom and recovery.

I would be in prayer, and take a personal inventory of everything that you have in your life, asking God and the Holy Spirit to teach you from scratch, how to live, and what things you should incorporate into your new life, and what things you should discard.

1. **Anything associated with drugs, alcohol, tobacco, including souvenirs and paraphernalia.**

2. **Photos, postcards, pictures, letters, and objects of sinful memories, and events that describe chaos, trauma, and places of hurt. Not every memory, but the ones that give you a sense of pride or extreme hurt.**

3. **Get rid of your phone, or change your number. Destroy all contacts from your past that have anything to do with people who use, or that are involved in illegal drug trafficking, or people who were a source of tempting desires and sinful lust. Stay free and clear from any source of temptation.**

4. **Until you are safe, strong, and trustworthy, having completed at least 30 days of sobriety, give the keys to your automobile to someone else and never travel to a place that will have things that will tempt you, or memories that will create temptation or lead to a confrontation of your past until**

you are strong enough to handle it, and the stronghold has been broken in your life. Do not travel alone.

5. Simplify your life just to include the things you need that strengthen you spiritually. You will be surprised at the freedom you will feel once the weight of all unnecessary stuff is gone.

6. All pornography, access to pornography, magazines, books, and things that promote an unhealthy imagination.

7. Turn away from anything that comes from the occult, eastern false religions, idols that usually relate to and are connected with seducing spirits. Stop burning candles or any form of incense. Get rid of any created object that takes away from the real power of God that comes from His presence within you. False idols such as statues of Greek gods, Buddha, and items associated with witchcraft, voodoo, black magic, and talking to the dead, must be destroyed.

8. Any cd's, music, songs, or records that give you urges you should not have, or create an atmosphere that produces temptation, or emotions that lead to defeat, or depression.

No soldier goes to battle carrying un-useful equipment, baggage, and clothing. They strip down to the bare essentials of survival equipment and weapons, lest they get distracted in the battle and worn out from the weight of carrying them.

Hebrews 12:1 (KJV) says, "Wherefore seeing we also are compassed about with so great a cloud of witnesses, let us lay aside every weight and the sin which doth so easily beset us, and let us run with patience the race that is set before us."

11

THE KILLER'S TARGET, YOUR BODY

> METHADDICTSHELP, FACEBOOK POST
> APRIL 10, 2017
> *IF SATAN CANNOT GET YOU ANY OTHER WAY, HE WILL*
> *THROUGH DESTROYING YOUR BODY. DRUGS ARE ONE OF HIS*
> *WEAPONS OF CHOICE. PLEASE DO NOT MAKE ONE OF HIS*
> *WEAPONS YOUR DRUG OF CHOICE, ...MESSAGE US IF YOU*
> *NEED ENCOURAGEMENT OR PRAYER..........TPC. (UNEDITED)*
> 109,377 PEOPLE REACHED
> 6,500 LIKES
> 1,793 SHARES
> 406 COMMENTS

*R*evelation 9:11 (MSG) says, "They had a king over them, the Angel of the Abyss. His name in Hebrew is *Abaddon*, in Greek, *Apollyon*—"Destroyer."

If Satan cannot infect your mind any longer with the disease of untruth and propaganda, he will try to attack your body. When Satan entered the garden, he came in the form of a serpent, cunning, and crafty, that he might deceive Eve. His first target was the mind. But, Satan comes as a roaring lion to destroy your body. If the child of God learns how to overcome his deception, he then must deal with Satan as the destroyer, seeking to harm him physically.

1 Peter 5:8 (KJV) says, "Be sober, be vigilant; because your adversary the devil, as a roaring lion, walketh about, seeking whom he may devour."

I was skin and bones when God saved me. My mouth was filled with abscesses. My teeth hurt and my body was simply beginning to wear out from the inside. It was the nature of the drug. There were times that my prostate would swell up, and I was bed-ridden for several days due to a bad batch of crystal meth. There were many times after being up for days, I slept for days and couldn't get out of bed. But as soon as I could get moving, I was on a binge, living on the edge, running, never stopping, going from one motel to another and from one girl's house to another, never staying more than a couple of days anywhere. I would close down strip clubs, bars, and go to the beach in the middle of the night. When nothing was open, we would go to an all-night drug store like Walgreen's. I remember spending a couple of thousand dollars in Walgreen's on vibrators, body massagers, cologne, perfume, battery operated toothbrushes, and food. You would be surprised what a person high on meth would do and buy. This lifestyle was designed by Satan to weaken and destroy my body.

Satan uses drugs like meth to kill the body

The drug results in increased physical activity, lack of rest, over-indulgence of toxic chemicals and adrenalin, adding stress on your physical body, creating a slow death. Meth was designed specifically to disrupt the normal flow of hormones, like serotonin, and dopamine. It floods your brain and glands with as much as a 1400% increase in hormone secretion throughout your body. Meth destroys your internal organs eating you from the inside out. People cannot control their emotions properly while on this drug. It can be very dangerous to threaten, insult, or agitate a person who is high on meth. People make extremely bad decisions while high, such as spending thousands of dollars at Walgreen's, only to give it all away the next day, because you did not need the items you bought. It has a two-edged sword effect. It is exciting and chaotic at the same time.

You can get stuck for days in a motel room, while your whole life is going to ruin on the outside. You can easily forget everything else in your life while using, including your children, home, automobile, job, wife, or husband. It doesn't start out that way, but it escalates to that kind of behavior in time. It was a full out war, an assault on my mind, and body. Everyone in addiction and many families have witnessed former addicts who are dis-func-tional, and handicapped by the effects of the drug abuse and its lifestyle. Many of you reading this book are having health prob-lems because of your past life in addiction. Drugs, alcohol, tobacco, and hard, fast living, without proper food and nutrients, have hurt your health. That was Satan's objective, to destroy you. It is God's objective in recovery to restore your health and heal your body.

If it wasn't for God's forgiveness, and healing power, I would not have a healthy mind and body today. I wouldn't be able to put thoughts like these together in a cohesive style. But, Jesus healed my body and my mind. After spending twelve years in addiction, God has totally restored my sanity and health.

Psalm 103:2-4 (KJV) says, "Bless the LORD, O my soul, and forget not all his benefits: Who forgiveth all thine iniquities; who healeth all thy diseases; Who redeemeth thy life from destruction; who crowneth thee with lovingkindness and tender mercies"

During the entire process of reading this book, if you will absorb, and take in each day what God is teaching you, I believe that you will be healed as well. God is very much invested in the healing of your body.

Isaiah 53:5 (KJV) says, "But he was wounded for our transgressions, he was bruised for our iniquities: the chastisement of our peace was upon him; and with his stripes we are healed."

Jesus did not go to the cross to pay for our sins only. He also went to provide healing for our bodies, Isaiah says with His stripes we are healed. I have personally witnessed healings of cancer, mental disorders, broken vertebrae, and all kinds of miracles since I have been saved, even the removal of heroin withdrawals. A lot of people that come to me for help suffer panic attacks and hear voices after extreme drug use. They all have been healed and set free by the miracle-working power of Christ. Everywhere Jesus went, He healed those that were sick. His whole purpose was to restore man's mental, physical, and spiritual well-being. He desires for us to have a healthy mind, body, and spirit. If you are really looking for God's perfect will concerning sickness and disease you need not go any further than the Garden of Eden. There was none, no sickness before man sinned. What about heaven? Nope, none there either. No sickness in heaven. *Revelation 21:4 (KJV) says, "And God shall wipe away all tears from their eyes; and there shall be no more death, neither sorrow, nor crying, neither shall there be any more pain: for the former things are passed away."* God's perfect will for man is to be spiritually healthy, and physically healthy, set completely free from the consequences of sin. Jesus not only died on the cross for our sins but also our diseased or sick bodies. Jesus fulfilled the prophecy of Isaiah in His death, and also in the example of the way He lived on earth. He just ordinarily, practiced miracle healing to all that came to Him. *Matthew 8:16-17 (KJV) says, "When the even was come, they brought unto him many that were possessed with devils: and he cast out the spirits with his word, and healed all that were sick: That it might be fulfilled which was spoken by Esaias the prophet, saying, Himself took our infirmities, and bare our sicknesses."* We also see the dual purpose of Christ's ministry found throughout scripture. The word of God is clear, all scripture is unified describing sickness as something God does not wish upon us. *3 John 1:2 (KJV) says, "Beloved, I wish above all things that thou mayest prosper and be in health, even as thy soul prospereth."*

1 John 5:14-15 (KJV) says, "And this is the confidence that we have in him, that, if we ask any thing according to his will, he heareth us: And if we know that he hear us, whatsoever we ask, we know that we have the petitions that we desired of him."

James 5:15 (KJV) says, "And the prayer of faith shall save the sick, and the Lord shall raise him up; and if he have committed sins, they shall be forgiven him."

The evidence is real. The facts can be presented in open and plain view throughout God's word, that it is His will, and wish for you to be healed, healthy, and productive. It is undeniable that anyone can have confidence and faith that God will hear their prayer and heal their body if they just ask and believe. If you are in pain, or sick in your body, God wants to heal you. He desires to heal you. He even paid the price for your healing on the cross or died so that you might be healed. He commissioned the church to pray for your healing. It would seem ludicrous or absurd, for God to go to all of that trouble if He Himself was not sincere. Don't you think it is time for you to accept your healing and believe God for it? God is trying to talk to you, and get your attention. He is saying to you that He loves you, and did not forget about your pain, but carried it to the cross to bury it, and destroy it so that you might be healed.

Stress is the body's number one killer and Satan's primary weapon of destruction

This is my labor of love to you, I have been a sojourner. I was where you are and have great compassion for my brothers and sisters who are in recovery. **All of us were facing the fear of an unknown future, and the stress that it brings. We can be overwhelmed at the mere thought of getting our lives back, and the possibilities of how to achieve it.** Many of us have court battles, custody hearings, no job or automobile, and maybe homeless. We have come into recovery without good support. Most of us have burned all our bridges.

When I spent time in jail, where the thoughts in my mind were speaking to me, I would think that the police in Calcasieu Parish were going to keep me there without bail. I felt that I would never get out, and eventually be imprisoned for years. Those words and circumstances put me alone with God, looking at four blank walls. **These law enforcement agencies had previously come at me in force. The Louisiana State Narcotics Division had kicked my walls in, and the FBI Surveillance Team had surrounded me, and the Lafayette Impact team had busted my doors down. I was arrested and charged several times. They had pictures of me on their walls, and now that they had me, I just figured my life, as I once knew it, was over.** I would spend many years in prison. I did not think I had anyone who would post bail, or help me.

This scenario became a conversation between God and me, and those blank prison walls, which produced who I am today. Mental stress and the physical fatigue it produces can destroy your health. It can destroy your will to pursue life and the future. The hopelessness of our unmanageable lives produces a platform for failure and relapse. Many children of God, a child of God, or infant in God's kingdom are pushed into aborting their mission to rise above addiction by the stress that problems bring. Having no coping skills to overcome it, Satan defeats us.

It was then, on January 15, 2013, that God began to incorporate His grace, or the ability to bear the burdens of life in me. I am reminded of the words that God gave me then, that I still live by today. I have had to live by them every day from that day forward. I told you basically what He told me in our first conversation we had in jail. From that conversation, He began to remind me of specific things in His word when I would feel threatened and bombarded with doubt and confusion.

Stress is pressure. It is a mental and emotional strain. It is tension resulting from adverse and very demanding circumstances. Stress produces fear, anxiety, fatigue, and is a contributing cause of many diseases. Stress gives motivation to unbelief, and doubt, which promotes drug use, and in turn, drugs kill. As reported in an article from *Web*MD, stress contributes to obesity, heart disease, Alzheimer's disease, diabetes, depression, gastrointestinal problems, and asthma. Stress is evil. Satan uses it to destroy our bodies and weaken our resolve.

Jesus' words became my words, and they are now my words to you.

Matthew 6:31-34 (AMP) says, "Therefore do not worry and be anxious, saying, what are we going to have to eat? or, what are we going to have to drink? Or, what are we going to have to wear? For the Gentiles (heathen) wish for and crave and diligently seek all these things, and your heavenly Father knows well that you need them all. But seek (aim at and strive after) first of all His kingdom and His righteousness (His way of doing and being right), and then all these things taken together will be given you besides. So, do not worry or be anxious about tomorrow, for tomorrow will have worries and anxieties of its own. Sufficient for each day is its own trouble."

The words of Jesus would comfort my thoughts, and ease my tension. They would encourage me and create hope in a beaten down body, and fatigued mind. The pressure and stress that Satan would attack me with folded under the authority of the words of Christ. **He would say to me, "Don't worry, or be anxious, I am with you, I know what you need, don't even think about it, I watch the tiny birds, and you are my most valued creation, I** know what you need before you ask, seek me first, Tim, and all these things will be added to your life." Truly God was with me and steadied my course. Those words in Mathew 6, along with the Lord's prayer, would speak volumes of encouragement to the man I was, the man that had been crushed under the weight of sin and Satan.

Inside those four walls, I found freedom from myself. When my inner demons tried to come home to rest, they found a new standard at home. My burden bearer had come to carry my burdens for me. Jesus was carrying the weight, and load of my previous sins and mistakes. He also carried the weight of tomorrow and all my concerns. I believed in Him. He alone carried me with those words. **Like a hungry starving man, I readily and eagerly digested and filled my mind and heart with Him. That's what believers do. That's why we persist. We don't cave under pressure. Because our mind is on Jesus, His kingdom, and doing His will in our lives. We had no peace before, and now with that witness and transformation comes faith, faith in the words of Jesus.**

1 John 5:4 (KJV) says, "this is the victory that overcometh the world, even our faith."

The one thing prison or jail cannot take from you is your choice to believe. The one thing you have that destroys fear and anxiety is Jesus telling you that He will take care of it. Your future is secure, and the problems you face will be taken care of, just seek His kingdom, and His righteousness and all these things will be added to your life. **While writing these words, I am overwhelmed with emotion and am in tears. God has come through with all the promises He made to me in jail, while sitting on a small bed, with no friends left, and a family that did not believe in me, not so long ago.**

God is talking to you right now about your worries and fears. All the things that are adding pressure to your life. Will I ever get my kids back? Can I ever pay my fines back? Is there anyone that will have enough trust in me to hire me again? I never really was a success at anything before, how will I be able to become one now? Will any of my family respect me again? These are some of the very thoughts Satan would speak to my spirit, also. But, God is saying to you, at this moment, not to worry, these are the very things I care about too, your cares are my cares.

1 Peter 5:7 (KJV) says, "Casting all your care upon him; for he careth for you."

Keys to overcoming stress

The word of God in five short verses gives us the keys to over-coming Satan's most powerful weapon, stress. It contains the most valuable insight and tools for personal growth and maturity the world has ever heard. It is a unique message written two thousand years ago by the Apostle Peter and inspired by the Holy Spirit. Peter was a fisherman. A normal, average, common man, and was uneducated. But just as you and I, when partnering with God, we become extraordinarily wise, above and beyond the ability and wisdom of all the sciences of humanity. This is the almighty, potent, and powerful word of God for you. It holds the key to spiritual rest and growth in the fourth dimension, the kingdom of God.

1 Peter 5:6-10 (KJV) says,

[6] Humble yourselves therefore under the mighty hand of God, that he may exalt you in due time:

[7] Casting all your care upon him; for he careth for you.

[8] Be sober, be vigilant; because your adversary the devil, as a roaring lion, walketh about, seeking whom he may devour:

[9] Whom resist steadfast in the faith, knowing that the same afflictions are accomplished in your brethren that are in the world.

[10] But the God of all grace, who hath called us unto his eternal glory by Christ Jesus, after that ye have suffered a while, make you perfect, stablish, strengthen, settle you.

Humble yourself before God

The first key is in verse six, to just humble yourself before God. **When I lifted myself up I failed and was brought down, when I let God lift me up, I was exalted.** All the things that you need to accomplish in your life will require God's help. Surrender, the first principle in this book applies here, to surrender everything to God, your wants, needs, problems and entire life, is the first step in humility. The often-quoted saying found in A. A., "Let go and let God," means you must let go of your control, and come humbly before God in need, allowing God's power to accomplish these things in His time. **When He has finished the work that success requires in you, He will at the right time, lift you up in honor.**

It is His process. **He is making you strong enough to be able to handle success. He is preparing you for achievement and honor so when it comes you will not fail at it.** A man's pride will get ahead of God. Seek things that could be dangerous to his overall success and health. You cannot let your human pride seek promotion of self. You will be brought low. Humbling comes under the mighty hand of God. It requires submitting to God. When I lifted myself up I was brought down, when I let God lift me up, I was exalted. You too will come to your own place, a place of strength and not weakness, strong financially, and healthy, both physically, and mentally. He is purifying you, and breaking chains of bondage in you now so that the Refiner's Fire of God can create the gold that will not perish, or lose its luster once God promotes and blesses you.

Cast your cares on God

The second key is in verse seven, to cast our cares on God.

Casting your cares upon Christ gives you the opportunity and freedom to care for others. When I quit taking care of number one, myself, and sought God, He provided. Peter is still talking in the present tense connecting it with the previous thought. You must always cast your cares upon Christ when faced with them in the present world. We attain humility by casting or throwing all our wants and needs upon the Lord. Give all your cares and worries over to God! Why? Because He cares about your cares. That's exactly what I did. I was tired of worrying about them anyway. Besides, there was nothing I could do about them anyway. Most all of them required a miracle from God. It takes faith and humility to throw your cares upon God. Putting it in God's hands requires patience and trust. *Hebrews 10:35-36 (KJV) says, "Cast not away, therefore, your confidence, which hath great recompense of reward. For ye have need of patience, that, after ye have done the will of God, ye might receive the promise."* The devil will try to remind you of them, and create fear and anxiety in your heart, but you must keep your concerns buried in trust before God. Peter then tells us how to do that, in the next few verses, by sober thinking, resistance, perspective, and endurance. Stress will always be present in this world but through biblical coping skills, you can live where it will not affect your health and productivity.

I accepted what God would provide for me, and where He would lead me. Doing things my way, and seeking the things of this world did not bring me happiness, even when I had them. The longing for meaning and purpose was only filled when I turned to God. That settled it for me. I would give my life and direction to Him. When I began to fill the needs of others, fulfilling my higher calling, and primary reason for existing, God began to provide in a supernatural way. I remember being so enthused about others, that I never prayed much about my own needs. It was God who stepped in and blessed me.

Be sober and vigilant

The third key is in verse eight, we must be sober and vigilant. Satan and demonic spirits attached to things, people and places, are trying to stop the progress of God in your life. Peter gives us soldiers a two-fold command. He says just be ready and prepared. This is where victory over Satan begins. First, we are to be sober. To be sober means to be discreet, cautious, and practice self-control, careful in our thoughts and actions with the idea of discernment, the ability to judge between truth and a lie. With the discernment of the word of God, and the Holy Spirit leading us, we can be sober enough, ready enough, to expose all the lies of Satan, not letting them affect our emotions and decisions.

Second, we must be vigilant, which means to be watchful, attentive, alert, and "on your toes" so to speak, taking a close examination of your thoughts, the people, and things around you, being on guard, ready to use the word of God, and faith to destroy Satan and your own previous positions of unbelief. Satan and his demonic counterparts use tools, such as people, places, and things, that create emotions, thoughts, and desires that affect your decisions. You must have the mind of Christ and His word in your heart to be able to know who and what to listen to. *It would be very hard for you to have a great deal of stress and anxiety if you believed in the healing, and prosperity of the believer. No lies equals no stress. No pressure.*

Philippians 4:8 (KJV) says, "Finally, brethren, whatsoever things are true, whatsoever things are honest, whatsoever things are just, whatsoever things are pure, whatsoever things are lovely, whatsoever things are of good report; if there be any virtue, and if there be any praise, think on these things."

Hebrews 4:1-2 (KJV) says, "Let us therefore fear, lest, a promise being left *us* of entering into his rest, any of you should seem to come short of it. For unto us was the gospel preached, as well as unto them: but the word preached did not profit them, not being mixed with faith in them that heard *it.*"

Identification and perspective

The fourth key is identification and perspective. Having the right perspective makes the unbearable bearable. When you identify the problem and you see it is doable, then you can bear the wait. Peter says your enemy is Satan, and what he is doing to you is nothing different than he is trying to do with your fellow travelers in the world. Verse 9b says that the same afflictions you are facing are being experienced by others. That view is life changing. **Because, once you see that others have overcome him while facing the same obstacles you have, you know it can be done. You can relax, or rest your fears.** We must be aware that Satan is an evil being who wants to hurt you. The source of your attack isn't people or God. God is on your side, and people can be ignorant of their position. People can be a help, or they can hurt you, and feed you thoughts of failure. You must select the right people in your life. Clarification of your enemy can save you valuable time, and difficulties.

Acknowledging God as your help restores confidence and peace of mind. Now that you know others have overcome the same problems you have, you can now rest and trust God to do the same for you. You are no different than the rest of us.

Resist the devil in the faith

The fifth key is to resist the devil in the faith. Your faith is bigger than your enemy. What is important to see is that the writer is talking about your position in Christ. He says, "in the faith." He didn't say by faith, or with faith. He was talking about resisting Satan with the entire embodiment of the practical applications of what the word says you are and how it says you are to live. Our religion, our faith, the entire working of the Christian faith is all we need to defeat Satan. **Practice Godliness, and there is nothing in you that he can attack.** The word resist is a military term. It means that you are in a battle of life and death and that your faith or conduct is the weapon that defeats the enemy. The word steadfast means to be fixed and firm in everything we believe and that our defense is so solid we don't have to worry, or fear Satan. In Luke 10:19, Jesus gave us authority over all the power of Satan.

Ephesians 3:17 (KJV) says, "That Christ may dwell in your hearts by faith; that ye, being rooted and grounded in love,"

We must grow and continue in the faith, become rooted and grounded in the depths of love. So that Satan cannot have any means to attack you, or penetrate your armor of Godliness.

Endure hardship

Finally, **the sixth key to overcoming stress is to endure hardship and wait patiently in confidence, knowing that God is in control and will come through for you in the end. Enduring grants the favor of God.** Verse 10 says that after you endure, God's grace or favor will work on your behalf by strengthening you, establishing you and settling you. God will restore the losses you have suffered as a result of addiction and sin. He will confirm, complete you, and ground you securely, settle you firmly on a good foundation. **That in real life terms is like saying you will have transportation, a job, finances, a home, your family back, or at the very minimum their respect, and your mental and physical health back. God is telling you that after you have suffered, He will establish you, or give you a start, and eventually set you up with the things you will need to survive.**

God is telling you the truth about suffering. Suffering is a present reality. Suffering is the one element that we will all face. The righteous will go through suffering and the unrighteous also. **But, when His children suffer, it has its limits. It will not last, and it produces achievement and eternal success.** God also grants us peace and joy in the Holy Ghost as we go through suffering. God is not talking about suffering from His hands. He is talking about suffering from the pressures and problems that come from living in a world that has been contaminated by sin and rebellion, a world that has Satan in it. He is talking about the suffering of the battle between your flesh and spirit. This battle governs the mental and physical health of your body also. Jesus was not exempt from suffering. We certainly will not be either.

Suffering produced such humility, joy, and peace in me that it is unexplainable to those who have not been surgically exposed and bared open in an environment that rendered you helpless to overcome by yourself. I relied only on God. I had no one else, and it freed me of myself. Suffering will de-clothe you, undress you. It leaves you exposed without the excess baggage you have relied upon for comfort. It reveals what you are lacking spiritually so that you will reach for it with your whole heart. Because you know you cannot survive without it. Everything is gone except what is necessary to live by. It opens you up to greater meaning, it leaves you naked, without the extra baggage, and the clothing you were carrying around, and really didn't need anyway. Suffering will get you to a place where you are relying on the only thing that will get you through, which is the sole basic ingredient of life found in Christ, the Bread of Life.

You must die to whatever process that God has allowed in your life so that in His hands you might be made perfect. There is a suffering or fire that God uses to develop and strengthen faith and purity in you. Sometimes there are things that you are using for comfort that are distractions, and there are parts of your flesh that you are relying on that will, later on, cause you to fail. God removes some of the comforts in your life to reveal to you greater truth and privilege in His kingdom. We must die to self and live unto God. We submit to God and whatever the process that He has us going through so that we may always be a victor, and never become the victim of Satan and sin again. In 1 Corinthians 15:31 (KJV), Paul says, "I die daily."

Hebrews 12:27-28 (ESV) says, "This phrase, "Yet once more," indicates the removal of things that are shaken—that is, things that have been made—in order that the things that cannot be shaken may remain. Therefore, let us be grateful for receiving a kingdom that cannot be shaken, and thus let us offer to God acceptable worship, with reverence and awe,"

There is a principle of God removing anything in the earth that has the seed of death and sin. These are temporal things that do not belong to us and must be removed so that His everlasting and unshakable kingdom is what remains in us. We then become unshakable, strong, durable and there is nothing in us left for Satan to tempt us with. Which removes all worldly stress and pressure in our lives.

Hebrews 12:1-2 (KJV) says, "Wherefore seeing we also are compassed about with so great a cloud of witnesses, let us lay aside every weight, and the sin which doth so easily beset *us*, and let us run with patience the race that is set before us, looking unto Jesus the author and finisher of *our* faith; who for the joy that was set before him endured the cross, despising the shame, and is set down at the right hand of the throne of God."

There is in all of us a weakness, and a special sin, or place where we continually miss the mark, and that keeps us from reaching our full potential. We must lay it aside, and run with patience so that we may attain the prize, and walk in mental and physical health, spiritual dominance, and financial well-being.

Once you have that knowledge, Satan has no place in you to tempt. Jesus becomes your food, and the necessary, primary, and only sustenance needed. He gives you joy, even while enduring.

There is no greater strength than this. It cannot be found anywhere but Christ. That alone gave me strength and faith to face any set of circumstances. I abandoned all my own inhibitions. Forgiveness freed me from a feeling of being unworthy to act on God's behalf, and faith gave me the courage to move forward abandoning my fears. I was no longer self-conscious, about what put me there, but aware that I was on God's timing and His path. I found meaning in obeying God and helping others. My suffering did not create emotional pain but allowed me to experience hope and rest. **When you come to the realization that what you feared losing the most wasn't really needed for peace of mind and well-being, you are at the very beginning of freedom.**

2 Timothy 2:3 (AMP) says, "Take [with me] your share of the hardships *and* suffering [which you are called to endure] as a good (first-class) soldier of Christ Jesus."

We must endure the suffering like a soldier in battle, knowing the fight will be over, and victory will be won through the miracle power of Christ.

Hebrews 5:8 (NLT) says, "Even though Jesus was God's Son, he learned obedience from the things he suffered."

Jesus was always obedient, and obedience requires effort, and work. It involves sacrifice, hardship, and suffering. But He also witnessed the rewards of obedience first hand. He learned through experience that the suffering was part of obedience, but paid big dividends. He had learned through being obedient a thousand times before, that the reward far outweighed the cost, and it laid the groundwork or prepared Him for His greatest test, the cross. In which Jesus endured, so He could experience the joy that it would bring.

Hebrews 12:2 (KJV) says, "Looking to Jesus the author and finisher of our faith; who for the joy that was set before Him endured the cross, despising the shame, and is set down at the right hand of the throne of God."

If you can endure, and be obedient, then you will experi-

ence great victory in your life. Casting your cares upon God. Enduring, resisting, and being sober-minded is stress-free. How could you be tormented if there are no lies to believe, and you are dead to sin? The very knowledge that others have resisted, and God has established them and prospered them, is all you need to have the right perspective of faith that will overcome stress.

Why does Satan want to destroy your body?

The primary reason Satan wants to destroy your body is that your body is God's temple. His Spirit lives there. It is God's Spirit in you representing His presence on earth. Our bodies belong to God, and our bodies were intended to bring honor to God, and establish peace, righteousness, and harmony on earth, which Satan hates.

1 Corinthians 6:19-20 (NLT) says, "Don't you realize that your body is the temple of the Holy Spirit, who lives in you and was given to you by God? You do not belong to yourself, for God bought you with a high price. So, you must honor God with your body."

Here are a few more reasons why Satan would like to destroy your body:

1. You are an ambassador for Christ in His stead. The word ambassador means that you are Christ's official representative from heaven and the Kingdom of God. How could you do that in full force if you are in a sick body, one that could not speak, hear, or move around? It would limit your service, and render you less effective. 2 Corinthians 5:20 (NLT) says, "So, we are Christ's ambassadors; God is making his appeal

through us. We speak for Christ when we plead, "Come back to God!"

2. We become less successful and productive over all because our lives are shortened.
3. The people we could reach are no longer reachable and helped.
4. It destroys the faith of others to see people's lives destroyed before it is time.
5. Suffering in your body helps destroy your will to live and serve God.
6. Your body is God's treasury for grace and strength. You are the only visible, tangible, evidence of God anyone will ever see. 2 Corinthians 4:7 (KJV) says, "we have this treasure in earthen vessels, that the excellency of the power may be of God, and not us."

Not all sickness is from a specific attack from Satan

Some sickness is not a personal attack per se, but just a general, customary assault upon all of humanity. All sickness is a direct result of sin, the original sin of Adam, and the cursed environment of sin in the earth. All bacteria, viruses, and other forms of sickness, and genetic defects come from the curse of death and the contamination of evil in general. It is a part of the atmosphere. When Adam sinned, he fell from grace, purity, and the ability to live forever in his physical body. Sin brought about death and the curse, we are born in it, it is part of our journey, and we are exposed to its harsh environment. It is part of the judgment and the law of God upon Adam's sin. It was placed here on this earth to produce limitations and consequences for sin.

If we did not have these limits, mankind would run amok, straight into hell itself without any warning. Indirectly Satan is the destroyer, but Adam was the responsible party, and now we are ultimately responsible. Why? We have a free will and the ability to walk in the wisdom of God or not. Sometimes we do not rest, eat, and exercise properly. We also choose certain destructive habits in our lives that directly cause sickness and stress. This is our responsibility. We also have God's word, and promises, along with the sacrifice of Christ, that we can believe and live by, which is the only true source of healing, deliverance, and restoration of the mind, body, and spirit.

Hebrews 2:3-4 (KJV) says, "How shall we escape, if we neglect so great salvation; which at the first began to be spoken by the Lord, and was confirmed unto us by them that heard him; God also bearing them witness, both with signs and wonders, and with divers miracles, and gifts of the Holy Ghost, according to his own will?"

Our defense and protection from Satan's attack of sickness or any other illness

1. The promises of God

God has promised us physical health as we live on earth. 3 John 1:2 (KJV) says, "Beloved, I wish above all things that thou mayest prosper and be in health, even as thy soul prospereth."

1. He has also guaranteed protection and immunity if we meet the conditions in His word. Exodus 15:26 (KJV) says, "And said, If thou wilt diligently hearken to the voice of the LORD thy God, and wilt do that which is right in his sight, and wilt give ear to his commandments and keep all his statutes, I will put none of these diseases upon thee, which I have brought upon the Egyptians: for I am the LORD that healeth thee."

2. He has given us the promise of prayer that will heal the sick, by laying on of hands and anointing with oil. James

5:14-15 (KJV) says, "Is any sick among you? let him call
for the elders of the church; and let them pray over him,
anointing him with oil in the name of the Lord: And the
prayer of faith shall save the sick, and the Lord shall
raise him up; and if he have committed sins, they shall
be forgiven him."

3. He promises to heal all of our diseases. Psalm 103:3
   (KJV) says, "Who forgiveth all thine iniquities; who
   healeth all thy diseases;"

4. He promises to protect us from plagues. Psalm 91:10
   (KJV) says, "There shall no evil befall thee, neither shall
   any plague come nigh thy dwelling."

5. He promises to restore our health. Jeremiah 30:17
   (KJV) says, "For I will restore health unto thee, and I
   will heal thee of thy wounds, saith the LORD; because
   they called thee an Outcast, saying, This is Zion, whom
   no man seeketh after."

6. He promises rest for our bodies. Hebrews 4:9 (KJV)
   says, "There remaineth therefore a rest to the people
   of God."

These promises are ours. All we must do is believe, meet
their conditions, and expect a miracle from God. As we
studied earlier, our sense knowledge might contradict the
word of God, but our trust is in God, and His promises. We
live accordingly, trusting God's character, His will for our
lives, and in prayer, and fasting.

1 Corinthians 3:22-23 (KJV) says, "Whether Paul, or Apollos,
or Cephas, or the world, or life, or death, or things present, or
things to come; all are yours; And ye are Christ's; and Christ
is God's."

2 Corinthians 5:7 (KJV) says, "(For we walk by faith, not
by sight:)"

Mark 11:22-24 (KJV) says, "And Jesus answering saith unto

them, Have faith in God. For verily I say unto you, That whosoever shall say unto this mountain, Be thou removed, and be thou cast into the sea; and shall not doubt in his heart, but shall believe that those things which he saith shall come to pass; he shall have whatsoever he saith. Therefore I say unto you, What things soever ye desire, when ye pray, believe that ye receive them, and ye shall have them."

Mark 16:18 (KJV) says, "they shall lay hands on the sick, and they shall recover."

2. There are things that we can do that prevent disease and sickness

First, we must recognize the biblical importance of our body, who does it really belong to, and who ultimately is responsible for it. Keeping in shape, and eating healthy is a spiritual discipline. The Holy Spirit lives in your body. God created it, and Jesus died for its healing and well-being. If God cares that much about our physical well-being, we should place the same value, and investment on it also.

1 Corinthians 6:12-20 (NIV2011) says, "I have the right to do anything," you say—but not everything is beneficial. "I have the right to do anything"—but I will not be mastered by anything. You say, "Food for the stomach and the stomach for food, and God will destroy them both." The body, however, is not meant for sexual immorality but for the Lord, and the Lord for the body. By his power, God raised the Lord from the dead, and he will raise us also. Do you not know that your bodies are members of Christ himself? Shall I then take the members of Christ and unite them with a prostitute? Never! Do you not know that he who unites himself with a prostitute is one with her in body? For it is said, "The two will become one flesh." But whoever is united with the Lord is one with him in spirit. Flee from sexual immorality. All other sins a person commits are outside the body, but whoever sins sexually, sins against their own body. Do you not know that your bodies are temples of the Holy Spirit, who is in you, whom you have received from God? You are not your own; you were bought at a price. There-fore, honor God with your bodies."

1. *"You are not your own."* Your body is God's property and belongs to Him. It must be respected and taken care of, as anything that God has loaned us. It is meant for God to live in. We cannot defile it, through sexual sins, and immorality. If we do, we jeopardize our fellowship with God and his dwelling in us. It is His spirit that dwells in us and protects us from the unseen world of sickness and disease. If He is not in control and leaves, where is our defense? Our first defense is to flee immorality.

2. *"I have the right to do anything."* A lot of things are permissible, but not everything you do is beneficial to your body. A lot of foods are edible but can cause an unhealthy body. Drugs, and alcohol, sometimes are permitted but are not healthy when used the wrong way. Tobacco has no healthy purpose at all, drugs can be used as medicine with limits and guidelines, and wine can be used for the stomach's sake in moderation. But, none of the things we eat should master us, or control us, because, then they can destroy something very precious to us, our bodies.

3. *"Your bodies are the temples of the Holy Spirit."* If you were walking down the street and saw someone vandalizing a synagogue or building you would probably call the police. What if they were destroying your home where you and your children sleep? If you regularly vandalize, and disrespect your body, by polluting it with filth, over-eating, and poison, don't you think that would make God angry? If you would do something about your home, I am sure God will do something about His. I would rather have God's blessing in my life, illustrated

in a healthy body than live in a cursed body falling apart, wouldn't you?

So, in conclusion, the promises of God, the prayer of faith, our diet, and being free from any dangerous habit like overeating, drugs, alcohol, and tobacco is our strong defense. That along with fleeing sexual sins is the best defense.

We must remember our bodies are important to God

If we view our bodies the way God sees them, it will help us to remember how important they are to God. Seeing how valuable of a tool they are in God's hands, gives new meaning to the care of our bodies. It also allows us to see it from the perspective of God's watchful protection. He protects what He values. This gives us faith and the ability to trust Him when things go wrong. His greatest investment to us is our physical bodies that carry our mind, soul, and spirit. It also carries His presence. That is why He provides healing and restoration to our physical bodies.

We are visible to all of God's creation. We were made in His image. He made us extremely well and perfectly formed, to honor, and glorify Him. We are His testimony of power and creativity. Our bodies are still a marvel to modern science.

Psalm 139:14 (KJV) says, "I will praise thee; for I am fearfully and wonderfully made"

As the word says, we were made wonderfully or brilliantly. We were created to bear His image in our earthly bodies. To disrespect our bodies is to disrespect His image. Tattoos and body piercings often take away from the beauty and exquisite features of our bodies, accenting the creativity of man rather than God. If you have already honored man, family members, the

dead, and many other things by tattooing and marking your body, remember that God has forgiven you, and that, now you must just glorify God in your body in a way that brings honor to Him, the one who created it. A lot of us innocently have done many things before we came to Christ, and unknowingly dishonored God. God is not concerned with your past. He is concerned about your future and the present. Your past is forgiven, and God is providing you with insight to restore, protect, and glorify Him in your body. He is doing this because He cares about you.

Leviticus 19:28 (NLT) says, "Do not cut your bodies for the dead, and do not mark your skin with tattoos. I am the LORD."

Romans 12:1 (KJV) says, "I beseech you, therefore, brethren, by the mercies of God, that ye present your bodies a living sacrifice, holy, acceptable unto God, which is your reasonable service."

Genesis 1:27 (KJV) says, "So God created man in his own image, in the image of God created he him; male and female created he them."

Our bodies were bought, or redeemed at a tremendous cost. It cost Jesus' life. The price was paid so that we could glorify God in our bodies. God is invisible, the world cannot see Him, but we can be seen. It is our conduct and actions that glorify God in our bodies. It is what honors Him, it is His witness on earth through us.

1 Corinthians 6:20 (KJV) says, "For ye are bought with a price: therefore glorify God in your body, and in your spirit, which are God's."

We proclaim the superiority of God's healing and miracle power in our bodies. It is where God puts his treasure, in our bodies, the treasure of spiritual giftings and talents. He also has put the gospel in us to reveal it to the lost.

2 Corinthians 4:7 (KJV) says, "But we have this treasure in earthen vessels, that the excellency of the power may be of God, and not of us."

Finally, our bodies are instruments or tools that God uses

to minister to a dying, lost world. We are tools of right-eousness, praying for others, witnessing to others, building ministries, and bringing the Gospel to the world. Our bodies are a living example that you can live free from sin, or any other bondage such as drugs, pornography, lust, greed, and gluttony.

Romans 6:12-13 (KJV) says, "Let not sin therefore reign in your mortal body, that ye should obey it in the lusts thereof. Neither yield ye your members as instruments of unrighteousness unto sin: but yield yourselves unto God, as those that are alive from the dead, and your members as instruments of righteousness unto God."

In conclusion, our bodies bring glory to God, and when they are under the attack of Satan, through stress, sickness, disease, addiction, or even emotional and mental disorders, that limits our productivity. God wants to give us grace, and healing so that His glory can be revealed in and through us.

12

GOD'S MARVELOUS GRACE

> METHADDICTSHELP, FACEBOOK POST
> FEBRUARY 15, 2017
> *BUT FOR THE GRACE OF GOD. MY RECOVERY APPEARS TO BE A GIFT NEITHER EARNED NOR DESERVED, BUT AS A GIFT FROM A GRACIOUS GOD. ANNE SMITH, " IT TAKES THE WHOLE POWER OF CHRIST TO DO THE SMALLEST OF THINGS."......TPC. (UNEDITED)*
> 88,583 PEOPLE REACHED
> 7K LIKES
> 622 SHARES
> 417 COMMENTS

*A*lthough we are saved by faith through grace, it is clear our rewards will be according to our actions. Regeneration is by faith and evaluation by works. Salvation is by faith and graduation is by works. Promotion comes from effort, commitment, and faithfulness. I do not work for promotion. My goals are to reach as many people as I can for God, help as many as I can, get my hands dirty, my knees calloused, my time and resources spent for Jesus. I enjoy doing it. I want to, desire to, and can do nothing else. It is my *duty, my honor, my privilege, and all I think about. It is because His grace overwhelms me, His love astonishes me, and His help was indispensable to me. It is who I am, Whose I am, and what I am. A product of God's marvelous grace!*

One of the things that caused my fall from God was my faulty, religious understanding of grace. Being tempted to sin is not the same thing as sin. Bad thoughts of anger and lust do not become sin until you accept them as your own and embrace them. Acting on sinful thoughts or allowing them to control your emotions and decisions is sinful.

I lived in a religious world filled with laws, legalism, and rules. Many of them would not be considered as sin if it was the Holy Spirit calling the shots and not religious leaders. It can become impossible to live up to the standards that others place on you. People often require perfection, and we sometimes seek perfection from within ourselves. Perfection is unattainable, that is why God provides grace.

After my wife left me, I was battling all types of issues, issues that dealt with my flesh. My flesh was grieving, hurt, angry, and I was helpless. I had never felt so much pain before. I was not prepared for it, who could be? I stood basically in uncharted territory. I was a baby when it came to that kind of pain. I had overwhelming, uncontrollable urges of hate, and I was contemplating murder. When a man thinks that his wife of 23 years could be having sex with another man while pacing sleepless floors, it is a horrifying experience. Just thinking it, not knowing for sure if it is happening is damaging enough. She was with him, that's enough to hurt you immeasurably. No one in their right mind would believe anything else. When her car is parked at his house, hidden in the backyard, on an early Sunday morning while you are at church, it is demoralizing.

I hated them for putting me through that. Whatever they were doing put these thoughts in my head, even if they were not true. I had thoughts of anger toward God for allowing this to happen.

How could I worship? I concluded that I was caught in the sin of hate, even thoughts of murder. I could not bear it. I was emotionally a wreck. My theology had no room for that kind of weakness in it. No grace. How could I explain such contradicting ideas of thought? How could I reconcile those thoughts of unbelief and hatred with God's love and grace? When the pain is so difficult that all you can do is suffer and nothing else, you cannot pray, or read, or work. Having that kind of spiritual battle, without having God's grace is like living in a dead zone.

Everyone religious would say things that made no sense to me. Like, "in time you will heal." Really, you mean before I kill someone, or drive my car off a cliff? Or, "God will give you someone else." So, you actually think I can replace 23 years of investment and loving someone, their mind, and body, just by going down to a meat market and getting another pound of hamburger? You guys need more help than I do if you think that is possible. The ridiculous sayings like, "It's her loss" or "just believe God," drove me insane. The more other people got involved, the more ridiculous it got. To a person who is completely empty inside, with no self-control, that could not sleep and was filled with the most horrifying lack of assurance and faith, their words made no logical sense. I felt like a worthless sinner, with no sign of God anywhere. The scriptures say there is no peace for the wicked. Paul said, "O wretched man that I am, who shall deliver me from this body of death?" That was me.

What I needed was someone to explain the grace of God to me. Had I known, what I know now about God's marvelous and wonderful grace, I could have survived. If someone had told me that God's grace is with me, and in my worst moments with feelings of anger, God wasn't throwing me out with the bath water of impure thoughts and helplessness. It would have made a difference. If someone in plain words would have said that God wasn't going to cancel out my salvation during my greatest temptations, then I could have relaxed. Temptations that led me to abandon good rational behavior and to be overtaken by irrational thoughts were tormenting me. The recognition of God's grace being a sufficient source of the favor of God during my extreme emotional swings might have given me the incentive to weather the storm. Those emotional swings ranged from hate and anger to love and forgiveness and eventually led to me wanting to kill myself. The information that God certainly was not planning to leave me during my moments of weakness and trial, would have saved me, and at the very least allowed me to come back to Him sooner.

If I could have understood that His grace or His undeserved favor would stay and would carry me until I was strong enough, well enough, and stable enough to pursue life normally, I could have survived. That is why it is so valuable for us to understand God's grace, that it produces mercy in your life. It is God's favor based on Christ, and apart from your behavior. When I am weak, I am still strong because God still loves me. It allows me to stand in Christ, and live by His righteousness and faith. Habakkuk the prophet spoke of this while dealing with the self-reliant Jews in the same sort of dilemma I found myself in. In bondage and slavery under the Babylonians their lives became unmanageable. While dealing with the idol worshipping Babylonians they became puffed-up, and arrogant in their own works. Their indictment was a heart that needed faith.

Habakkuk 2:4 (KJV) says, "Behold, his soul which is lifted up is not upright in him: but the just shall live by his faith."

Romans 1:17 (KJV) says, "For therein is the righteousness of God revealed from faith to faith: as it is written, The just shall live by faith."

Really, all that is required is to be humble enough to put your faith in Christ, and not yourself. God understands thoughts of rejection, hurt, and loneliness. He also understands our weaknesses in the flesh. He knows we have the capacity to feel and think bad thoughts. That's why He sent us Jesus, full of grace and truth.

Hebrews 4:15 (NLT) says, "This High Priest of ours understands our weaknesses, for he faced all of the same testings we do, yet he did not sin."

Jesus came in the form of a man, to be tempted, and was acquainted with pain and suffering. He understands you, and the overwhelming odds you face. **When we suffer He carries us with mercy, never leaving us, but staying in the struggle until we get better. I needed to hear that.** I needed to know that faith is all I need to be righteous. If I could have continually placed my faith in Jesus, I would have been fine, because God was not judging me, and was not going to leave me. His grace is really what it is, undeserved, and unearned favor when I am incapable. I just thought He left me. After feeling like He left, I had nowhere to turn but to hate, bitterness, and anger, anger toward God and everyone else.

It is important to know that you might face a mental and emotional battle so strong that it leaves you with a complete inability to cope and manage your life. And, in that battle, all rational behavior and thoughts abandon you. It embarrasses you. You are ashamed of yourself. How can I be so helpless? It leaves you without control, breathless, exhausted, and can be relentless, offering no relief. Most of all, there is nothing you can do about it. You have no regulator over it. Your emotions are in disarray. There is no thermostat, or switch to turn it off. They are running amok, mocking you, laughing at you, as Satan himself would. **It is then, at that moment in your life, that you need God's grace the most when all control and hope has left you.** If and when this occurs, I want you to know that God's grace has you. God is not leaving, and it is not your righteousness that will get you through, but the righteousness of Christ. When you do not have the power of God within yourself to keep it together, that is when you need His favor and grace the most, until you are well again.

The God that I have come to know will not leave you during your greatest weaknesses and your greatest hurt. But, it is precisely at that moment when the greatest gift of God, His marvelous grace works the best. It is overlooking your weakness and staying, remaining for the journey. You are saved, and standing righteous before God until you can be strong again. The God I have come to know now in an intimate fashion could not hold anyone responsible for thoughts and uncontrollable feelings if they continue to trust in Christ's righteousness. **It is not a license to commit wrong, but it is mercy, forgiveness, and the compassion of your heavenly Father that allows for the battle to continue without judgment, for as long as it takes for you to heal.**

What is grace?

In every loan agreement made between a loan institution and someone, there will always be a grace period in meeting the required installments, usually a period of 5 or 10 days. So, if you pay it within the grace period, it is considered on time, and the obligation is met without any penalties. If men can show grace, certainly God will. There are a lot of things children do that are wrong, but we do not throw them out of the house. There are certainly a lot of wrong things we do as children of God, and He doesn't throw us out of the house either. We see parents that let their children get away with a lot of things with no punishment, and even when they do correct them, it is done with love. That's grace. They do not throw them out of the house, or starve them, and chain them in a cellar, why? They love them.

Mothers hold small, screaming toddlers, carefully, with warmth, all the while, softly speaking to them, whispering love messages, and at the same time, changing their dirty, soiled diaper, washing and adding powder to their precious baby. That's grace. That is favor. That is what God does as we scream in hurt, disgust, and anger. He holds us in our panic, and says, "I love you." Grace allows for mistakes, messes, disobedience, and failure. If humans, who can be so vile and corrupt, calculating and evil, cruel and violent, have the capacity to give grace, certainly God does. God's grace ministers to us in spite of our imperfection. God's grace comes from a place of perfection. That place of perfection is in Christ. Just like a mother holds her child, the grace of God holds us and cares for us through all of our inabilities, weaknesses, and limitations. It comes in the form of time given to me just to get it right. It becomes a freedom from the penalty of being late in meeting His requirements. It is patience, and longsuffering when I am sick, sick in sin, through disobedience, or sick in my body, and I am irritable. That is the grace of God.

We are saved by the grace of God. We will stay saved by the grace of God. Grace is unearned favor. It is when someone gives you favor undeserved, in this instance, eternal salvation. It is important to know that a simple mistake does not affect your salvation. If you have a relapse or breakdown in your walk with God, it is very important to know that God doesn't cross you off his list, or cancel your salvation. Some people live in fear, guilt and torment over an impure thought, and a mere slip of the tongue. You must understand the power of grace if you are going to grow in strength and maturity. Our right standing with God, or in Biblical terms, our righteousness, is based on Jesus and His righteousness. We live by His righteousness. It is imputed or given to us. It is credited to our account, no charge and paid in full by Christ's blood.

Jeremiah 23:6 (KJV) says, "In his days Judah shall be saved, and Israel shall dwell safely: and this is his name whereby he shall be called, THE LORD OUR RIGHTEOUSNESS."

Romans 4:6 (KJV) says, "Even as David also describeth the blessedness of the man, unto whom God imputeth righteousness without works"

It clearly states in the word of God that Jesus is our righteousness, and our salvation is not based on our works but given to us, or imputed, or ascribed to us on the account of what Jesus has done, His works of righteousness. The impartation of eternal life is a free gift to the sinner who trusts Jesus Christ as his personal Savior and is by faith apart from works. We must remember all deliverance, healing, and answered prayer comes from God's grace, and cannot be earned.

Romans 3:23-25 (KJV) says, "For all have sinned, and come short of the glory of God; Being justified freely by his grace through the redemption that is in Christ Jesus: Whom God hath set forth to be a propitiation through faith in his blood, to declare his righteousness for the remission of sins that are past, through the forbearance of God;"

Romans 6:22-23 (KJV) says, "But now being made free from sin, and become servants to God, ye have your fruit unto holiness, and the end everlasting life. For the wages of sin is death; but the gift of God is eternal life through Jesus Christ our Lord."

Philippians 3:9 (KJV) says, "And be found in him, not having mine own righteousness, which is of the law, but that which is through the faith of Christ, the righteousness which is of God by faith:"

2 Corinthians 5:21 (KJV) says, "For he hath made him to be sin for us, who knew no sin; that we might be made the righteousness of God in him."

1 Peter 2:24 (KJV) says, "Who his own self bare our sins in his own body on the tree, that we, being dead to sins, should live unto righteousness: by whose stripes ye were healed."

Romans 6:17-18 (KJV) says, "But God be thanked, that ye were the servants of sin, but ye have obeyed from the heart that form of doctrine which was delivered you. Being then made free from sin, ye became the servants of righteousness."

Romans 5:1-2 (KJV) says, "Therefore being justified by faith, we have peace with God through our Lord Jesus Christ: By whom also we have access by faith into this grace wherein we stand, and rejoice in hope of the glory of God."

1 Corinthians 1:30 (KJV) says, "But of him are ye in Christ Jesus, who of God is made unto us wisdom, and righteousness, and sanctification, and redemption:"

Romans 10:9 (KJV) says, "That if thou shalt confess with thy mouth the Lord Jesus, and shalt believe in thine heart that God hath raised him from the dead, thou shalt be saved."

The word of God is clear about these facts in the scriptures above:

1. We all have sinned.
2. We are justified freely by grace, not works.
3. Justified clearly through redemption found in Christ.
4. Righteousness and justification are given us through His blood.
5. We declare His righteousness, not ours.
6. Our sins are remitted, forgiven, and behind us, now in our past.
7. We had no right standing with God before this.
8. We gain righteousness through faith in Christ.
9. He was made to be our sin on the cross who had no sin.
10. He took our sins and was punished for us, on the tree, or cross.
11. He did that to make us the righteousness of God, or His righteousness.
12. He made us perfect in God's eye through His perfect sacrifice for our sins.

13. We were a slave or a servant of sin and now are free and a servant of righteousness.
14. Jesus was made to be our righteousness.
15. We are justified by faith and forgiven by faith, all through undeserved favor, or grace.

Now that is wonderful and great news! So, Jesus who knew no sin, became our sins, paid the penalty for our wrongdoing on the cross with His blood, and set us free from the slavery of our sin, was made to be our righteousness, giving us everlasting life, through confessing Him Lord, and being redeemed, and justified free of charge, by believing in what He has done, through faith by grace which is by no merit of our own, or good deeds, to become His righteousness, not our righteousness, and are justified, redeemed, set free, saved, and are holy with eternal life by **faith through grace!**

Our effort does not have to be perfect or sinless. His grace is permanent.

Grace is God's favor toward you. It is predisposed, and available for free, no charge, unearned favor. Most people have a tough time with that, mostly about the free part. Few people center in on God's benefits package, grace. They fail to see what the favor of God provides. The only thing that grace requires is a heart of faith, a pure heart. I mean a heart with a pure discipline of strengthening one's faith. Grace is connected intimately with your faith, and your ability to believe God. Without faith, there is no experience of grace. God's favor can be attained by only one thing, a 100% trust in Jesus Christ. So, if you let doubt creep in, it can frustrate the grace of God. Faith must be undefiled by fleshly, human effort, and works of humanity, and must be found only in believing and relying upon God in complete surrender. Pure in the process of accepting forgiveness, dedicated to not living by one's own accomplishments, keeping your eyes on Jesus, His sacrifice.

After making a mistake, you look upon Him who was wounded for our transgressions, with a repentant heart, in confession, admitting to God whatever it is, and receiving his benefits. Mercy, forgiveness, reconciliation, healing, power, patience, and the peace of God are the benefits of grace. Grace demands an effort, and nowhere in scripture does God look favorably upon anyone that does not make an effort. We do not receive forgiveness based on our works, but we do on our effort of faith. Our salvation and new life now become a battle of faith, a trial of faith, and not a battle of works. Our works could never measure up to the perfection of Christ and His perfect sacrifice. God does not look at your works. He measures your heart. He is not looking at your imperfections today, He is centered in on the real you, not your weaknesses, strengths or talents, but your heart and will. If your heart is pure and you choose Him, or have a strong will to follow Him, He gives grace. That inward effort is what God blesses, not our outward performance. God blesses a strong desire to serve Him and faith in the blood of Jesus.

The only thing that grace demands is that you believe. It requires you fight the good fight of faith. Grace requires at the very least, a continual look at the work of Jesus. Grace blesses pure intentions of the heart, a heart that wants God. That even when failing, wants to please God. That is the type of a pure heart Jesus was talking about in the Sermon on the Mount. He wasn't talking about pure works, perfect lives, and accomplished, talented, beautiful, handsome people. He was talking about a heart clean in motive, and sins forgiven, undefiled by sinful intentions, and the pride of life. He didn't say that you would see God if you had great accomplishments. He didn't say that you would see God if you had worked hard.

Matthew 5:8 (MSG) says, "You're blessed when you get your

inside world—your mind and heart—put right. Then you can see God in the outside world."

Psalm 51 is a notable example of this. It is a love letter to the one David had wronged, the God of Israel. David had a heart after God. He had a soft heart, one that God could work with, a repentant heart. He made mistakes, but he held the key to God's heart. He was humble and lived in confession.

Psalm 51:1-17 (MSG) says, "Generous in love—God, give grace! Huge in mercy—wipe out my bad record. Scrub away my guilt, soak out my sins in your laundry. I know how bad I've been; my sins are staring me down. You're the One I've violated, and you've seen it all, seen the full extent of my evil. You have all the facts before you; whatever you decide about me is fair. I've been out of step with you for a long time, in the wrong since before I was born. What you're after is truth from the inside out. Enter me, then; conceive a new, true life. Soak me in your laundry and I'll come out clean, scrub me and I'll have a snow-white life. Tune me in to foot-tapping songs, set these once-broken bones to dancing. Don't look too close for blemishes, give me a clean bill of health. God, make a fresh start in me, shape a Genesis week from the chaos of my life. Don't throw me out with the trash, or fail to breathe holiness in me. Bring me back from gray exile, put a fresh wind in my sails! Give me a job teaching rebels your ways so the lost can find their way home. Commute my death sentence, God, my salvation God, and I'll sing anthems to your life-giving ways. Unbutton my lips, dear God; I'll let loose with your praise. Going through the motions doesn't please you, a flawless performance is nothing to you. I learned God-worship when my pride was shattered. Heart-shattered lives ready for love don't for a moment escape God's notice."

In those scriptures, we have an inside view of David's heart, and we see his broken spirit, his regret, repentance, and confession.

1 John 1:9 (KJV) says, "If we confess our sins, he is faithful

and just to forgive us our sins, and to cleanse us from all unrighteousness."

In the scripture above, we see that if we sin and confess our sin, He forgives us.

James 4:17 (KJV) says, "Therefore to him that knoweth to do good, and doeth it not, to him it is sin."

All God cares about are the sins you know about, not some unknowing freakish minuscule mistake, or accident. Sin must be a premeditated act of disobedience, you know it's wrong, and you do it anyway. Any other sin is not a sin to you. Accidents really don't count as sin. Just like David, our conscience is freed through confession and repentance of any **known sin**. It is called living the repentant life and having a deep reverence for God. God looks at your heart while the world looks at your actions. Once any mistake is dealt with through confession, you must immediately move on, God does. You must have an attitude of faith, faith in the character of God. God does not want you to live in torment and defeat, but in victory through His forgiveness.

God finds beauty where beauty is real, in a pure heart, in a heart that wants and desires to worship and love God, a heart that wants to do the right thing. God wants us to do the right thing, for the right motives and reasons, not for glory, fame, money, prestige, or honor, but out of love and compassion. **Grace is God rewarding the intentions of your heart. If you are trying and reaching out to God, God will work with you, until you get it right.** Grace provided through Christ enables God to reward intentions before they can even be developed into works. Jesus is saying, I am standing with you, through all your struggles, efforts, and failed works. So, keep working at it, make the effort, God will never leave you, as long as you desire Him, and have a heart that is in the fight, the fight to keep believing.

When your works don't measure up, you must with undying faith accept Christ's work. Faith in Christ alone, the product of a heart after God, is your salvation. Your fight reaches far beyond failure, and your pure, uncompromising heart relies upon Christ and His works. **The heart of faith doesn't care what your wife, husband, or friends might be saying about you.** The heart of faith is looking to God. God is looking at your heart. If your heart is still in the fight, albeit still in a tussle, a battle to do right, in a war, but not giving up, then Jesus is saying that He is with you in that struggle, standing with you, never leaving you, and blessing you for making that effort, that honest, pure effort. And, thank God, He is not blessing us according to our works and our performance. He is blessing us based on His perfect performance.

Ephesians 2:8-9 (NKJV) says, "For by grace you have been saved through faith, and that not of yourselves; it is the gift of God, not of works, lest anyone should boast."

The benefits package that comes with grace

Romans 5:1-2 (KJV) says, "Therefore being justified by faith, we have peace with God through our Lord Jesus Christ: By whom also we have access by faith into this grace wherein we stand and rejoice in hope of the glory of God."

Ephesians 2:8-9 (NKJV) says, "For by grace you have been saved through faith, and that not of yourselves; it is the gift of God, not of works, lest anyone should boast."

Hebrews 4:16 (KJV) says, "Let us therefore come boldly unto the throne of grace, that we may obtain mercy, and find grace to help in time of need."

2 Corinthians 12:9 (KJV) says, "And he said unto me, My grace is sufficient for thee: for my strength is made perfect in weakness. Most gladly therefore will I rather glory in my infirmities, that the power of Christ may rest upon me."

2 Corinthians 9:8 (KJV) says, "And God is able to make all

grace abound toward you; that ye, always having all sufficiency in all things, may abound to every good work:"

We have access to this grace (the favor of God) by faith. So now, by simply believing in Christ we have the favor of God in our lives. We would otherwise fall flat on our backs, but now we stand. It is because God favors us. His favor gives you the edge you have always needed to make it in this world. We have salvation through grace, favor that includes healing, deliverance, and being made whole. If we have a need, we now can approach God boldly and find God's favor waiting on us to supply all our needs. Grace is the foundation for answered prayer. When we are weak, we have the perfect strength of God to endure hardship, as Paul did. When we face limitations, we have access to unlimited strength, endurance, patience, and longsuffering. God's grace makes you sufficient in all things. Whatever you are doing, it will be done well through God's favor in your life. Paul prays for God's grace to be active in your life so that you may abound, flourish, and prosper in every good work.

We are saved by grace and rewarded for our works

Having the favor of God gives you the confidence to work for God. It grants you approval and gives you inspiration. The whole point of grace is to enable you to work for God. God's favor gives you access to His strength, and power, the power to live a life free from sin, and inspired for good works. When Christ forgave me, He freed me from the feeling of being unworthy to facilitate the good works of my heavenly Father in this life. What would be the point of grace, or God's favor, if it was useless, had no real function, or purpose, if there were no fruit from it? It is the truth of the Gospel that brings forth fruit. What is the Gospel? It is the good news of salvation by faith through grace. The Gospel is the love of God reaching out to humanity. It is love. When we love we become compassionate. We respond to the needs around us, all of this is part of what the grace of God in truth produces.

Colossians 1:4-6 (KJV) says, "Since we heard of your faith in Christ Jesus, and of the love which ye have to all the saints, For the hope which is laid up for you in heaven, whereof ye heard before in the word of the truth of the gospel; Which is come unto you, as it is in all the world; and bringeth forth fruit, as it doth also in you, since the day ye heard of it, and knew the grace of God in truth:"

We do not work to produce the grace or the favor of God. But, it is the favor or grace of God that produces work in us. The power of grace produces a strong work ethic in the hearts of everyone it has truly affected. This is proven out every day in my work with former addicts, and those who have been healed from emotional pain and suffering. I have never come across one that was set free by the grace of God, who did not have a fervent desire to take this message to everyone they knew. Every one of them begins to work hard at it and strives to develop their skills to be an effective witness. Most of them became tireless in their effort to bring it home where they live and thrive. **So many Christians are bamboozled into thinking of works in a negative light, that they never envision the silver lining or the goodness of works.** They are kept from the possibilities of the Christian life, and the enormous effects that doing the works of God accomplishes in the world.

Works are a good thing. While we strive to work, our salvation is not based upon our works. But our joy is hindered, and our sense of meaning is altered when we do not incorporate helping the lives of others in our walk with God. We, of all people, should be recognized by our zeal, and enthusiasm, coming from such a place of bondage as we once were. We should be the achievers of this world, powerfully work orientated, giving it our all, and loving our work for God so much, as for it not to shrink in the light of death, persecution, hardship or trials. After all, our cause is great. And we alone have the only answer, and that is the saving grace of God. **Work should define us. It clarifies and reveals what we are committed to. The devils believe, but they are not committed, and hell's flames are reserved for the devil and his angels.**

James 2:18 (KJV) says, "Yea, a man may say, Thou hast faith, and I have works: shew me thy faith without thy works, and I will shew thee my faith by my works."

James 2:20 (KJV) says, "But wilt thou know, O vain man, that faith without works is dead?"

Works are the only thing that your fellow humans will see. They don't even care about what's in your heart. Why should they? I don't even care about what's in your heart. I care about your commitment. A pure heart is something only God can see. Your works are the light of God seen in the world. Knowing God is not interested in performance frees you to work for Him in purity. Whereas a guilty conscience destroys your zeal, grace that allows God to forgive, sets you free to work. If you are committed and dedicated, then you can be of immense value to God's work, and to yourself. **Jesus even encouraged you to demonstrate works where they could be seen by others, it is our duty. Works make others feel important and loved. Work is light, and love in action.**

Matthew 5:16 (KJV) says, "Let your light so shine before men, that they may see your good works, and glorify your Father which is in heaven."

Works that have the right motives and intentions carry the grace of God. It is His favor in you reaching out to a dying world. Jesus said that good works glorify God, reveal your love toward God, and are meant to expose your personal testimony of His saving power. **Your works inspire others and give them faith and encouragement.** Works are what the world needs. It is His grace in your life that produces the desire to work for Him.

Grace says, "Work because you are qualified." Satan says you are not qualified, you have sinned, you are too imperfect to work or witness for God. It is the right standing with God that is produced by grace that encourages us to cross the bridge of imperfection, and reach out to humanity with grace's very own message—Jesus saves!

Works provide the activity that transforms your life from being dull, unsatisfying, and without meaning, to a rewarding, purpose driven life, filled with joy, and the eternal satisfying experience of doing what you were created to do. The completion of your responsibilities as a husband, wife, citizen, son or daughter, or child of God, fills your heart with a sense of accomplishment, and eternal reward. That produces rest and the peace of God in your life. Why else would Jesus describe it like this in His word?

Matthew 11:29 (KJV) says, "Take my yoke upon you, and learn of me; for I am meek and lowly in heart: and ye shall find rest unto your souls."

Works are important and valued by God. To downplay works as so many snowflakes that melt at the sign of the slightest temperature change, when the word work is mentioned, is dangerous. They need to know that we will be rewarded for our works when we get to heaven. To simply find an excuse not to do God's will in your life is weak faith, and not relying on the grace of God to achieve the greatness you were designed for. I have spent hours studying, meditating, and seeking God in writing this book. It has required a great effort and work discipline to get it done. The effort was there for God to bless it with His grace.

Where there is no effort, there is nothing to bless. I would just sit down, and write for hours, as the Holy Spirit would remind me of things that have happened in my life, and then He would inspire me with thought patterns, and revelation, not a new revelation that I had not been living, but, revelation in how to communicate it to others. These words are His inspiration, they make me cry, and I have found myself engulfed in the power and presence of God's Spirit throughout this experience. When I obeyed His voice, He provided the grace. It takes hard work to get anywhere in this life. To cop out, or fold under pressure, will not bring real satisfying joy in your life, and eternal reward. You might make it to heaven, but without rewards.

1 Corinthians 3:14-15 (KJV) says, "If any man's work abide which he hath built thereupon, he shall receive a reward. If any man's work shall be burned, he shall suffer loss: but he himself shall be saved; yet so as by fire."

2 Corinthians 5:10 (NLT) says, "For we must all stand before Christ to be judged. We will each receive whatever we deserve for the good or evil we have done in this earthly body."

Revelation 22:12 (KJV) says, "And, behold, I come quickly; and my reward is with me, to give every man according as his work shall be."

13

DILIGENCE IN PRAYER

 METHADDICTSHELP, FACEBOOK POST
MARCH 15, 2017

IF YOU ARE WILLING TO FIGHT FOR IT. IF YOU ARE WILLING NEVER TO GIVE UP. IF YOU ARE WILLING TO GRAB A FIRM HOLD OF GOD AND NEVER LET GO. THEN YOU ARE READY TO BE SOBER. TPC (UNEDITED)

126,405 PEOPLE REACHED

10K LIKES

1,674 SHARES

487 COMMENTS

*P*rayer is the fundamental and essential discipline needed for all spiritual transformation, strength, and power. If you are not willing to spend time in prayer, then you are wasting your time with any other spiritual discipline in your life. The most potent powerful tool available to humanity is prayer. I get hundreds of mothers who contact me to pray for a son or daughter who is in addiction. God spoke to me during one of those heart-wrenching moments. While listening to her desperate cries for help, and hearing the hopelessness in her voice,

God said, "Tell her that there is something more valuable than a mother's hugs, and that is her prayers."

A mother contacted me through the internet about her daughter who had run away from home and was using drugs. She was experiencing great concern, anxiety, and fear. But, she was praying and was a child of God. Her daughter was steeped in addiction, and its lifestyle. Her health was deteriorating rapidly. She hadn't heard from her in days, was worried, and extremely upset. So, I immediately responded with a prayer video. I started praying, it was about 5:00 a.m. As I began to pray for her daughter, the Holy Spirit stopped me, and said, "Tell her I have heard her prayers, and her daughter is on her way home as we speak." I began to rejoice and gave her the message. I hurriedly hit the send button. Within a few minutes, I got a message back from the most excited, overwhelmed mother, full of thankful praise to her heavenly Father. She said she had listened to my prayer and begun to weep when her phone rang a few minutes later. It was her father, her daughter's grandfather. He said that he had heard from her daughter, he was in another state, and he drove all night, picked her up, and would be there shortly.

The greatest opportunity for change we have is prayer. Prayer changes things. It changes you, and everyone around you. Prayer changes you and your circumstances. I have had hundreds of encounters with people I have never met before, except to pray for them. I have witnessed miracle after miracle in these calls. They have changed my entire character, and personality. It has matured faith in me and changed the very dynamics of my relationship with God.

When someone is presenting themselves to you as spiritual, you would automatically think that they are a person who specializes in communication with God, or prayer. This is an assumed position. How could one be intimate with God, and not be spiritually strong? How could someone be spiritual and not pray? It is impossible. Prayer equals power. Show me a person who prays, and I'll show you someone who has real power. There are a lot of people professing to know God, have His power, and be spiritually adept, but really can offer you nothing. They are Christians with no fruit of the supernatural in their life. Why? Because they have no prayer life.

The instructions of the Holy Spirit are that we are to "Pray without ceasing," 1 Thessalonians 5:17 (KJV). The disciples and the 120 in the upper room had been there ten days praying before any power fell. In Acts 12, we read where King Herod violently apprehended some of the church, murdered James, and then arrested and imprisoned the Apostle Peter. The church did not immediately hire a lawyer, protest, and start a civil war, but what they did was come together to bombard heaven in prayer. While Peter was being kept in prison, they were praying without ceasing, 24 hours a day. They all came together to the house of Mary, the mother of John. Every time you turn a page in the book of Acts, the history of the early church, you see people praying. While they were calling out to God, Peter's chains fell off him in prison, and he was set free. They prayed, and they had power, and that power resulted in a dramatic change of circumstances.

Enoch was a man of prayer. It is said that he walked with God for 300 years. He was a special man of prayer. It was evident and visible, and everyone knew he was walking with God. It was obvious he was in conversation with the invisible God. While in conversation with his friends and neighbors, no doubt he would pause a moment to speak to the invisible God he served. I can picture him in the closing of the day, walking on the side of a hill, as night is falling. In the shadows, he is talking, and someone is talking back, but that someone is invisible. I can hear them laughing and enjoying each other's company.

For Enoch to even be mentioned in the early stages of Biblical history, Enoch had to be an extraordinary, well known, and famous person. In a world without technology, word of mouth is all that they had. Enoch was so different than the others of his time that he became famous, and stood out. It is said that one day, possibly in the marketplace, or among his family, while talking to God he just evaporated, or disappeared. Everyone knew what had happened, no one even questioned it, they instinctively knew, he had joined his invisible friend, God. The New Testament says he was translated. He simply was and then he was not. Enoch prayed. Enoch had amazing power and influence with our supernatural God.

Elijah was a man of authority and power because he knew how to pray. He bounces off the pages of the Bible as some superhuman, in control of even the weather. He just announced to the wicked king Ahab, "As the Lord God lives, before whom I stand, there shall not be any dew or rain," and for the next three years, there was no rain. Elijah was standing with God as he spoke. He was in the inward posture of prayer and engaged in communication with God himself. The next thing you see him doing is providing miracle food for the widow of Zarephath and her son. While staying there her son died, and the "bigger than life" potent man of prayer, cried to his God and raised the dead. After many days of drought and no rain, in the third year, God spoke to Elijah to visit King Ahab and pronounce the coming of rain.

But, before the rain came, Elijah and God had some unfinished business to take care of. They had to deal with the wicked rebellion of Queen Jezebel, and her husband King Ahab. They also had to deal with the eradication of their false prophets, the 450 prophets of Baal, and the 400 prophets of the groves. They gathered on Mount Carmel and Elijah called down fire from heaven, and then Elijah slew the 850 false prophets at the brook of Kishon. Elijah then buried his face between his knees in prayer and cried out for rain. He prayed not once or twice, but seven times, face buried between his knees in prayer, kneeling on the bare earth before rain appeared in a cloud the tiny size of a hand. Then he stood up from kneeling on the ground to warn his servant to prepare the chariot, and get down from the mountain before the monsoon of rain would make it impossible to travel. Elijah knew the power of prayer and knew how to pray.

I believe with all of my heart that you might be an Enoch or Elijah in the making. That God has you reading this book because He is developing in you a desire to pray. The prophet Hosea says that prayer is planting a seed in the undisciplined callous heart that reaps a harvest of the favor and power of God. It is called right standing (righteousness) with God. A restored relationship of favor and friendship with your heavenly Father.

Hosea 10:12 (NLT) says, "I said, 'Plant the good seeds of righteousness, and you will harvest a crop of love. Plow up the hard ground of your hearts, for now is the time to seek the LORD, that he may come and shower righteousness upon you."

How to obtain answers through prayer

To gain entrance into the fourth dimension where God dwells and communicates, the spiritual realm, you must have an open, spiritual dialogue with God. That is prayer. Without an open, consistent, dialogue, and focused conversation with God, with no distractions from our three-dimensional world, you will never have entrance into divine impartation and revelation. The deeper the conversation, the longer the time spent with God, and the closer you get to Him, the greater the revelation. Just as in any relationship, the longer you spend with someone, and the more you are open to them, the more honest, and desiring of them, the closer you get, **the more you gain knowledge of them. The more access you have, and freedom you gain in God's presence, the more becomes available to you.**

It is a process of earned trust. **Effort, diligence, consistency, and hard work will always weed out the impure and ambi-**

tious. Only the pure in heart and those motivated by love will get to know God. God is looking for persistent devotion, tireless pursuit, and overwhelming desire. In that respect, we are like God. We desire the same thing from the people we let into our hearts, especially for intimate companionship. **What makes you think, that if you give less, God will give more?** What makes you think that less time spent with God will please God? What makes you think you will get more of what you need from Him, if you only speak to Him casually, and in a hurry, like while you are driving, or preoccupied with something else?

Jeremiah 29:13 (KJV) says, "And ye shall seek me, and find me when ye shall search for me with all your heart."

The prophet Jeremiah spoke to God's people when they were facing difficulties and hardship during their captivity. He gave them a word from the heart of God, a key to finding God in their situation. God says, "You will find me when you search for me with all of your heart." In this specific word from God, He gives us the key to finding him in this life. **To have an encounter with the supernatural, and experience the miraculous you must search for God with undivided focus and devotion, with all your heart.** All, with everything you have, all the energy, and time it will take. Then and only then will you gain access. Are you willing to exhaust all measures to acquire a close relationship with God?

If you want to have a life-changing transformation, then you must make a life-changing commitment to prayer. I talk to people from all over the world about their loved ones who are addicts and need God. The first thing I ask them is about their relationship with God. Do you have complete access to God's miracle power, and have an uncompromising relationship with Him personally? Are you willing to actively pursue God with your whole heart to gain power, and faith to destroy the enemy you are facing? If they are willing to spend time in prayer, then God will save their loved ones. The reason people have no miracles in their lives is that they give up too easily. They have no internal fortitude and are weak in faith. They are weak because of undeveloped spiritual muscles. Even Jesus acknowledged this type of inadequacy among His disciples.

Prayer and fasting, faith, and forgiveness are the three things that Jesus said were missing in the disciple's lives

Matthew 17:19-21 (KJV) says, "Then came the disciples to Jesus apart, and said, Why could not we cast him out? And Jesus said unto them, Because of your unbelief: for verily I say unto you, If ye have **faith as a grain of mustard seed**, ye shall say unto this mountain, Remove hence to yonder place; and it shall remove; and nothing shall be impossible unto you. **Howbeit this kind goeth not out but by prayer and fasting.**"

Mark 11:22-25 (KJV) says, "And Jesus answering saith unto them, **Have faith in God**. For verily I say unto you, That whosoever shall say unto this mountain, Be thou removed, and be thou cast into the sea; and shall not doubt in his heart, but shall believe that those things which he saith shall come to pass; he shall have whatsoever he saith. Therefore I say unto you, what things soever ye desire, when ye pray, believe that ye receive them, and ye shall have them. **And when ye stand praying, forgive**, if ye have ought against any: that your Father also which is in heaven may forgive you your trespasses."

Prayer and fasting

Jesus provides us with a process of order, and spiritual progression to obtain power, and faith, the ability to believe and not doubt. He gives us great insight into the art of not giving in, or giving up to doubt. **He starts out with power, and then says** you attain this kind of power through prayer and fasting. So, power is linked to the twin pillars of strength in the kingdom of God, prayer, and fasting. They work together, and are listed in unity, or bound together when seeking power. Christ is saying that they must be practiced together to have influence in the kingdom of God, to have power. This principle is illustrated in His own personal life. What is required in prayer and fasting is found in Jesus' personal life.

Matthew 4:1-2 (KJV) says, "Then was Jesus led up of the Spirit into the wilderness to be tempted of the devil. And when he had fasted forty days and forty nights, he was afterward an hungered."

Mark 1:12-13 (KJV) says, "And immediately the Spirit driveth him into the wilderness. And he was there in the wilderness forty days, tempted of Satan; and was with the wild beasts; and the angels ministered unto him."

- **When these two principles are combined, they create a unique set of priorities.** They require holiness, which is a separation "from" and "unto." A separation from all your activities unto God, giving Him your complete undivided attention and focus.
- Christ was moved, led, and compelled by the Holy Spirit to go to a remote place, alone with one singular purpose and objective. To fast, go without food, and pray, to talk with God. The Holy Spirit always will lead us in the same direction as He led Christ.
- There He talked with God alone, pursuing only Him and nothing else. He sacrificed and disciplined himself for forty days.
- He was persistent and diligent in His effort.
- He lived only by God, and the angels, as they ministered strength and truth to Him. He came out full of power and the Holy Ghost.

Luke 4:14 (KJV) says, "And Jesus returned in the power of the Spirit into Galilee: and there went out a fame of him through all the region round about."

Jesus is our example. We must follow Him and use His example as our model. If you want the power of the Spirit of God, you must be willing and yielded to the Holy Spirit, or there will be no power. **There must be a set time of prayer in your life, on a regular basis, where undistracted dialogue and conversation between you and your heavenly Father occurs, a separation unto Him, a dedication and a new priority that compels you to seek Him above all else.** This is true in all human experience, why would it not be with God? In every pursuit of man, there must be discipline, dedication, and effort. In education, training, relationships, and in the development of gifting and talents, there must be priorities set before one can achieve greatness. **If the flesh requires this, we should not be surprised that the spiritual realm requires the same determination. After all, it is the realm we are most unfamiliar with and traveled the least in. We certainly need to gain the expertise of operating in the spirit. We all have the desire, but do we all practice and pursue God with the dedication that He deserves?**

When a person is missing someone they love, because of death or separation, they often cannot think of anything else. Food becomes unimportant, and daily chores mean little to them. They often forget to shave and bathe. They are experiencing great loss and longing for the company and warmth of their loved one. They lose weight, look unkempt, and appear sickly. It takes them over. **This is very similar to a man or woman of God in hot pursuit of God's presence and power.** Nothing is as important as that chase, a chase or pursuit of God that will give everything necessary to find Him. That is how Jesus found the favor of God. He pursued Him in love and dedication. He desired Him above all else. He fasted and prayed. Fasting and praying are dedication in pursuit. If you do not fast and pray, then you are not dedicated. Really? Is there any other way to say it? Live it? There is no other way to live out your pursuit for God in total effort without fasting and prayer. It is our only way to communicate spiritually.

Can you imagine a man deeply in love with a woman, but not passionately pursuing her? Do you think she would just magically jump into his life without an effort on his part? Can you see her throwing herself at him, or jumping in his car magically at some point? That is just as ridiculous as the way some Christians think about God. They feel as though God will just magically push everything out of the way and visit them when He gets ready, with no effort on their part at all. Jesus says that you must thirst after righteousness, seek Him, ask from him, and knock on His door if you are to receive anything from him.

Matthew 7:7-8 (KJV) says, "Ask, and it shall be given you; seek, and ye shall find; knock, and it shall be opened unto you: For every one that asketh receiveth; and he that seeketh findeth; and to him that knocketh it shall be opened."

The power I walk in personally comes from that dedication and pursuit also. **Your power will always be measured by your quality of pursuit.**

Faith, or mustard seed faith

Faith comes from meditating on the word of God, understanding the character of God, and knowing His will for us. I discussed this in the chapters concerning faith previously, that it requires intimacy, which includes prayer and fasting. But in this context, we are talking about a faith here that doesn't give up.

Hebrews 11:6 (AMP) says, "But without faith it is impossible to please and be satisfactory to Him. For whoever would come near to God must [necessarily] believe that God exists and that He is the rewarder of those who earnestly and diligently seek Him [out]."

All you must do is believe and trust in God. Believe that He is, and that He will reward your time spent with Him. He is a rewarder of diligent faith, a person who consistently seeks Him, and makes a constant effort. Being earnest and sincere will always get God's attention. It is the most attractive quality God finds in a person. We come before Him to make us and shape us in the likeness of His Son, full of faith, power, grace, and truth. A diligent effort is one that keeps on coming, keeps on praying, and will not give up until the heavens are open, and our prayers are answered. **It is the effort that says until I receive an anointing or a word of faith from God, I will never quit, or give up, or surrender my will to the enemy. I will surrender only to prayer and fasting until God visits me.**

This is mustard seed faith, faith that is planted and requires effort to grow. It is the nature of this plant to continue to grow, even though it might be planted beneath hard surfaces such as large rocks. It is an example of determined effort. Its roots will continue to grow looking for an opening to get to the sun, so it can break the soil and get the light it needs to grow into a mature plant, and produce fruit. The mustard seed, though it is tiny, has the determination, and strength not to quit. Just like Elijah, and the way he prayed, mustard seed faith is the missing ingredient in a lot of people's lives.

James 5:16-17 (KJV) says, "Confess your faults one to another, and pray one for another, that ye may be healed. The effectual fervent prayer of a righteous man availeth much. Elias was a man subject to like passions as we are, and he prayed earnestly that it might not rain: and it rained not on the earth by the space of three years and six months."

In the original text, the emphasis on his prayer was not the words he prayed, but the effort he gave. The effectual fervent prayer or the earnest, heartfelt, continued, prayer is what avails.

The wording is bringing attention to the effort and persistence given in his prayer, not content or the wording of his prayer. What God is saying here, is that any prayer or petition made given with the same determination and persistence of Elijah will be answered. As further proof, the Holy Spirit says that the prayer was not honored by God on the merit of Elijah, for he was a man like us, with doubt, and fleshly passions. But his fervent prayer is what accomplished the work of God in his life. He just did not give up but persisted until all doubt was gone, and miracles stood in their place. Just think of how many marriages could be saved and people could be healed, if we could have the mustard seed faith of Jesus and Elijah.

Forgiveness

God cannot heal you, or grant you access if there is unforgiveness in your heart toward someone. To make one powerful who has some type of dominant sin in their lives would create the wrong foundation for success when ultimately the unforgiveness or sin in your life will cause you and others in your life to fail. By the way, God loves the people who have wronged you just as much as He loves you. Another reason for God dealing with us first is that maybe we are partly responsible for the failure we see in our children or others that we are praying about. And until that is dealt with, or removed out of the way, they will not listen to God.

A lot of our prayers require repentance, restitution, and effort on our part so that we can be effective Christians. The psalmist David said, "If I regard iniquity in my heart, the Lord will not hear me:" Psalm 66:18 (KJV). The answers to our prayers are often just a simple requirement of obedience on our part. When it is completed, we see miracles of salvation and healing around us and in us. So, He deals with it. It is His way to create life and restore healing and love in all our lives. It is what connects us to Him, and His miracle power to transform our situations. **I call it the river of life, healing, and power. Nothing should move in that river that can corrupt the flow. For you to be a conduit of that river you must be free of all obstructions that will prevent its free flow. You also can call it a branch of the vine of life. The scriptures below describe Jesus as the vine. Can you imagine a large branch not bearing fruit, but using up all the resources of the vine and starving the other branches? Unforgiveness will destroy all the other branches in your life. It will create anger, bitterness, and unbelief in your life, making it impossible to look upward and trust God. It can become the dominant controlling factor in your life.**

John 15:5-7 (KJV) says, "I am the vine, ye are the branches: He that abideth in me, and I in him, the same bringeth forth much fruit: for without me ye can do nothing. If a man abide not in me, he is cast forth as a branch, and is withered; and men gather them, and cast them into the fire, and they are burned. If ye abide in me, and my words abide in you, ye shall ask what ye will, and it shall be done unto you."

Psalm 66:18 (NIV2011) says, "If I had cherished sin in my heart, the Lord would not have listened;"

2 Chronicles 7:14 (KJV) says, "If my people, which are called by my name, shall humble themselves, and pray, and seek my face, and turn from their wicked ways; then will I hear from heaven, and will forgive their sin, and will heal their land."

So, God in an intimate way through the Holy Spirit will reveal weaknesses that affect the outcome of your prayers. We must cherish righteousness and desire change if God is going to take us seriously. If you are unwilling to live in power, how can you convince your son, daughter, husband, or wife to change? **It is the power revealed through you that promotes change in others.**

Powerful prayers come from people who have fasted, spent time with God intimately, asked in faith, and have

allowed God to show them the path of love. These qualities are the real and truthful essential attributes of answered prayer.

I have sent powerful prayers that changed entire communities, simply by praying according to God's word, as any ordinary believer can. I remember praying for a young wife in a small town in the Midwest. She was desperate and had nowhere to turn for help. Her husband was bound in heavy addiction, she said, "Can you pray for us?" I turned the webcam on and began to pray. A special anointing came upon me as I prayed. I was interceding on their behalf when suddenly I used the name of Jesus to command the illegal drug trafficking in her life to be shut down, and for God to send them all to jail. That is something I never do.

I have too much compassion in my heart ever to pray something like that. I always pray for salvation and deliverance. I never pray for someone to be arrested. But, I had spoken under the anointing and the words came out before I could get them back. I continued my prayer of deliverance. I then prayed for God's protection aimed at everyone in her family, they all were addicts. I sent the video and began praying for someone else. The next morning there was a message awaiting me from this young lady. "Last night the police raided the only drug dealer's house in our city and community. They all went to jail. There is no other drug connection around here unless you drive hours away." God answers prayer.

One day I received a message from a sixteen-year-old boy. He was addicted to pain pills he was getting off the street. It was one of the most heartbreaking addictions I have encountered. He was taking a large number of pills to maintain a certain amount of sanity and functionality. At some point in opiate addiction as your tolerance level increases, your dosage must increase appropriately to experience a high, and at some point, you don't even get a high. You medicate to stay alive. He was at that point. He had been selling drugs full time, and quit school to pay for his habit. He was a scared and tormented young Spanish American teenager from Florida.

Detox was not a choice for him. He had been to a medical facility and went through it a couple of times before. The horrors of withdrawals were too much for him to even think about going through it again. Some of the withdrawal symptoms are intense cravings, bone pain, diarrhea, agitation, sweating, vomiting, insomnia, weakness, extreme fatigue, and tremors can be present along with tormenting dreams, and mental stress. Detox was too scary, and painful of a process. I gave him my phone number, and he called me. I said, "Son is there anyone at home with you?" He said, "Yes my mom." I said, "Does she know about your addiction?" He said, "Yes." I said, "Can I speak with her?" He said, "Yeah, but, she doesn't understand English very well, I'll have to interpret for her." "That's fine," I said. "I know you are high right now because it would have been too hard for you to call if you weren't, am I right?" He said, "Yeah, me and my mom were talking about calling you, but I had to wait till I felt better, because I can't think very well, or talk worrying about it."

I said, "Ok, I know, I was an addict myself, God doesn't care if you are high, God loves you, He's just glad you are reaching out for help. I'm going to pray with you, and Jesus, our Savior, is going to set you free." I explained salvation, faith, and grace to them, while he relayed everything to his mother. I asked, "Are you guys ready for that?" He and his mother agreed, so we prayed the sinner's prayer, and we all began to weep as the precious Holy Spirit filled our hearts with love, acceptance, and hope.

And boldly under a heavy anointing, I prayed "Lord, I ask you to deliver him from all withdrawals, I declare him to be completely made whole from this day forward." And then the prophetic voice of God spoke to me, He said, "Tell him, that although he is high, I have removed the effects of the drug from him forever, and that a heavy restful sleep will fall on him, as though he is not high, and he shouldn't worry, I am going to let him rest tonight." I told him, "You are going to sleep until around 2:00 P.M. tomorrow, and when you wake up there will be no withdrawals."

As I relayed that message, we all were weeping, and I could barely say the words as the power of God was all over me. I told his mother to watch over him, and said, "You don't have to worry anymore, God's got this! You guys call me tomorrow, and let me know how things went." The next day about 2:30 P.M., he called me, and he was ecstatic and overjoyed. He said, "It was just like you said, I fell asleep, and rested, I had not rested like that in a long time. I can't even remember the last time I rested like that! It was so relaxing, and peaceful. And, I'm feeling great!" He would call me every hour for the next few hours to say how well he was doing. He just kept saying, "It's a miracle, it's a miracle, thank you, God."

Prayer involves you personally with the supernatural miracle power of God, and transforms, grows and matures your faith

Jude 1:20 (KJV) says, "But ye, beloved, building up yourselves on your most holy faith, praying in the Holy Ghost."

I have prayed with women who were suffering panic attacks, and couldn't even speak on the phone. Some of them were hearing voices and having withdrawals. But God who is no respecter of persons delivered many of them. Right in a casino, a fifty-year-old man was delivered at the slot machine, the power of God hit him so strong that he started crying, loudly, uncontrollably, as Satan left his body. Several men and women were touched in these unusual places as God ministered to them. Prayer works. God works. The miracle power of God cannot lose.

The more I prayed with people, the more I witnessed God's miracle power. My faith got stronger, and my prayers

became relentless. **I grew an inward, stubborn, resolve to persist until I heard from God.** If any person wants Christ and His power, they can have it. God is always available. What God has done for me, is now being done through me for others. All through prayer.

God has no limitations. Space, matter, and time are only human boundaries. Prayer is fourth dimensional. There is no medical doctor alive today that can administer medicine through the thin air, instantaneously, and several hundred miles away through a phone conversation. Yet, that happens quite frequently with men and women who are of the Christian faith, who believe in the power of Jesus through prayer. **No other religion has the preponderance of supernatural phenomena as the Christian faith.** You could not find a warehouse big enough, or even build one large enough to store the books that record the testimonies of the miracle power of Jesus anywhere on this earth.

The actual testimony of firsthand credible witnesses of tragedies averted, storms changing their course in midair, protection in impossible circumstances, physical healing, cripples healed, blind eyes opened, deaf ears healed, vocal cords created, arms and limbs created, eyes created, people who can see without a natural eye (I have personally witnessed this, and many of these miracles have actually happened in my presence), depression and mental disorders healed, actual bullets stopped, guns firing but bullets are nowhere to be found, violent people rendered harmless, car accidents prevented, actual cars moved out of harm's way, automobiles running for hundreds of miles on empty tanks, wars won, and many millions of other miracles, which are too numerous to even record, or even try to list, all through faith in the name of Jesus as a direct result of Christians praying specific prayers of faith. In the word of God, we see Jesus performing these miracles. We do not have any superhero available that can go through buildings and protect people from avalanches, Pacific tsunami waves, blizzards, hurricanes, tornados, gale winds and any other natural catastrophes. But, in the word of God we see Jesus doing it.

In the Christian faith, death doesn't even have enough power to hold a person if God sees fit to raise him from the dead. We have recorded instances of people who were dead and men of God prayed, and the prayer of faith brought them back to life. **There is a recorded instance, highly documented with the most substantial of evidence recorded by missionary evangelist Reinhard Bonnke, who studied at The Bible College of Wales, of a man that was dead, and was brought to life, even after he had been embalmed. It happened during one of his mass evangelical meetings in Africa. It is on film.** The testimony of this man brings me to tears. **Faith in Jesus is the most authoritative, influential, conviction a man or woman can have. When used within the petitions of prayer, it is the open door or "blank-check" for a miracle.**

John 15:7 (AMP) says, "If you live in Me [abide vitally united to Me] and My words remain in you *and* continue to live in your hearts, ask whatever you will, and it shall be done for you."

14

THE POTENTIAL OF "YOU"

 *METHADDICTSHELP FACEBOOK POST*
MAY 18, 2017

GOD BELIEVES IN YOU. HE HAS INVESTED HIS BREATHE IN YOU, CREATED YOU, AND YOU ARE UNIQUELY DESIGNED. YOU ARE SO IMPORTANT TO HIM, AND HAVE SUCH GREAT POTENTIAL, THAT CHRIST DIED FOR YOU, UNWILLING TO LOSE YOU....THINK ABOUT IT...TPC. (UNEDITED)

122,937 PEOPLE REACHED
11,000 LIKES
1,854 SHARES
89 COMMENTS

We have an amazing future filled with possibilities and restoration. There are things born in us, seeds of greatness that originated from God's greatness. God's plans have been intricately woven within us. Your inspirational dreams of being a strong man or woman filled with faith, productivity and achievement were put there to bring God glory, and to fulfill your heart's desires. Your special DNA requires a plan designed to complement your creative characteristics birthed by God himself. There are no other means than a partnership with the Father of your design and purpose to reach this potential. The potential and possibilities of "you."

You are the only threat in your world to Satan's destructive power. You are Satan's worst nightmare. You were strategically placed by the hand of God into this world. If you can, imagine a spaceship carrying a capsule of human potential from a distant planet, light-years away. Sent to impregnate a small sphere of space for a moment in what is measured by time, sent by the Creator of the vast galaxies, stars, and different innumerable solar systems. That capsule, a tiny human seed, is you. Planned, created, designed to fit, and fill a divine purpose by the Father of Lights. In your cocoon-like capsule, you are being formed and shaped along the way. You could not hear the rumbling engines and feel the speed at which you were traveling, and the urgency with which you arrived. But your timing was more important to your coming than the ride that got you there. Your mission was too important to abort, and others were waiting on you. For the light was ever burning low in the place where the Prince of Darkness had invaded.

All the galactic created beings and soldiers of light were gathered around Him, the Father of Lights, and His right hand the Brilliant One, the Son-light, and the Comforting One, the Revealer and Exposer of light, who is the Holy Spirit that stands next to the throne. You are their child and come in their image, to express their concern for those in need of their love and help. They watched in awe and expectation at your arrival, all ready to stand with you at a moment's call. After a tumultuous landing, and abrupt instantaneous birth, you are here. You are the only one in your personal world that has the power to overturn the enemy of that sphere of influence. God would not have gone to all that trouble to send you if you were not qualified. Basically, you are that capsule, or package, specially sent by God himself, to a world that needs you.

You are a gift of inspiration, ability, and intelligence designed specifically to inhabit a world that needs you. You represent the best that God has to offer the world you will inhabit. You have a special time slot to fill, a space to occupy and matter to work with. You are eternal and possess a soul that will never die. You are a fourth-dimensional being, placed in a specific time, in a certain space (earth), within matter (your body), and also a spirit which can communicate outside of time, space, and matter. You are extremely valuable in the scheme of things, and God's overall plan of creation. You are God's man or woman, and within your genetic DNA is that potential. The potential to develop into what you were designed to be. That potential comes from the power of God, the Father of Lights, and the authority comes from the name of Jesus the Son of God, the Light of the world. The gifting to reach that potential comes from the comforting presence of the Comforter, the Teacher, the ever-illuminating teacher of light and truth, the Holy Spirit.

Everything good or evil starts with one man or one woman.

You have the potential to change the world, and affect the nations of the world.

I have heard it said that the world has yet to see what one man, completely sold out to Jesus, can accomplish. I agree.

You could be that man or woman.

I am writing this for you. I have a burning desire in me. **To make sure you do not fail, that you get what you need to become happy, productive, and live free from your past.** You are all I think about. I want what God has done for me to happen for you. I am a man on fire. On fire for others, who were hurting like me, and struggling to live a normal life. God put it in my heart, birthed it in my spirit to say these kind words. Words that the Holy Spirit wants you to hear. Words for you, about yourself. Words from God. Words that worked for me. Why? Because I know what it feels like to be broken. To be without faith, and not to believe in one's own potential. To have given up. That's why. I cannot bear the thought of other people feeling that they have no value, nothing to give and feel helpless. I felt like I had no real value, and was permanently damaged goods.

It is a miracle that these words are coming from me, a man that was in the clutches of such evil and spiritual deprivation. Who thought it was impossible at such a late moment in my life for anything to change. **But, at 55 years old, I had a major encounter in the fourth dimension,** an encounter with Jesus that created who I am today. A man who worships not the creation but the Creator. Who has no vices, and with no detrimental distractions. Filled with the power of God. With direction, vision, and influence. **When I had no car, no job, no money, no home, no real friends, addicted to methamphetamines and other drugs, filled with pain, with no self-respect, lonely, unproductive and at one point in my life, facing years in prison, God rescued me. It is my personal testimony and witness that the power of God, at any point in a human being's life, can transform anyone's life. From any place of devastation.** It is one man's truth to add to the truth of millions of others who are actively living in the fullest of their potential, and the untold stories of those that have left legacies of inspiration to their families before they left us for a new and better home. In which they now live, and are among the "cloud of witnesses" in heaven awaiting our arrival. The true and only truth that Jesus saves.

The word potential means having the capacity to become something in the future, or the power to develop into something in the future. Right now, you are beginning to walk in freedom with the seeds of God's word and salvation. The gifts and fruits of the Spirit are now at work in your life. You now have the ability and the tools of greatness to reach your greatest potential. There is no difference between you and me. There is no big variance or quality that is inconsistent in how we are made. We both have bodies, a spirit, and a soul. We are not different, even in sinfulness. We just have a different specified assignment and unique character traits that were instilled to complete it. The only things that make us different are our decisions, our faith, and our will. **Now that you have decided to follow Jesus and have faith, you must strengthen your will and resolve to reach your potential. It is the only thing that can catapult you into productivity and achievement.**

It is our free will that elevates us and gives us this potential of greatness. A cow or a sheep may prefer another pasture to graze in, but that does not make it a free will choice. That is just a matter of preference. One dog may like Purina Dog Chow, another may like Pedigree. Does even the dog have a free will? Not really, in essence, the dog doesn't even know why his preference may be different, it just is. The term "free will" refers to the type of decision that is uniquely human: a moral choice, the ability to choose right or wrong. To know the difference between good and evil is a product of free will.

The potential to fail or succeed, try or not to try, live or die, is our unique choice. The free will of man decides what is right for himself. You will not live long if your will to live is destroyed. Our will grants us tremendous power and potential. So many of us never utilize or exploit its power. We overlook the potential in us, and the strength of our will. Circumstances and failure can wear down and reduce the strength of our will. Our solemn resolve can all but disappear. If Satan can control your will, he can control you. You can be made to believe you are powerless over habits, weaknesses, and many other things in life by just believing a lie. A lie about the potential of "you." The power of your will.

James 4:7 (KJV) says, "Submit yourselves therefore to God. Resist the devil, and he will flee from you."

Dr. Lester Sumrall said, "The will is the most potent force in the universe." James equates the human will with power in this verse. He says resist. In most Christian teachings, too much power is given to the opposing forces of Satan than is necessary. Here, the human will is vindicated, and lifted to its true potential, a potential that you possess. A power to resist the forces of hell itself. **You might feel you are helpless, and failure is just part of who you are. Maybe you were teased as a child, or told by people who were supposed to love you that you were worthless, and you don't have it in you to succeed.** But, that isn't true. I used to think I was just average, and mediocre. I could possibly do more but didn't have the heart in me for greatness. I was looking at a failed ministry and failed marriage with little insight. One of the contributing factors of my addiction and careless behavior was because I didn't think I had it in me to carry on. I just copped out, bailed, and gave up on life.

If you think in your heart you have no chance and feel your will, or inward strength, is inadequate, you have a reason not to try. Many people have been diagnosed by doctors as having a learning handicap, and are considered weak minded. But, yet they still have a strong will. They can have a rebellious will or willing, obedient one. Many of these unique individuals when accepting Christ become great intercessors and have a genuine Godliness about their behavior. You could not get them to do wrong using the strongest of persuasion. God has given you the same resolve and inward strength through redemption of your will. Through Christ, you can beat the odds and overcome the failure of the past.

1 John 4:4 (KJV) says, "Ye are of God, little children, and have overcome them: because greater is he that is in you, than he that is in the world."

Everything that has hindered your inward strength and weakened your will has been destroyed through Christ. Greater is He that is in you than he that is in the world. You were born with the spark of enthusiasm. You were sent here with an assignment, and are not an accident. God would not have sent you into this world without a strong enough will to complete your assignment.

John 20:21 (KJV) says, "Then said Jesus to them again, Peace be unto you: as my Father hath sent me, even so, send I you."

God sent Jesus into the world with a mission, just like you were sent here for. Do you think God sent Jesus into this hostile environment filled with sin, sickness, and adversity ill-prepared? Do you think God sent Christ to be born as a man and to be tempted by Satan without equipping Him for the battle? Is there any loving father that would ever send their son or daughter into battle without being properly weaponized to face the enemy? Of course not. God sent Jesus into the world with enough strength and favor to overcome the enemy and handle all of life's difficulties. His willpower was strong enough to complete His assignment. Even when facing the cross in the Garden of Gethsemane. His will was the only thing that was tested. He was under extreme pressure. He was facing for the first time in His life the separation of Him and His father, which would be the consequence of taking the sins of the world upon Himself.

During the testing of His will to be obedient to His assignment, Jesus experienced **hematohidrosis**, a rare condition that can occur through excessive exertion. According to the physician Luke, "He prayed and being in anguish He prayed more earnestly and His sweat was like **drops of blood** falling to the ground." Yet Jesus submitted to God, and said, **"Nevertheless not my will but thine be done." (Luke 22:42 KJV)** So, Jesus had enough inward willpower to do extraordinary things when facing extraordinary circumstances. God gave Jesus willpower and inward strength. He was born with the seed of greatness in Him. Jesus sends you and me out with the same willpower and inward strength that His father sent Him into the world. He said, "My father hath sent me, even so, I send you." Jesus, God's Son, sends you and me with the same impartation of power and fullness of spirit as His Father gave to Him. (Jn. 7:37-39; 14:12; 17:18; 20:21; Lk. 24:49; Acts 1:4-8; Mt.18:18)

The Apostle Paul had the willpower to keep going when facing testing and trials. Paul pressed toward the goal to win the prize. His will overpowered the pressure of the outside forces of the world. He made his mind up that he would go forward, no matter what he faced. He decided not to let the past affect him.

Philippians 3:13-14 (NLT) says, "No, dear brothers and sisters, I have not achieved it, but I focus on this one thing: Forgetting the past and looking forward to what lies ahead, I press on to reach the end of the race and receive the heavenly prize for which God, through Christ Jesus, is calling us."

Jesus promised us that He would not allow any testing that could destroy our will to accomplish our purpose

1 Corinthians 10:13 (NLT) says, "The temptations in your life are no different from what others experience. And God is faithful. He will not allow the temptation to be more than you can stand. When you are tempted, he will show you a way out so that you can endure."

You have only one option in Christ if you want it, if you desire it. The only option you have that is promised is to succeed, nowhere in scripture does God promise ever to let you down, or destroy your willpower. But to the contrary, He promises to protect your will. It is valuable and precious to Him. If you give in to the pressure around you and quit, you will not be able to blame God. God said your temptation is not unusual or more difficult than anyone else's. God even promised grace to Paul to be able to endure his trials and adverse circumstances.

2 Corinthians 12:9-10 (ESV) says, "But he said to me, "My grace is sufficient for you, for my power is made perfect in weakness." Therefore, I will boast all the more gladly of my weaknesses, so that the power of Christ may rest upon me. For the sake of Christ, then, I am content with weaknesses, insults, hard-

ships, persecutions, and calamities. For when I am weak, then I am strong."

Your potential becomes unlimited when you partner with Christ. The following scriptures promise us the power to reach greater potential than was humanly possible before our conversion.

John 14:12 (KJV) says, "Verily, verily, I say unto you, He that believeth on me, the works that I do shall he do also; and greater works than these shall he do; because I go unto my Father."

Philippians 4:13 (ESV) says, "I can do all things through him who strengthens me."

Romans 8:35-37 (KJV) says, "Who shall separate us from the love of Christ? shall tribulation, or distress, or persecution, or famine, or nakedness, or peril, or sword? As it is written, For thy sake we are killed all the day long; we are accounted as sheep for the slaughter. Nay, in all these things we are more than conquerors through him that loved us."

Romans 8:38-39 (KJV) says, "For I am persuaded, that neither death, nor life, nor angels, nor principalities, nor powers, nor things present, nor things to come, Nor height, nor depth, nor any other creature, shall be able to separate us from the love of God, which is in Christ Jesus our Lord"

Mark 11:22-24 (KJV) says, "And Jesus answering saith unto them, Have faith in God. For verily I say unto you, That whosoever shall say unto this mountain, Be thou removed, and be thou cast into the sea; and shall not doubt in his heart, but shall believe that those things which he saith shall come to pass; he shall have whatsoever he saith. Therefore I say unto you, What things soever ye desire, when ye pray, believe that ye receive them, and ye shall have them."

Our amazing future

Philippians 3:13-14 (NLT) says, "No, dear brothers and sisters,

I have not achieved it, but I focus on this one thing: Forgetting the past and looking forward to what lies ahead, I press on to reach the end of the race and receive the heavenly prize for which God, through Christ Jesus, is calling us."

We have an amazing future filled with possibilities and restoration. There are things born in us, seeds of greatness that originated from God's greatness. God's plans have been intricately woven within us. Your inspirational dreams of being a strong man or woman filled with faith, productivity, and achievement were put there to bring God glory, and to fulfill your heart's desires. **Your special DNA requires a plan designed to complement your creative characteristics birthed by God himself.** We must press forward, never looking back, make up our mind, strengthen our will, and resolve to complete our final mission, to reach our full potential of greatness. **How could anything that was born from God be anything less than great?** To achieve this, we must use our will to press spiritually toward all that God has for us. We must use our God-given will innately born in us to attain spiritual prowess, gifting, and fruit. We must be brave, courageous, unrelenting, resilient, and press with purity seeking to honor God in everything we do.

2 Corinthians 4:16 (KJV) says, "For which cause we faint not; but though our outward man perish, yet the inward man is renewed day by day."

Our outward man is flesh. It is facing the pressure of the corruption that is in the world. Our bodies are dying from it, and the mental stress that it causes. But, our inward man is empowered by the Spirit of God and is renewed by God's Spirit. No one is exempt from this warfare of the flesh. We all get frustrated in the flesh while pursuing our dreams. We must realize that every attack of Satan is always on our flesh and the weakness that is existent through the flesh. What stands between you accomplishing your goals is resistance aimed at your flesh, your only weakness.

None of us are exempt from this pressure or resistance. It is placed on us pressuring our nerves, intensifying stress and fatigue, mentally and physically. **Maturity and experience do not escape the attack of the enemy.** There is only one thing that relieves and destroys this pressure. That is the power of the Holy Spirit. You must practice faith, and be in constant communication with God, set spiritual boundaries that keep you out of harm's way, and arm yourselves with the Word of God. God tells us that we are to suffer in the flesh, even Christ suffered in the flesh. But, arm yourselves. Christ was victorious, completed His mission, pleased God, and you are destined to do the same.

1 Peter 4:1 (AMP) says, "So, since Christ suffered in the flesh for us, for you, arm yourselves with the same thought and purpose [patiently to suffer rather than fail to please God]. For whoever has suffered in the flesh [having the mind of Christ] is done with [intentional] sin [has stopped pleasing himself and the world, and pleases God],"

Christ could please God, because of the faith He had in His mission, and the joy that would come as a result of completing it.

Hebrews 12:2 (KJV) says, "Looking unto Jesus the author and finisher of our faith; who for the joy that was set before him endured the cross, despising the shame, and is set down at the right hand of the throne of God."

If you can keep your eyes on the goal and its reward, then you can endure anything. The ability to do that comes from the most potent power in the universe. Your God-given will to press on. Jesus' reward was filled with fruits of joy. It created companionship and intimacy, and a new relationship created between Him and His bride, the church. It accomplished the destruction of His greatest adversary the devil and catapulted Him upon His eternal throne at the right hand of God. The verse says that Jesus is the author and finisher of our faith. That means He is our Leader and Source of what we believe, and the Finisher that brings it into maturity and perfection.

So, we must look away from all that distracts us and look to Him who strengthens us. He will strengthen you if you have willed it, made up your mind to receive His strength and wait for it. The word also tells us that we are to walk in this newness of life. How? By deciding to. It is within your will and power to do so, to decide. You have a free moral will to walk where you choose. Don't ever forget it. It is the potential of "you" that threatens Satan. If Satan and the pressure of this world diminishes your desire and convinces you that you are weak-willed, then it is over. God says you are not. He says you have the power to resist.

1 Peter 5:9 (KJV) says, "Whom resist stedfast in the faith, knowing that the same afflictions are accomplished in your brethren that are in the world."

Romans 6:4 (KJV) says, "Therefore we are buried with him by baptism into death: that like as Christ was raised up from the dead by the glory of the Father, even so we also should walk in newness of life."

God has set you free from sin, and your flesh is crucified with Christ giving you more freedom, and power to choose. We are raised a new man in the power of His resurrection.

Romans 6:5-8 (KJV) says, "For if we have been planted together in the likeness of his death, we shall be also in the likeness of his resurrection: Knowing this, that our old man is crucified with him, that the body of sin might be destroyed, that henceforth we should not serve sin. For he that is dead is freed from sin. Now if we be dead with Christ, we believe that we shall also live with him:"

The Greek word used for sin in this verse *hamartia* was used because of its overall understanding of the unified teachings of sin in the original Hebrew and Old Testament. The entire teachings given to us about sin are represented in this Greek word. It is important to know what you are freed from, and just what God is referring to as sin in its rawest form. The word means to miss the mark or goal, to fall short of a standard, and from this to err, to make a mistake, to sin. In the New Testament, the world understands sin in its fullest revelation, in the light of the self-revelation of God in His Son. Through the revelation of God in Christ, you are freed from living a lie. Christ shows us by example how to live. He frees us from living the wrong dream, and we are strengthened to live the life that God has planned for us. You are free from failing God and yourself by chasing the wrong dreams and having the wrong goals. These mistaken dreams are what put you in addiction, and created trauma in your life.

You are also made free from the damage of others that you have received in your life as the result of their misguided sin. Our missing the mark is revealed in honest through what we were intended to be, as it is revealed in the perfect man, Jesus of Nazareth. In His life, we see what our potential is. The real potential of "you." Not a distorted image of man and the failures of Adam. Not your distorted image of yourself either. Our example and leader is now Christ, and our strength is His, and our will is God-given to choose that life. If King David can "encourage" himself in the Lord so can we. We also can recover everything the enemy has stolen from us.

1 Samuel 30:6 (KJV) says, "And David was greatly distressed; for the people spake of stoning him because the soul of all the people was grieved, every man for his sons and for his daughters: but David encouraged himself in the LORD his God."

1 Samuel 30:8 (KJV) says, "And David enquired at the LORD, saying, Shall I pursue after this troop? shall I overtake them? And he answered him, Pursue: for thou shalt surely overtake them, and without fail recover all."

Your potential is to recover all—to achieve your dreams, accomplish your goals, and have that ability in a variety of God's strengths and attributes including the power of "you." When David asked God if he should pursue his dreams and overtake his obstacles, God emphatically said yes. **Only you can stop you.**

You control the destiny of you. It is up to you, and the responsibility lies within your own determination and desire to continue on that path. This book has spoken about powerful tools, gifts, and principles, which if practiced will get you there. I am praying for you, and fasting for God to bless every person that reads this book. God put it in your hands. It is information that you needed. Nothing can stop you now. No weapon or attack from the enemy can prevent you from reaching your full potential in Christ.

Isaiah 54:17 (KJV) says, "No weapon that is formed against thee shall prosper; and every tongue that shall rise against thee in judgment thou shalt condemn. This is the heritage of the servants of the LORD, and their righteousness is of me, saith the LORD."

God bless,

Tim

ABOUT THE AUTHOR

Tim Cormier is the son of missionaries and pastors, Paul and Alice Cormier. He is a multi-functional dynamic speaker, and the founder of Recovery Ministries, Inc., Hope Recovery Center, and the Facebook page Methaddictshelp. He has been involved with hundreds of addicts and their recovery from all over the world.

For more information, go to:
recovery-ministries.org/
office@recovery-ministries.org

CPSIA information can be obtained
at www.ICGtesting.com
Printed in the USA
FFHW02n1251070818
47696312-51328FF